AF600244

The Laws of the State of Texas Affecting Church Property

This dissertation was approved by the Reverend John J. McGrath, A.B., LL.B., J.C.D., as director, and by the Reverend John Rogg Schmidt, A.B., J.C.D., LL.B., and the Reverend Romaeus W. O'Brien, M.A., J.C.D., as readers.

THE CATHOLIC UNIVERSITY OF AMERICA
CANON LAW STUDIES
No. 405

The Laws of the State of Texas Affecting Church Property

A DISSERTATION

Submitted to the Faculty of the School of Canon Law of The Catholic University of America in Partial Fulfillment of the Requirements for the Degree of Doctor of Canon Law

BY

REVEREND DONALD C. MCLEAISH, B.A., S.T.L., J.C.L.
Priest of the Diocese of Austin

THE CATHOLIC UNIVERSITY OF AMERICA PRESS
WASHINGTON, D. C.
1960

Nihil Obstat:

John J. McGrath, A.B., LL.B., J.C.D.
Censor Deputatus

Washingtonii, die 1ª Junii 1959

Imprimatur:

Ludovicus J. Reicher, D.D.
Episcopus Austiniensis

Austin, die 15 Junii 1959

Printed by
Von Boeckmann-Jones Co.
Austin, Texas

Dedication

Sacratissimis Cordibus
Jesu et Mariae

FOREWORD

Studies in comparative law are increasing in number. Not only do they teach, by the light of costly experience, what is to be avoided, but the statement has been made that: "the affirmative and educative worth (of comparative studies) is the revealing, and increasing of common international perspectives and agreements."[1] It is hoped that this study will contribute to revealing the laws of the State of Texas to churchmen while placing the laws of the Catholic Church before lawyers and legislators. To the churchman, be he Catholic or non-catholic, the law of the State affecting the property rights of his flock will be of practical value. To the lawyer, it will be a source of information concerning the law of the Catholic Church as well as that of the State. To the legislator, it is hoped that the information contained herein will assist him to continue the munificent policy of the State towards the Christian religion.

The plan of the book is to touch only the major aspects of property law in the jurisprudential systems of the Church and the State. The laws of the Church affecting property are given more complete treatment. The historical synopsis which comprises Chapter I gives the general background upon which Church-State relations are founded in Texas. Before a treatment can be had of the acquisition and the administration of church property, it is necessary to understand the legal status of the Catholic Church in the State of Texas. The final chapter on tax exemptions illustrates most lucidly the public policy of the State of Texas towards religious societies and their educational and charitable projects.

One fact will be patent to the reader at the conclusion of this book. That is, the State of Texas has at all times upheld the natural and indefeasible right to worship God according to the

[1]Jerome Frank, "Studies in Contrastive Law," 104 *University of Pennsylvania Law Review* 887.

dictates of each man's conscience as promised in the Bill of Rights. Because of this, the Catholic Church has greatly prospered and has contributed much to the magnificence of the Lone Star State. However, in the final judgment of the laws of the State, it will be seen that the legislature has not fulfilled the duty imposed upon it with respect to all religions. The Bill of Rights asserts that:

> It shall be the duty of the legislature to pass such laws as may be necessary to protect equally every religious denomination in the peaceful enjoyment of its own mode of public worship.[2]

For this purpose, the knowledge of the laws of the Catholic Church will be of value.

The bibliography includes numerous works on Church Law in the English language. These works were used instead of the numerous Latin books on the subject in order that the readers might know more of the law of the Church. In many cases, the specialized dissertations concerning church property are of much more value for the conditions in the United States. The writer wishes to express his thanks to His Excellency, the Most Reverend Louis J. Reicher, D.D., Bishop of Austin, for his encouragement in these canonical studies and to the Faculty of the School of Canon Law of the Catholic University of America for their kind assistance.

---

[2]*Vernon's Annotated Constitution of the State of Texas* (3 vols. Kansas City, Mo.: Vernon's Law Book Co., 1955) I, Article I, section 6. (Hereafter cited by Article and section only.)

TABLE OF CONTENTS

CHAPTER I

CHAPTER II.

CHAPTER III

CHAPTER IV

CHAPTER V

CHAPTER I

HISTORICAL SYNOPSIS OF CHURCH-STATE RELATIONS IN TEXAS

Texas is the only state that was an independent republic, recognized by the United States, before being annexed to the Union. Over Texas has flown the flags of Spain, France, Mexico, the Lone Star Flag of the Republic, the Confederate States and the United States. The following is a summary presentation of Texas history from the time of its discovery in 1519 to the present. Events of major importance in the secular and religious history of the State are included.

1519 Alonso Alvarez de Pineda, of Spain, explored and mapped the coast of Texas, and mapped the mouth of the Rio Grande.

1541 Coronado led his troops in search of the cities of gold. He was accompanied by Franciscan missionaries, among whom was Father Juan de Padilla, Protomartyr of the United States.

1659 The first Mission was founded in El Paso.

1685 Robert Cavelier, Sieur de la Salle (generally called La Salle) founded Fort St. Louis to protect a French colony.

1690 Mission of San Francisco de los Tejas, the first mission in East Texas, was founded.

1691 Texas became a Spanish province by official decree.

1793 The first decrees of secularization of the Missions in Texas were issued by the Cortes in Madrid.

1803 The United States purchased Louisiana. A period of filibustering by American adventurers began with this purchase.

1821 Mexico gained its independence from Spain, and Texas was made part of the State of Coahuila.

1827 The Constitution for the new Mexican State, Coahuila-Texas, was enacted.

1835 June 30, Texans began skirmishes with Mexican troops in Anahuac; October 1, settlers took Gonzales in the first battle of the Revolution.

1836 March 2, Texas formally declared itself independent from Mexico. April 21, Independence was won by the battle of San Jacinto.

1845 The Republic of Texas became the State of Texas by being annexed to the United States of America.

1847 The Diocese of Galveston, first Roman Catholic Diocese in the State, was established.

1861 Texas seceded from the Union.

1870 Texas was readmitted to the Union.

1948 The seventh and most recent Roman Catholic Diocese, the Diocese of Austin, was established.[1]

The unique history of the State of Texas has contributed considerably to the relations that exist between the State and religious societies. The passing of the "Catholic" regimes of Spain and Mexico with the advent of the Republic of Texas that eschewed religious affiliation has proven to be a blessing. This is a historical fact that has no regard for the theoretical advantages of the system that preceded the Republic of Texas. Further, it will be seen that the Republic of Texas, and the State which followed it, gave full credit to the need of religion. Belief in God permeates the governmental documents and history of Texas.

A true understanding of the present relations that exist between the Roman Catholic Church and the State of Texas will be had only after a study of the historical beginnings of these relations. Neither the government of France nor the Confederate States had any real effect upon these relations. However, Church-State relations under the Spanish regime and the Mex-

[1] *Texas,* Compiled by Workers of the Writers' Program of the Work Projects Administration in the State of Texas, W. E. Gettys, Director (New York: Hastings House, 1940), pp. 671 ff; *The Official Catholic Directory, 1953* (New York: P. J. Kennedy & Sons). (Hereafter cited *The Official Catholic Directory, 1953.*)

ican government have definitely influenced the present relations that exist between the Church and the State of Texas.

Article I. Spanish and Mexican Rule

Section 1. The Church under Spain

The Spanish dominion over Texas lasted from 1519 to 1821. In the beginning, the explorers were moved as much by desire of spiritual conquests as of temporal. From the years of the explorers until the founding of the permanent missions at the end of the Seventeenth century, approximately 92 expeditions were sent to explore the vast area. However, not until 1691 did Spain consider Texas of such importance that a province was officially declared to exist for the territory.

The mission of San Francisco de los Tejas that had been founded in 1690 was moved to San Antonio in 1718. This led to the founding of more than a dozen missions in the area in the ten year period until 1731. At this time, the Spanish regime in Spain was being infected with a false political philosophy that greatly weakened its far-flung dominion. The age-old harmony that had existed between the Church and the State was replaced by discord.[2]

In 1753, a concordat was entered into between the Church and the Spanish monarchs. By this concordat, Spain gained practical dominion over all ecclesiastical temporalities and extensive powers over spiritual matters. For the first century after the discovery of America, Spain had conducted herself in a just manner towards the temporal and spiritual rights of the Church. In the 17th century, a gradual encroachment began that was culminated in the concordat of 1753.[3]

Historians assert that in the first years of the New World,

[2]Carlos E. Castaneda, *Our Catholic Heritage in Texas* (7 vols., Austin: Von Boeckmann-Jones, 1950), Vols. 1-6; W. E. Gettys, *Texas* (New York: Hastings House Publishers, 1940), pp. 36 ff; W. F. McCaleb, *Spanish Missions of Texas* (San Antonio: The Naylor Co., 1954). (Hereafter cited Castaneda and Gettys, respectively.)

[3]R. S. Lamadrid, *El Concordato Espanol de 1753*, Doctorate Thesis at the Gregorian University (Rome, 1937), pp. 102 ff. (Hereafter cited Lamadrid.)

the conquistadors were a boon to the missionaries, but in later years, their cooperation became chains that bound the Gospel. The Church was ever present to contribute a strong influence to the colonization and evangelization of the land and its peoples. However, the strict surveillance of the Spanish Viceroys impeded the proper functioning of the missionaries. As a consequence, the Indians repelled the many attempts to establish colonies at a distance from the missions. Thus, the Spanish never successfully colonized the vast territory. Nor did the missionaries successfully spread the Gospel to the savage tribes in Texas.[4] In fact, at the end of the Spanish Rule, there were less than 3,000 people in Texas and a total of only 11 missions.[5]

Not only did the government interfere with the functions of the ministers of the Church, but covetousness for the lands that belonged to the missions bred a greater evil. The missions had been in the hands of the Franciscan missionaries who had trained the pagan Indians in the ways and means of cultivating the lands. Government officials had hopes of obtaining funds from a public sale of these lands and in 1793, the first decree to secularize the missions was issued.[6]

Secularization meant that the mission property was surrendered into the hands of the civil authorities and a division of the agricultural lands was made. This division apportioned a part to those Indians who had some title to the land and the remainder was placed before the public for sale. Secular priests, instead of the religious, were charged with the spiritual interests of the people. The government refused to give ear to the pleas of the Church that there were no secular priests available to be sent to those areas. The government did not force the removal of the missionaries but it did refuse funds for the support of the missionaries. It must be remembered that the missionaries were supported by the government, not by the vol-

[4]Sister Mary Angela Fitzmorris, *Four Decades of Catholicism in Texas 1820-1860* (Washington, D.C.: The Catholic University of America, 1926), p. 2. (Hereafter cited as Fitzmorris.)

[5]Gettys, p. 37.

[6]Castaneda, V, 310.

untary offerings of the faithful. Unfortunately for the government, there were no interested buyers. The missions proved to be materially poor and few petitions were filed for the lands.[7]

The decline of Spanish power continued. In the early part of the 19th century, groups of filibusters invaded Texas from the new territory of the United States, Louisiana. One group succeeded in capturing a few Spanish outposts in East Texas.[8] These American filibusters were successfully ejected from the territory but only with difficulty. At this time, the huge rift that had long existed between the rich and the poor in Spanish territories expanded even more. Governmental leaders were not mindful of the temporal welfare of their subjects. The native clergy, most of whom were from the more impoverished classes, used the training they were given as priests to supplant the temporal leaders. These priests did not seem to understand that their spiritual leadership of the people was not intended to be transformed into a revolutionary leadership. Consequently, Miguel Hidalgo, a priest, was the leader of the first revolution against the Spanish government.[9]

At this time, in the year 1813, the Monarchy issued another decree to secularize the missions. This decree insisted in the removal of the religious missionaries. As a result, Texas was practically without priests during the revolutionary period.[10] Hidalgo did not succeed with his revolutionary attempt and was executed in 1814. His companion-priest in the revolution, Jose Antonio Gutierrez, did not end up before the firing squad. He continued to seek ways in which the people of Mexico might be freed from Spain. The movement was successful in 1821 when Spain capitulated to the demands of the combined revolutionary forces.[11]

Before the successful completion of the revolution, an American named Moses Austin sought to bring settlers from the

---

[7]Fitzmorris, p. 3; Castaneda, V, 317.

[8]Gettys, p. 37 ff.

[9]Castaneda, V, 317.

[10]*Loc. cit.*

[11]*Loc. cit.*

United States into Texas. Austin was a citizen of Spain by virtue of having lived in Louisiana while it was under the Spanish government. He had moved to Missouri in order to gain more wealth from the lead mines. In this, he was sorely disappointed. He therefore decided to return to the Spanish province and establish a colony. In December 1820, he traveled to Bexar, now the city of San Antonio, which was the capital of Texas at the time. Not only was his petition rejected, but the Spanish ordered him to leave the province. The filibustering Americans did not make Moses Austin's task any easier. Fortunately, a friend appeared, the Baron de Bastrop, who successfully convinced the Spanish governor that Austin did possess Spanish citizenship. After the governor gave him a hearing, Austin was sent to Mexico City with the petition to settle 300 families. After being granted the petition, the long trek to Missouri began. Exposure to the elements and loss of his supplies in a torrent so weakened Moses Austin that he soon succumbed to pneumonia after reaching home. He obtained a promise from his son, Stephen, that an attempt would be made to fulfill his dream of colonizing Texas. In July of 1821, Stephen Austin and the Spanish commissioner, Erasmus Sequin, explored the Colorado and the Brazos rivers in order to find a suitable place in which to establish the 300 families. Stephen Austin returned to bring the first settlers to settle on the Brazos in December, 1821.[12]

A. Actual Status of the Church

The brief history of those things that led to the downfall of the Spanish dominion over Mexico indicated a worsening of the condition of the Church. At the beginning, the Church was recognized as possessing all those rights that had been given it by Christ, as well as being its due by natural law. The Papacy had been generous to the Spanish monarchs who sought to spread the faith while increasing the strength and riches of their dominion. Papal grants of exclusive rights of coloniza-

---

[12]*Laws of Texas, 1822-1905* (Gammel, H.P.N., 10 vols. and index, Austin: 1906), I, 4 ff. (Hereafter cited in the following manner: 1 Gammel 4ff., etc.)

tion to Spain over certain areas of the world assured the Spanish of peace in Europe while seeking to acquire the hidden treasures of the New World. Further, the Papacy gave the monarchs a mission to convert the pagans of the New World, then called the Indies, and assured them of those means necessary to effect conversions. For this reason, rights of appointment and presentation, rights to tithes and obedience were given the monarchs. As a consequence, the Hierarchy and subordinate clergy in the dominion saw greater power in the Monarchs than in fact existed.[13]

During this period, Spain never ceased to recognize that the Roman Catholic Religion was the religion established by Christ for the salvation of all men. Consequently, the universal church was considered to be a society perfect in itself and to an extent, independent of the power of the State. To what degree Spain recognized the complete independence of the Church in religious and temporal matters within the Spanish dominion is not definitely settled. Until the era of the modern concordats that began in 1753, the Church enjoyed a favored status in Spain. Even before this concordat and definitely after, the State usurped rights, privileges and property that belonged to the Church. It has been concluded that Spain recognized the Church as a juridical entity apart from the papal state, but that because of a confusion of the temporal and the spiritual in that time, the Church in the Spanish dominion was held subject to the State.[14] An erroneous opinion asserts that the Church made the Spanish monarchs both the temporal and spiritual rulers of the Church in the New World. A brief study of the papal donations and the effects of these donations will illustrate the sources of this error.

---

[13]R. Gomez, *Las Leyes de Indias y el Derecho Ecclesiastico en la America Espanola e Islas Filipinas* (Medillin, Columbia: Ediciones Universidad Catholica Bolivariana, 1945), pp. 1-66. (Hereafter cited as Gomez.)

[14]L. Perez, *Iglesia y Estado Nuevo, los concordatos ante el moderno derecho publico* (Madrid: Ediciones Faz, 1940) p. 362. (Hereafter cited as Perez.)

B. Papal Donations

Spain made great strides in the latter part of the 15th century towards establishing itself as a major power of that time. The Moors eventually lost the upper hand in the Iberian peninsula and found themselves cornered in the southeastern part of the united kingdom of Castile and Aragon. A marital union of the two monarchies placed the renowned pair, Ferdinand and Isabella, over the Spanish peninsula. Shortly after their ascendancy into power, Christopher Columbus discovered America on behalf of the new monarchy.[15]

Within a year after this momentous discovery, the Holy See acted to establish the rights of Spain in the newly discovered lands, called the Indies. This action of the Holy See was taken in order to preserve peace and to forestall possible discontent on the part of other countries of Europe. Therefore, the request made by Spain that the Pope grant the Spanish government a commission to spread the faith in the "indies" was answered by the Bull, *"Inter Coetera."* In this Bull, Alexander VI stated:

> Therefore, we commend your holy and laudable proposal to bring the name of Our Savior, Jesus Christ, in those parts . . . We exhort you in the Lord and by holy baptism which has obligated you to an apostolic mandate . . . to lead those peoples to the Christian religion . . . We command you in virtue of holy obedience to send proven men who fear God to those Islands and lands above described (part of the Bull had delineated the territory for Spanish exploration) to instruct the people in the Catholic Faith.[16]

---

[15]W. H. Prescott, *Ferdinand and Isabella* (1st ed. 1837; new and revised edition by J. F. Kirk, Philadelphia: Lippincott, 1883), pp. 172, 491 ff. (Hereafter cited Prescott.)

[16]Javier Hernaez, S.F., *Collection de Bulas Breves* (2 vols.; ed. A. Vromont, Brussels, 1879), I, 12 citing the Latin texts:

> Nos igitur hujusmodi vestrum sanctum et laudabile propositum plurimum in Domino cemmendantes . . . ut nomen Salvatoris Jesu Christi in partibus illis inducatur, HORTAMUR VOS IN DOMINO QUAMPLURIMUM ET PER SACRI LAVACRI SUSCEPTIONEM qua madatis apostolicis obligatis estis . . . populos . . . ad

On the same day, May 4, 1493, Alexander VI issued another Bull, *"Eximiae Devotionis"* that conceded to the Spanish monarchy those privileges, favors, exemptions, faculties, immunities and liberties that had been conceded to the Portuguese in their vast exploratory expeditions.[17]

These two Bulls placed Spain on a level with the Portuguese kingdom in so far as the right to conquer and to spread the faith were concerned. The only privilege that the Spanish now desired was that of universal or Royal patronage.

The monarchs encountered far greater expenses than they expected in fulfilling their grandiose plans for the spiritual conquest of the New World. Alexander VI issued another Bull entitled *"Eximiae Devotionis"* on November 16, 1501. The monarchs were permitted to exact tithes from the rectors, the bishops, the pastors of churches and from all ecclesiastics in order to support the Church in the New World. The Bull explicitly stated that these means were for the spreading of the gospel, the building of churches, oratories, and other ecclesiastical buildings, and the support of the missionaries. This support of the missionaries was to begin in their formative years and to continue when they were in the missions. The effect was to give the monarchs a more extensive control over ecclesiastical temporalities.[18]

Alexander VI died in August of 1503. His successor, Pius III, reigned only a month and was succeeded by Julius II who was to reign until 1513. The saintly Queen, Isabella of Spain, died in this same period. King Ferdinand began to petition the new Pope, Julius II, for greater power over church property in the Spanish dominion. On July 28, 1508, the Bull, *"Universalis Ecclesiae,"* granted full Royal Patronage to the Spanish monarchy. This meant that the King had the power

---

cristianam religionem inducere.

Mandamus vobis in virtute sanctae obedientiae ad terras firmas et insulas praedictos viros probos et Deum timentes, . . . ad instruendos . . . in fide catholica . . . destinare debeatis . . .

(Hereafter cited as Hernaez.)

[17] *Ibidem*, p. 15.

[18] *Ibidem*, p. 20.

to concede or deny privileges, to build churches, to present and approve all beneficiaries in the "Indies." The Pope retained the power to determine boundaries for the beneficiaries of a diocesan status.[19] A subsequent communication from the Holy See to the Spanish monarch freed the monarch from making the payments of the "diezmos" or tithes to the Holy See. In this communication of April 8, 1510, the Pope refused to permit the King to judge those causes that arose in the colonies and touched upon the extension of Royal Patronage.[20]

A final note in this matter is that the King made a re-donation of his right to the "diezmos" (tithes). In a concordat entered into with the Bishops of Spain, King Ferdinand relinquished this right together with the right to appoint the beneficiaries in minor benefices. However, the Bishops were obligated to use the "diezmos" for those purposes designated in the Bull of 1501.[21]

C. *Interpretation of the Papal Donations*

In 1848, the Supreme Court of Texas had occasion to pass judgment upon the effect of these acts that took place between the papacy and the Spanish Monarchy. Judge Lipscomb spoke for the court in asserting that:

> In most catholic countries, the Pope, as the head of the church claims rights of property in himself . . .; . . . he claims the right, independent of the temporal sovereignty to levy tithes and to regulate the collection of fees for the various services of his clergy . . . the right was universally acquiesced in at the period of the discovery of our continent, by the greater part of Christiandom.[22]

The judge then observed that this claim, which extended to the right of dispensing of all newly discovered countries, was relinquished to Ferdinand and Isabella. He meant that Alexander VI relinquished the tithes, collections and independence

---

[19]*Ibidem*, p. 24.

[20]*Ibidem*, p. 26.

[21]*Ibidem*, p. 21.

[22]Blair v. Odin, 3 Tex. 288 (1848).

by granting Royal patronage that included absolute disposal of all ecclesiastical benefices. Therefore, Judge Lipscomb said that: the Spanish monarchs became in effect, the heads of the Catholic Church in their American possessions.[23]

The court rested heavily upon the historical work of W. H. Prescott in coming to this conclusion. This well-documented work by an able historian came to the conclusion that as a result of these papal donations, the Spanish Monarch was placed "at the Head of the Church with absolute disposal of all dignities and emoluments . . ."[24] This was a source of astonishment to the author; he solved his astonishment by viewing the donations as political gifts from Alexander VI to his fellow-countrymen, Ferdinand and Isabella. In fact, Prescott implies that the matter was practically forced upon the Pontiff. He does not say that the Pope gave up all right to temporal possessions so that he kept only a usufruct interest and relinquished the absolute title. Prescott did not consider the redonation of Ferdinand to the Bishops in 1812. It may be that he did not know of this act. If he had, it seems that his conclusion would have been different.

An extensive treatment of these pontifical donations and subsequent interpretations by jurists in the Latin American countries in the centuries preceding the concordat of 1753 was made by Rafael Gomez in 1945.[25] He asserts that because of the numerous privileges and powers conceded to the monarchs, the missionaries came to consider the Royal patron as a type of religious superior. By force of this attitude, a natural argument evolved that the spiritual powers of the missionaries emanated from the monarchs themselves or at least that the monarchs were the dispensers of powers coming from the Roman Pontiff. A pernicious conception arose that the monarchs participated in ecclesiastical jurisdiction in the spiritual as well as the temporal realm.[26]

This theory was first advanced in 1574 by a learned Fran-

[23]*Loc. cit.*

[24]Prescott, p. 172.

[25]Gomez, pp. 1-66.

[26]*Loc. cit.*

ciscan and was subsequently broached by vast numbers of the Latin American jurists who had received their appointments from a hierarchy presented by the monarchy for their respective sees. Finally, in the works of Don Juan de Solorzanay Pereira, the proponents of this theory advanced into open Regalism. The interference of the Royal Consuls in ecclesiastical matters was justified by Don Juan in a threefold way. First, the monarchy had the right by force of the pontifical concessions to act in ecclesiastical matters. But since this was not definite, he proposed: second, that the immemorial custom of more than a hundred years of such interference became law by tacit consent. However, the fact was that opposition had been voiced. Therefore, he stated that in any event, the kings had a certain innate right to mix into ecclesiastical matters.[27]

This work was immediately attacked and the reigning pontiff, Urban VIII, issued a decree on the 20th of March, 1642, putting the author's work on the Index. The monarchs of Spain recalled the decree from its provinces so that the book effectively dispersed the false concept of regalism throughout the territory. As a result, the ideas have prevailed in those areas even to this day. Gomez proposes the works of at least seven authors after Solorzanay who treat of this question and, as all are Latin American jurists, all justify lay interference in ecclesiastical matters. None, however, express the theory of regalism in such a brazen manner as Solorzanay had done. A Jesuit is cited as presenting the prevailing theory on the papel donations with these words:

> Our Kings are delegates of the Holy See by the Bull of Alexander VI and as such, delegates and Vicar Generals, they have the right to exercise ecclesiastical and spiritual government, authority and jurisdiction touching all matters both religious and ecclesiastical (meaning material or temporal?) in their kingdom . . . with full and absolute power to dispose everything as seemed more convenient to their wills.[28]

---

[27] *Loc cit.*

[28] *Loc. cit.*

Gomez criticizes these theories and asserts that the Popes could not concede such full power of jurisdiction because it touches the essence of jurisdiction that by divine establishment can be exercised only by those in the clerical state. Yet, the monarchs received some sort of delegation from the Roman Pontiffs to carry out the mission they had been given. The laws of the Viceroys concerning ecclesiastical matters were considered valid. If those laws were in conflict with the legislation of the universal church or the laws of the particular dioceses in which they were promulgated, the laws were invalid.[29]

Gomez agrees with Prescott that the donations were political acts intended to settle dissension that might arise amongst the Christian nations concerning the exploration and the evangelization of the new continents that were discovered. Suarez and Bellarmine are cited to support this contention. However, the monarchs never had reason to conceive of themselves as legitimate heads of the Catholic Church in their dominions by the very fact that they were obliged to continue to have recourse to the Holy See for the purpose of increasing their privileges. Further, the monarchs never obtained the fullness of the power they considered necessary for the proper maintenance of religion by the State.[30]

These criticisms of Gomez are the most accurate and extensive that have been made upon the many theories concerning the effect of the Papal donations. Consequently, it must be held that the donations of certain privileges, rights, powers and duties by the Papacy to the Spanish monarchy in the years 1492-1513, did not have the effect of making the monarchy the head of the Catholic Church in things temporal as well as spiritual.[31]

Section 2. The Church under Mexico

The various revolutions that had begun in 1811 were ter-

[29]*Loc. cit.*

[30]*Ibidem,* pp. 31-32, where it is stated that King Ferdinand sought the privilege of defining the limits of all the dioceses, but that this was denied. On one occasion in Spanish history this was conceded, namely, to Emperor Charles V by Pope Leo X.

[31]Cf. Perez, pp. 32 ff; Lamadrid, pp. 102 ff.

minated in the collapse of the Spanish domination by the Treaty of Cordoba in 1821. The expulsion of numerous leaders both of the secular and ecclesiastical realms led to a state of confusion. The conquering general, Iturbide, assumed the rank of Emperor but the numerous elements that united to win the Independence did not permit this Emperor to remain in power. The Church in Mexico was accorded the same recognition that it had received under Spain. Therefore, the Church in Texas remained under the Bishop of Durango who was unable to supply the territory with priests. The colonization grant that had been awarded to Stephen F. Austin insisted upon the immigration of Catholic families.[32]

To renew this colonization grant which the Spanish government had first awarded to his father, Stephen F. Austin went to Mexico City in April, 1822. A new colonization grant was made by Iturbide in 1823. Austin was about to depart for Texas when close friends advised him that the grant would have to be renewed if Iturbide fell. Therefore, Austin waited for the establishment of a stable government which renewed the grant and permitted his return. Hence, in April, 1823, after spending a year in Mexico City, Austin returned to Texas with the power to settle colonists in a determined area and to establish a government for the colony in accordance with the laws of the United States of Mexico.[33]

A. The Church in the Colonies

Stephen F. Austin is called the Father of Texas. This title is justly attributed to the man who paved the way for the immigration of the vast majority of American settlers and who was the mastermind of the governmental system in the new colony. His attitude to the Catholic Church during this colonization period indicates the true position of the Church in relation to the Mexican government.

It must be remembered that of the more than 7,000 families brought into Texas between 1821 and 1831, Austin had settled

[32] I Gammel, 4 ff.

[33] *Loc. cit.*

approximately 5,600.[34] The debt which Texas owes to this man has not been overvalued. When not journeying to Mexico to arrange for favorable legislation or for new grants of colonization, he was governing the colony and keeping up correspondence in order to keep the inquisitive well informed. He stated in a letter to a General Gaines that "the prosperity of Texas has been the object of my labors, the idol of my existence. It has assumed the character of a religion for the guidance of my thoughts and actions in the last fifteen years."[35]

As a consequence, Austin never married although he had a great desire to have a family and a large colonial plantation. He expressed the feeling that as the leader of the colonists in the new territory, his life was too difficult to share with a wife.

Austin was a man of extremely high character who attempted to fulfill to the letter his agreements both with the Mexican government and the people that came to colonize the State of Texas. He realized that a breach of trust on his part in the matter of religion might bring on unnecessary reprisals. Therefore, he constantly besieged the Mexican government for priests. However, he found that the ecclesiastical authorities were unable to act because of the restrictive legislation of the government. Therefore, the constant desire of the colonists, as expressed by Austin, to learn about the Catholic faith, receive the sacraments, especially Baptism and Marriage, were thwarted.[36]

Still Austin insisted upon obedience to the laws of the land and the practice of the Catholic faith required by those laws. At the same time, he expressed the sentiment that the day would come when there would be a toleration for all religions. However, he expressed a fear that a few fanatic and imprudent preachers would come in and upset the equilibrium of the colony. In his correspondence, even the most personal, he paid reverent respect to the religion of the land so that one could

[34]Getty, pp. 39 ff; E. C. Barker, *The Father of Texas* (Austin: The Steck Co., 1935), pp. 55-58. (Hereafter cited Barker.)

[35]Barker, p. 80.

[36]Fitzmorris, pp. 24-30.

justly conclude that he favored the faith. The only loss of respect for the Catholic religion seems to have come from the manner in which he saw it practiced in Mexico and used as an instrument by the Mexican government.[37]

On one occasion, a vicar of the Bishop of Coahuila, Father Juan Nepomucen Pena, answered Austin's pleas that something be done to remedy the dire state of religion in the colony. The letter of Austin to Father Juan is indicative of his understanding of the Catholic faith and his intention that it be practiced in the colony. A Franciscan was sent to the colony to serve the area around the Brazos, now called Austin. The priest did not speak English and he was ill received. Coupled to this fact, the colonists had not prepared a living quarters nor a church for the priest and he therefore departed.[38]

The mentality of the regime in Mexico erected definite obstacles to the practice of the faith by the people of Texas. Foreign priests began to seek entry in order to supply for the extreme need of the people but their entrance was strictly forbidden. An Italian priest was refused permission to stay and work with the Texans because of the hostility that the Mexican government bore toward the Papal States and the fear that he was an emissary of the papacy to the colonists.[39] A priest from Louisiana was refused entry because of the fear that he was the first to infiltrate from the United States and that unauthorized American colonists would follow in his path. The colonists greatly desired English-speaking priests but there were few occasions upon which they were blessed to meet them.[40]

There was a priest who did extensive work amongst the colonists. He was a Father Muldoon. Father Muldoon is a mystery to the historians. There is no record of where he came from nor where he definitely settled upon leaving Texas. There are no records in Ireland, the supposed place of his origin, that

---

[37] *Loc. cit.*

[38] *Loc. cit.*

[39] Castaneda, VI, 300.

[40] Fitzmorris, p. 25.

he was ordained. There are no records of his saying Mass in Texas, although he did baptize and marry many of the colonists. One of his "converts" was Sam Houston. It is known that he reported to the diocese of Durango upon leaving Texas and interceded with the Mexican government for the colonists when he was in Mexico City. However, there seems to be no reason to doubt that Father Muldoon was a priest in good standing.[41] Father Muldoon did give the colonists a taste of the Catholic religion in their native tongue. Austin and others expressed their admiration for him and requested the Mexican hierarchy for more priests of his caliber. But Father Muldoon seems to have been an inconstant character and instead of remaining with the colonists and assisting them in their times of trial, he sought new fields in which to work. Later, Bishop Odin was to express distrust for those whom he termed "Muldoon" catholics and he observed that the seeds planted by Father Muldoon did not bear much fruit. Thus, the four years work of Father Muldoon, from 1830 to 1834, were not to have much effect upon the catholicity of the new Republic of Texas.[42]

Of the other empresarios (colonizers) in Texas at the time, Martin de Leon seems to be the only one worthy of note as far as religious matters are concerned. He found it difficult to bring up the Mexican families that he was instructed to settle. They did not adapt themselves to the hardships of the area as readily as the Anglo-American settlers. However, in the townsite that was established, De Leon did not make use of the land set aside for a Catholic Church. Because of the lack of families, he built the church upon his own land and kept a priest there to administer to the needs of the people. This fact was later to contribute to a court decision that permitted the land dedicated to the use of the Catholic Church to be diverted to the use of another religion.[43]

From this it can be seen that there was no oppression of the

---

[41]Castaneda, VI, 308; Fitzmorris, p. 28. Castaneda questions the fact that Father Muldoon was a priest.

[42]Fitzmorris, p. 28.

[43]*Loc. cit.;* cf. Blair v. Odin, 3 Tex. 288 (1848).

colonists by the Catholic religion. It is understandable that the law of the land which required that the colonists become Catholics in order to protect their property rights was not well accepted. This is especially true when one considers that the Mexican government hindered the Church in presenting itself to the colonists so that a rational and wholehearted acceptance of the faith might be effected. The law remained as an ax over the head of the colonists so that their property rights were always in peril. It seems that there were approximately five priests in the vast territory when the colonists entered, none of whom spoke English. By the time the colonists revolted in 1836, there were only two priests and these were not in good standing.[44]

Many other problems plagued Austin at the time. The constant changes of governments and the consequent fickleness of policy with regard to the colonists planted the seed of discontent. Not a few unscrupulous settlers sought to give growth to that discontent in order that Texas might be independent. The fear of Austin and the more prudent leaders was that the colonists would suffer disastrous defeat at the hands of the large Army which the Mexican government would be able to send against them. The approximate population of Mexico at this time was six million, that of Texas, 40,000. The hope that the United States would intervene in favor of the colonists proved to be unfounded.[45]

B. Legislation Affecting the Church

When Stephen F. Austin had returned from Mexico City to the colonies to establish the settlement on the Brazos, he had the authority to administer justice and to preserve good order as required by the original grant of colonization.[46] Austin

---

[44]*Loc. cit.;* C. G. Deuther, *John Timon* (Buffalo, 1870), p. 42, who cites a letter of the first Prefect Apostolic of Texas, John Timon, to the Sacred Congregation of the Propagation of the Faith in 1838, saying: "No catholic priests are to be found in Texas."

[45]Gettys, pp. 36 ff; Barker, pp. 78 ff.

[46]E. Markham, "The Reception of the Common Law of England in Texas and The Judicial Attitude toward that Reception, 1840-1859,"

had been trained in the common law of England and by virtue of his long stay in Mexico seeking the passage of the colonization laws, he became well versed in the civil law. Common law had certain advantages; the civil law others. Consequently, Austin set up a court system, methods of procedures, and a concise civil and criminal code, using the best of both the common and the civil law.[47] The importance of this system will become evident when the struggle for the adoption of the common law is discussed.

The numerous governments that ruled over Mexico in these few years did not vary from the pattern that had been begun in Spain. The Church was the object of both praise and vilification, of legal assistance and restrictions. The colonization law that consisted of thirty-two articles treated of the catholic religion in two articles:

> Article I. The government of the Mexican nation will protect the liberty, property and civil rights, of all foreigners, who profess the Roman Catholic Apostolic Religion, the established religion of the empire.
>
> Article XVI. The government shall take care, in accord with the respective ecclesiastical authority, that these new towns are provided with a sufficient number of spiritual pastors, and in like manner it will propose to Congress a plan for their decent support.[48]

The "Federal Constitution of the United Mexican States," commonly known as "The Constitution of 1824," divided the territories of the Mexican Republic. Texas was made a part of the state of Coahuila. The state of Coahuila was to govern itself and to make a law that would govern its colonies. A Texan, Baron de Bastrop, exerted tremendous influence in the organization and the formation of the new Mexican Republic and was a member of the legislature of the state of Coa-

---

Texas Law Review (The University of Texas Publication of the School of Law: Austin) Vol. XXIX, October, 1951, No. 7, pp. 904 ff. (Hereafter cited 29 *Texas Law Review* 904.)

[47]Gilmer, "Early Courts and Lawyers of Texas," 12 *Texas Law Review* 435.

[48]Colonization Law of 1823, 1 Gammel 28.

huila. Baron de Bastrop had immigrated to Texas early in the century and he knew the value of favorable laws for the colonists. The word "Catholic" in the original grant was changed to "christian."[49] This action made the law more amenable to probable immigrants from the north who were swamping Austin with objections to the religious requirements.

The restrictions upon the Catholic Religion was even more numerous than the assertions of favors and privileges. The decrees of secularization were reaffirmed and as a consequence, the remaining missionaries were withdrawn. The regime had exiled the Bishop from the ecclesiastical province to which Texas belonged and for ten years the Church was leaderless. Governmental decrees re-emphasized the policy of oppressing the Church. The decree of the Spanish Cortes abolishing all entail and primogeniture and mortmain in March, 1821, was adopted by the Mexican government. This prevented the Church from acquiring property in its own right.[50] One decree read:

> . . . the founding of edifices built by charitable donations under any denomination whatever is hereby absolutely prohibited; no person shall dispose of more than one-fiftieth of his property in benefit to his soul; the intervention of ecclesiastical authority in affairs purely civil is prohibited; also, the testament visit in the state by the bishops of the diocese.[51]

Other decrees forbade the execution of orders of bishops and other spiritual authorities without permission from the government and the publication of pastorals and edicts were forbidden. Disobedience by curates of this decree meant exile for two years and the loss of the benefice.[52] Finally, the Mexican Republic determined that religious differences should not hinder the sale of public land. A law regulating the public sale of public land provided that "no person should be molested for

[49] 1 Gammel 40; cf. Castaneda, VI, 198.

[50] 1 Gammel 350.

[51] *Loc. cit.*

[52] 1 Gammel 363.

political and religious opinions provided that the public order was not disturbed."[53]

Thus, it can be seen that not only did the Mexican government put the Catholic Church at an extreme disadvantage by virtue of the fact that it was considered the "State" religion but further, the doorway was being opened to freedom for those practicing other religions. Not that this is not desirable, but the anomaly is patent. It cannot be questioned that the government recognized the Church as a juridical entity, distinct from the State. But it must be admitted that the government did not permit the Church to function freely. The right to acquire, hold and administer property independently of the State was not permitted.

Article II. The Republic and the State of Texas

The Republic of Texas came into existence as a result of the successful revolution against Mexico in 1836. This government lasted until 1845 when Texas sought and obtained annexation to the United States. It will be seen that little of the adverse legislation made under the Spanish and Mexican regimes continued to affect the Church. The acquired rights of the Church received recognition by the Republic and the State, but the restrictive legislation was not kept in being. Texas adopted a legal system peculiarly its own in some respects but closely resembling that of the states in the United States for the most part. There was no change in this system when the Republic became a State.

Section 1. General Church-State Relations

The Papacy was fully aware of the sad state of religion in Texas while under the Mexican domination and it was quick to accord a quasi-recognition to the new Republic of Texas. This came about in the following fashion. A communication was given to the Bishop of New Orleans requesting that he provide for the great number of Catholics solicitous for their religion in Texas. The best that Bishop Blanc could do was to

---

[53] 1 Gammel 358.

send Father John Timon, C.M. to obtain a true report for the Sacred Congregation of the Propaganda of the Faith.[54]

The report of Father Timon induced the Sacred Congregation of the Propaganda to give him an appointment as Prefect Apostolic. The Cardinal prefect addressed a letter to the President of the Republic presenting Father Timon as the representative of the Holy See. In the letter, the Cardinal congratulated the President and Congress for the kindness shown to the ministers of the Church that had been sent to re-establish the faith. A recommendation was made that whatever property that had been in the hands of the Church before the revolution be returned to Father Timon as the head of the Church.[55]

Father Timon did not find President Lamar upon his arrival at the Capitol but the letter was presented to the Vice-President, Burnet. The Vice-President sent a reply which stated that it was an honor to receive the distinguished priest, and expressed good will toward the Church. He acknowledged the fact that there was property that belonged to the Catholic Church and asserted that it would be restored to sacred uses as soon as possible. At the same time, Burnet commented on the fact that there were large numbers of Protestants in the Republic and that the freest principles of religious toleration were in effect.[56]

The abilities and the personalities of Fathers Timon and Odin planted seeds of confidence in the minds of the authorities and respect for the Catholic Church which they represented. On January 5, 1839, Father Timon was invited to preach in the House of Representatives. His sermon was attended by the whole Congress and by many of the Protestant ministers who

[54]John Timon was born on February 2, 1797, in Conevago, Pennsylvania, of Irish parents. He was ordained in 1825 and became visitor to the Congregation of the Missions in 1835. Bishop Blanc sent him as the "envoy" to Texas on December 24, 1838. On April 12, 1840, he was made the Prefect Apostolic for Texas with the power to confirm, and was given Jean Marie Odin, C.M. as Vice-Prefect. When Timon returned to be a visitor for the Congregation of the Missions in 1842, Odin was made the Vicar Apostolic of Texas. Cf. Deuther, pp. 2 ff.

[55]Fitzmorris, p. 52. The letter is quoted in full.

[56]*Ibidem*, p. 53. The letter is quoted in full.

had come into Texas. The testimony of the time avers that a deep impression was made by his words.[57] The two priests used all the influence they could muster to obtain the passage of a bill for the return of the property of the Church. In 1841, a special bill was proposed to the legislature requesting that the lands that had belonged to the Church be returned to the Chief Pastor of the Church in Texas. An objection was made to the inclusion of the Alamo. The Alamo was thereby excluded from this Bill by mutual agreement and the grant was passed unanimously. Two days later, General Sam Houston earnestly pleaded that the generosity of the Republic of Texas be made manifest in a complete restoral of church property. In consequence of this talk, the Alamo was granted to the Church in a special Act.[58]

Before these official acts that occurred between the Church and the Republic of Texas, a French nobleman had sought to establish a Catholic colony in July, 1837. The plan was to include a definite religious clause for those belonging to the colony. The plan included the raising of Texas to the rank of an Archbishopric with the purpose of freeing Catholics in Texas from the jurisdiction of a Mexican Bishop. Further, he wished that there would be a public grant of land for the Church and its schools so that there would be no possibility of State control. The protection of the government was expected and freedom for the Roman Catholic faith was to be had in all parts of the State. President Houston correctly replied to the nobleman

---

[57]*Ibidem*, p. 43.

[58]Fitzmorris, p. 55. Sam Houston, a veteran of Andrew Jackson's Indian Wars and a Governor of Tennessee and a U. S. Representative for that State, had come to Texas in 1834, apparently to forget an unhappy marriage. He was baptized by Father Muldoon. Although he stood for the Church in this instance, he later aligned himself with the Know-Nothing Party in 1853, in order to oppose the Democratic stand on the Kansas-Nebraska bill. He became a Mason and later remarried outside the Church. In Texas he was the First President, 1836-1838, and President again in 1841-1844; U. S. Senator, 1846-1859; Governor, 1859-1861, from which he was removed because he refused to consent to the secession and join the confederacy. He died in 1863. Cf. *Columbia-Viking Desk Encyclopedia* (2 vols., New York: Viking Press, 1953), I, 572.

that it would be good to see a separation of religious ties with the Mexican hierarchy and that freedom had been granted to Roman Catholics. However, he rightly denied that he had the power to make a special grant of privileges of land to any religion. The plan was abandoned but at least one historian has interpreted the move as an attempt to establish Cathholicism as the religion of the State.[59]

The Church has experienced fabulous growth in the more than a century that it has been under the government of the Republic and the State of Texas. The annexation of the Republic to the United States did not affect a substantial change in the relations that had existed. The freedom that the Church enjoyed under the Republic of Texas and the consequent growth that had begun during that period, continued to advance. Father Jean Marie Odin had been consecrated a Bishop and made the Vicar-Apostolic of Texas in 1842. When the diocese of Galveston was founded in 1847, Jean Marie Odin became the first Bishop in Texas. He encountered many physical difficulties and experienced personal rebuffs but his tenacity and tact firmly established the Church in the land.[60]

Section 2. The Legal System

Much has been written concerning the relative merits of the common law and the civil law and the differences between the two. This is not an attempt to enter into the debate which has even flourished amongst the justices of the Supreme Court of Texas. However, for a true appreciation of the present law in Texas affecting church property, some knowledge of the history of these legal systems in the State of Texas is desirable.

As a province in the Spanish dominion and a State in the Mexican Republic, the territory of Texas was governed by the civil law of Spain and the decrees and orders of the Royal government. The Viceroy of Mexico augmented this body of

---

[59]H. Yoakum, *History of Texas* (2 vols. New York, 1856), II, 220-222.

[60]Fitzmorris, pp. 60 ff. The author narrates the numerous problems that faced the bishop, and the manner in which he solved or accepted them.

laws with particular decrees and orders. When the Viceroyalty of Mexico become the United Mexican Republic in 1821, Texas was considered a part of the State of Coahuila. In 1827, the State was called Coahuila-Texas. The legal system in the government was that of the civil law, that is, the system of jurisprudence held and administered in the Roman empire, particularly as set forth in the compilation of Justinian and his successors, as distinguished from the common law of England and the canon law.[61]

The colonists were familiar with the common law of England and certain groups of the colonists insisted upon the introduction of that system. There was a loud clamor for the trial by jury which was felt to be constitutive of a free government. The laws of the Mexican government tended to perpetuate the civil law system and to forget the sentiments of the Texans. The fact that the seat of the State government was Coahuila and that of the national government was Mexico City did not help to change the situation. The civil law was not readily accepted, not so much because of the variant elements in the system as because of the language obstacle. Because the immigrants did not know Spanish, they failed to understand the civil law system and in particular, the laws that were passed were neither known nor understood.[62]

However, it should be remembered that Stephen F. Austin had been empowered to administer justice and to preserve good order in the colony by virtue of the original colonization grant. Austin had been a student of the common law in the United States and observed the civil law during his sojourn in Mexico City. As a consequence, the court systems, methods of procedures and civil and criminal code that he set up were adopted in an eclectic manner from the two systems.[63]

In 1827, the colonists sought remedies to the civil law system so that there would be more conformity with the familiar

[61]H. C. Black, *Black's Law Dictionary* (3. ed., St. Paul: West Publishing Co., 1933), p. 332, "civil law." (Hereafter cited *Black's Law Dictionary.*)

[62]E. Markham, 29 *Texas Law Review* 904.

[63]Gilmer, 12 *Texas Law Review* 435.

common law system of trial by jury. The constitution of the State of Coahuila-Texas in 1827 stated:

> One of the main objects of attention of Congress shall be to establish the trial by jury in criminal cases, to extend and even to adopt it in civil cases in proportion as the value of this valuable institution becomes practically known.[64]

It seems that this expressed intention never reached a concrete state while Texas was under Mexico. This can be easily understood since the jurists were Mexicans who had not much appreciation for the jury system whereas the constitutional enactment was made by politicians who did not understand the status of the question.[65]

The Republic of Texas sought the adoption of the common law in so far as "applicable to the situation of the Republic and in so far as it is not inconsistent with this constitution."[66] In 1840, legislation was passed that made this article of the constitution effective. The law read:

> An Act to adopt the Common Law . . . to repeal certain Mexican laws . . .
>
> Section 1: Be it enacted . . . that the Common Law of England (insofar as it is not inconsistent with the constitution or the Acts of Congress now in force) shall, together with such acts be the rule of decision in this Republic, and shall continue in full force until altered by or repealed by Congress.
>
> Section 2: . . . that all laws in force in this Republic, prior to the 1st of September, one thousand eight hundred and thirty-six (except . . . such laws as relate exclusively to grants and the colonization of lands in the State of Coahuila and Texas and . . . to the reservation of Islands and lands, . . .) be, and the same are hereby repealed.[67]

Later, the Congress of the Republic adopted the civil law on

[64] 1 Gammel 449.

[65] E. Markham, 29 *Texas Law Review* 904.

[66] *Constitution of 1836,* Article 4, section 13, 1 Gammel 1074.

[67] 2 Gammel 262.

petition and pleading in order to avoid the inequities contained in the formalized system then prevalent in the Common Law. Further, the law of marriages and community rights in marriage were enacted in accordance with the civil law. The lack of distinction between law and equity that prevailed in the civil law was made a part of the legal system of Texas in order that the judiciary would have broad powers to administer justice.[68]

This adoption of the common law by the Congress was not such that the value of the civil law was lost to the courts of Texas. The Supreme Court was composed of Justices who knew the common law and some who were cognizant of both the common law and the civil law. In consequence, the court tended to put into practice the usages of both law, with the common law predominating. In doing this, the Supreme Court adopted an ecleticism and chose the best substantive and adjective law they judged fit for the prevailing conditions in Texas without completely accepting or rejecting the common law or the civil law.[69]

Chief Justice Hemphill, one of the greatest jurists of Texas, had high esteem for the civil law and stated that:

> The rules of the Spanish Monarch, whether we consider the sound philosophy on which they are founded, or their intrinsic equity, would, to say the very least, not suffer in comparison with those in the common law, and are Sanctioned by judicial wisdom and authority.[70]

This esteem was not mutually shared by all the jurists of his day.

Because of the prevalence of the common law system, the famous principle of *"stare decisis"* became a part of the jurisprudential system of Texas. This principle means that the court stands by decided cases and maintains former adjudications as a rule for judging cases.[71]

> The doctrine rests upon the principle that law by which

---

[68] *Loc. cit.;* Cf. E. Markham, 29 *Texas Law Review* 904.

[69] E. Markham, 29 *Texas Law Review* 904.

[70] Means v. Robinson, 7 Texas 502 (1852).

[71] Benavides v. Garcia, 290 S.W. 739 (Com. App., 1927).

> men are governed should be fixed, definite, and known, and that, when the law is declared by a court of competent jurisdiction authorized to construe it, such declaration, in absence of palpable mistake or error, is itself evidence of the law until changed by competent authority.[72]

The Common Law which was adopted in Texas was declared to be that as held in England but as applicable to the local situation.[73] One court stated that the common law adopted was "that system as practiced by the several states of the United States; that is, that law in force in the United States of America at the time of the statutory provision."[74] In other words, at the time of adoption, the State did not intend to distinguish between the enactments of the legislature and that body of principles and rules of action, which derive their authority solely from usage and custom of immemorial antiquity, or from the judgments and decrees of the courts.[75] The law of Texas therefore, consists of those legislative acts now in force and the decisions of cases given by the courts of Texas.

Section 3. Attitude towards Religion

A. Documental History

The variant political-religious philosophy of the peoples of Mexico and those of Texas as regards religion is evidenced by the following:

> a) The Mexican Constitution of 1824, Article 3:
> The religion of the Mexican nation is and shall perpetually remain the Roman Catholic and Apostolic, which the nation protects by just and wise laws and prohibits the exercise of every other.[76]
>
> b) The Declaration of Rights of the Republic of Texas, 1836, Third: No preference shall be given by law to any religious denomination or mode of worship over another,

[72]Black's Law Dictionary, p. 1651, *"stare decisis."*

[73]Ford W. Hall, "An Account of the Adoption of the Common Law of Texas," 28 *Texas Law Review* 801 (1950).

[74]Grigsby v. Reib, 105 Tex. 597, 153 S.W. 1124 (1913).

[75]Cf. *Black's Law Dictionary*, p. 368, "common law."

[76]1 Gammel 72.

> but every person shall be permitted to worship according to the dictates of his own conscience.[77]

The Republic of Texas did not reject the Catholic religion by this declaration of the rights of its citizens, but the Republic was expressing the view that the people of Texas, as a united whole, did not recognize any one religion as being the true religion. Nor does this declaration mean that the people of Texas recognizes all religious as equally true. The government merely desires that all religions be equal before it since it does not desire to tread into theology where it considers that it has no right to tread. It may be said that the state is merely granting equality in the interests of its own secular end, which, as St. Thomas has said, is the *unitas pacis* (unity of peace), which ultimately is the common temporal good.[78]

While the above statements concerning the intention of the peoples of Texas in making the Declaration of Rights are true in retrospect, the Declaration of Independence is definitely antagonistic in spirit to the Catholic religion. It has been said that the antagonism evidenced therein is more the result of a desire to give a moral cause to the revolution rather than to assert factual antagonism.[79]

However, it must be admitted that the close union of the Church and the State under the Mexican government, although not desired by the Church, led the people of Texas to feel that the Church was a partner to the actions of the government. They naturally failed to distinguish the Church from the government which feigned to protect and promote the Church. Therefore, the Declaration of Independence devoted three separate phrases to declare that religion was a cause of the revolution. The introduction claims that "every interest has been disregarded but that of the army and the priesthood." Later the Declaration maintained that there is left only "the cruel alter-

[77] 1 Gammel 1082.

[78] Jorge R. Coquia, *Legal Status of the Church in the Philippines* (Washington, D.C.: The Catholic University of America Press, 1950), p. 40.

[79] Fitzmorris, p. 57.

native either to abandon our homes, acquired by so many privations or submit to the most intolerable of all tyranny, the combined depotism of the sword and the priesthood." Finally, the Declaration asserted that "It (the government) denies us the right of worshipping the Almighty according to the dictates of our own conscience, by the support of a national religion calculated to promote the temporal interests of its human functionaries."[80]

Undoubtedly some of the colonists harbored sentiments similar to these but if they did, the sentiments were without foundation in fact. Perhaps resentment could have been present in the hearts of those who became Catholics in order to protect their property rights and not of their free will. However, there could have been no truth to the charge that the priests were despots for there were no priests to be despots. Getty asserts that there were few priests in colonial Texas and that the coming of a priest to a colony was one of the most pleasurable and exciting events in the lives of the colonists. He also observes that the mass marriages and baptisms performed by "Father" Muldoon were not forced but the vibrant personality of the man induced the people to accept the faith. A colonist, John Linn, is cited to confirm this sentiment when he says that not one in ten of the colonists were Catholics and there were no efforts made to secure the forcible subscription to the tenets of the Church.[81]

Either because the true situation has come to light or because of political reasons, the Inscription on the San Jacinto Monument erected in 1936, the centenary of the Declaration of Independence, reads as follows:

> The early policies of Mexico toward her Texan Colonists had been extremely liberal. Large grants of land were made to them and no taxes or duties imposed. The relationship between the Anglo-Americans and Mexicans was cordial. But following a series of revolutions begun in 1829, unscrupulous rulers successfully seized power in Mexico.

---

[80] 1 Gammel 1063.

[81] Getty, pp. 32 ff; pp. 106 ff.

Their unjust acts and despotic decrees led to the Revolution in Texas.

This seems a more accurate presentation of the causes of the revolution. From the history that has been presented, Catholics had a sufficient cause to seek to be freed from the domination of the Mexican government.

The Bill of Rights not only assured all of religious toleration but certain privileges were to be accorded ministers. The Constitution of 1836 states that:

> Ministers of the gospel being, by their profession dedicated to God and to the care of souls, ought not to be diverted from the great duties of their functions: therefore, no minister of the gospel or priest of any denomination whatever, shall be eligible to the office of the executive of the republic; nor to a seat in either branch of the congress of the same. . . .[82]

The Republic did not consider itself as showing any preference for religion when the property rights of the Catholic Church were acknowledged. The grant reads:

> That the churches at San Antonio, Goliad, Victoria, the church lot at Nacogdoches, the Churches at the missions of Concepcion, San Jose, San Juan Espada, and to the mission of Refugio, with outbuildings and lots, if any, belonging to them, be, and they are hereby acknowledged and declared, the property of the present chief pastor of the Roman Catholic Church in the Republic of Texas, and his successors in office, in trust forever, for the use and benefit of the congregations residing near the same, or who may hereafter reside near the same, for religious purposes and purposes of education and none other: provided, that nothing herein contained shall be construed as to give title to any lands, except the lots upon which the churches are situated, which shall not exceed fifteen acres.[83]

The Constitution of the State of Texas has undergone

[82] 1 Gammel 1075.

[83] 2 Gammel 492; 2 Gammel 496 gives the grant for the Alamo in similar words.

changes in view of the fact that the government has varied. The Constitution of 1836 was substituted by the Constitution of 1845. A Constitution was made for the State while in the Confederacy from 1861-1865. A new amended Constitution was adopted in 1867 with the fall of the Confederacy. This Reconstruction Constitution met with general disdain on the part of the people. With the passing of the Reconstruction era, a new Constitution was made and adopted in 1876 that remains today.[84]

The Constitution of the State of Texas illustrates a reverence for God with a consequent concern for the religious beliefs of its citizens. The Preamble to the Constitution states:

> Humbly invoking the blessings of Almighty God, the people of the State of Texas, do ordain and establish this constitution.

Subsequent Articles of the Bill of Rights assert:

> 1st, that no religious test is to be required for the holding of any office of public trust in the State and that no one is to be excluded from office on account of his religious sentiments, provided he acknowledge the existence of a Supreme Being.[85]
>
> 2nd, that witnesses are not disqualified because of their religious beliefs or lack of religious belief.[86]
>
> 3rd, that all men have a natural and indefeasible right to worship God according to the dictates of their own consciences. No man shall be compelled to attend, erect or support any place of worship, or to maintain any ministry against his consent. No human authority ought, in any case whatever, to control or interfere with the rights of conscience in matters of religion, and no preference shall ever be given by law to any religious society or mode of worship. But it shall be the duty of the legislature to pass

[84]*Vernon's Annotated Constitution of the State of Texas* (3 vols., Kansas City, Mo.: Vernon's Law Book Co., 1955), I, pp. i ff. (Hereafter citations from the Constitution of Texas will be indicated by Article and Section only.)

[85]Article I, section 4.

[86]*Ibidem,* section 5.

> such laws as may be necessary to protect equally every religious denomination in the peaceful enjoyment of its own mode of public worship.[87]
>
> 4th, that no money shall be appropriated, or drawn from the Treasury for the benefit of any sect, or religious society, theological or religious seminary; nor shall property belonging to the State be appropriated for any such purposes.[88]

These various sections of the documental history of Texas indicate the attitude of the government towards religion. Through the many changes in the governmental system, from the Republic to the State, from a State of the United States to a State of the Confederacy and after returning to the Union, the documental history consistently maintained a non-committal attitude towards religion. However, a general attitude of respect and reverence permeates these same documents. The judicial interpretation of this documental history and the judicial recognition given to religion remains to be treated.

B. Judicial Approach to Religion

The courts of the State have been meticulous in observing the precepts of the Constitution and the acts of the legislature concerning religious societies. The subsequent chapters concerning the acquisition of church property, its administration and taxation will illustrate the strict approach followed by the courts with regards to religious societies. This section presents the divisions that the courts have made of religious societies and the extent to which the court will interfere in the internal affairs of the religious societies.

Judicial recognition has been given to the fact that there are three forms of religious societies existing in the State of Texas. The three forms are: the prelatial form, Presbyterian (assembly) form, and the congregational form.[89] These forms are given

---

[87]*Ibidem,* section 6.

[88]*Ibidem,* section 7.

[89]Paul Martin, "Property Rights Among Factions in Independent Churches," 7 *Baylor Law Review* 425 (1955) (Baylor University publication of the School of Law: Waco, Texas.)

judicial recognition in other jurisdictions in the United States.[90]

The most common form is the congregational form wherein each church or religious society is independent of the whole group and is, in effect, without superiors.[91] The presbyterian system has a local church as a member of a larger organization and under its government and control, but the members function as a group in that the general assembly acts as a legislative, executive and judicial body.[92] Finally, there is the hierarchical system in which the episcopacy is over the whole body and possesses large powers respecting the temporal as well as the spiritual affairs of the church, with subordinate ministers under the office of the bishop.[93]

The law provides for the incorporation of these religious societies. When the religious society does incorporate, it is considered as a creature of civil law. This is in accord with the common law principle of England, that has consistently held that there can be no corporation which is not the creation of the civil law, and that all tenure of property requires civil authority.[94] Further treatment of religious societies as corporations will be given in the following chapter. It should be noted here that although the society may incorporate, the membership of the religious society is not reduced to the plane of membership in other voluntary societies.

---

[90] John J. McGrath, "Canon Law and American Church Law, A Comparative Study," *The Jurist* (Washington, D.C., 1941-—), XVIII (1958) 260-278; Cf. Watson v. Jones, 80 U.S. 679, 20 L. Ed. 666 (1871). (Hereafter cited McGrath.)

[91] Kelly v. Curry, 15 S.W. 2d 109 (1930); Fort v. 1st Baptist Church of Paris, 55 S.W. 402 (Civ. App.) modified 93 Tex. 215, 54 S.W. 892, 49 L.R.A. 617 (1898).

[92] Brown v. Clark, 108 S.W. 421 (Civ. App.) reversed on other grounds 102 Tex. 323, 116 S.W. 360, 29 L.R.A. (N.S.) 670 (1909); Methodist Episcopal Church v. Roach, (Civ. App. 1935) 51 S.W. 2d 1100.

[93] Blanc v. Asbury, 63 Tex. 489, 51 Am. Rep. 666 (1885); Gabert v. Olcott, 22 S.W. 286 reversed in 23 S.W. 985 (1893).

[94] Dignan, *A History of the Legal Incorporation of Catholic Church Property in the United States,* (1784-1932) (New York: Kenedy, 1935), p. 50.

The courts consider membership in religious societies to create a relationship that is on a higher plane than in other voluntary societies.[95] When one willingly becomes a member of a voluntary religious association, he subscribes to all of its rules and regulations, and consents to the exercise of such powers as are conferred on its officers.[96] This is to say that membership in a religious association is a compact between the members so that the constitution of the religious society is the expression of the terms of the contract. However, because of the nature of this relationship, civil tribunals will not interfere with the internal policies of religious organizations. Each society or body is left free to settle its own problems unless some valuable property right is involved.[97]

The courts have asserted that to interfere in internal matters would be a violation of the constitutional rights of the members. Judge Pleasants stated:

> If the courts assume jurisdiction to question the validity of a judgment of a church court upon a question of this character (doctrinal), the churches would be deprived of the right of construing and administering their church law, and our proud boast of religious liberty and our absolute separation of Church and State could no longer be proclaimed.[98]

In fact, the First Amendment of the Constitution of the United States has been interpreted to forbid the state to interfere in the internal affairs of religious societies. This interpretation construes the First and the Fourteenth amendments together.[99]

It has been said that:

> There is, therefore, now no country in which not only

---

[95]Minton v. Leavell, 297 S.W. 615 (1927).

[96]Clark v. Brown, 108 S.W. 421 (Civ. App.) reversed on other grounds 102 Tex. 323, 116 S.W. 360, 29 L.R.A. (N.S.) 670 (1909).

[97]*Loc. cit.*

[98]Minton v. Leavell, 297 S.W. 615, (1927).

[99]Watson v. Jones, 80 U.S. 679, 20 L.Ed. 666 (1871); Nance v. Busby, 91 Tenn. 303, 18 S.W. 874 (1891).

> religious liberty in general, but the property of religious bodies in particular, is as secure as it is in the United States.[100]

This statement has particular force in Texas, it seems. It is evident that the position of religion in general, and of the Catholic Church in particular, is considerably more secure than it was under the regimes that preceded the Republic of Texas.

---

[100] C. Zollman, American Church Law (St. Paul: West Publishing Co., 1933) p. 7. (Hereafter cited Zollman.)

CHAPTER II

LEGAL STATUS OF THE CHURCH IN TEXAS

The Catholic Church in the State of Texas is recognized as a voluntary association of people for a religious end. However, Texas follows the common law doctrine that there can be no tenure of property by a religious society without proper civil authority. Therefore, the question arises as to the legal capacity of the Catholic Church to acquire, hold and administer property in the State of Texas. The courts stated that "the Roman Catholic religion was reduced from the high privilege of being the only national church, to a level and an equality with every other denomination."[1] But the same court recognized the legal capacity of the Catholic Church to acquire, hold, and administer property. In this comparative study, it is important to understand the historical acceptance of the Church by civil powers.

ARTICLE I. HISTORICAL ACCEPTANCE OF THE CATHOLIC CHURCH

The Catholic Church is a divine institution that has received legal capacity from God Himself. This legal capacity has been given to the Church so that it may make use of those temporalities which are necessary for the fulfillment of its end, namely, the salvation and sanctification of men. It would not be possible for the ministers of the Church to sanctify the people, to rule and to teach them without material means. Because of this need, the Church has asserted its native right to acquire, hold and administer temporalities for these purposes independently of the power of the state.[2] The universal Church does not propose to acquire, hold and administer the temporalities necessary for the successful accomplishment of the ends of the individual

[1] Blair v. Odin (1848) 3 Tex. 288.

[2] Canon 1495, §1.

parts of the Church. However, the individual parts possess legal capacity to acquire, hold and administer temporalities by virtue of being established by the universal Church.[3]

At times, the desire to return to the pristine purity of the Gospel has led some into the error to deny that Christ would have permitted the use of temporalities by His Church. It has been denied that Christ and His Apostles had deigned to make use of material things. This misguided desire contradicts the facts for it is evident that Judas Iscariot was the treasurer for the small group with Christ, and as treasurer, he bought those things necessary for the group and distributed goods to the poor.[4] Similarly, the new-born Church held all things in common and the goods were distributed to those who had need.[5] Hence, while preserving the pristine purity of the gospel, the Church has made use of these temporalities which were necessary for the fulfillment of its end.

During the period of the persecution, it is certain that the Church held property, but it is debatable as to the manner in which this property was held. There are instances in which schismatics were ejected from property belonging to the Church. From this it is deduced that there was some recognition given to the legal capacity of the Church. It must be remembered that until the Edict of Milan under Constantine the Great (313), the Church as a religious society was illegal. However, during this same period, the Church received the offerings of the faithful and possessed property. From this it must be inferred that the Church was conscious, in some manner, of a legal capacity to acquire property independently of the Empire.[6]

During this period, some of the real property of the Church (the land and buildings) were held in the name of societies established to care for the needy or for the burial of their members. Other means of holding the property were in existence,

---

[3]Canon 1495, §2.

[4]John, XIII, 29.

[5]Acts, II, 44-45.

[6]Goodwine, *The Right of the Church to Acquire Temporal Goods,* The Catholic University of America Canon Law Studies, n. 131 (The Catholic University of America Press, 1941), p. 57 ff. (Hereafter cited as Goodwine.)

but these means have not been determined.[7] After dispossessing the Church in numerous persecutions, the Roman Empire had no success in exterminating christianity. The final persecution of Diocletian was the most complete and devastating. After this persecution, a change in policy was effected. The Edict of Milan ordered the restoration of property to the society of the christians and to "the churches." This Edict stands as a recognition of the fact that the Church had acquired, held and administered property independently of the Empire.[8]

Certain adversaries of the Church have declared that before the Edict of Milan, the Church had made no claim to temporalities. Both the local and general councils of the Church illustrate the inherent independent spirit of the ecclesiastical society. True enough, these councils are after the Edict, but the facts noted above sufficiently demonstrate that the Church possessed and administered property in the Empire. The decrees of the councils exhibit the perfectly sovereign attitude of the Church concerning the acquisition, possession and administration of the property.[9]

It is of historical interest to observe that the legal capacity of the Church did not present any difficulty to the jurisprudential system of the Roman Empire. Following the recognition of christianity by the Edict of Milan, the Roman law acknowledged the legal capacity of the Church as existing before the Edict itself. The Roman law seems to have understood that if the Church was to fulfill its divine mission, it must be permitted to have those means necessary to act in the world. Further, the Church was not hampered by the laws of the State.

---

[7] J. Abbo and J. Hannan, *The Sacred Canons* (2 vols., 2 ed., St. Louis: B. Herder Book Co., 1957) II, 705. (Hereafter cited as Abbo-Hannan.)

[8] Goodwine, p. 61.

[9] *Ibidem*, pp. 62-67: the canons of the councils relating to Church property are given consideration. These canons are to be found in councils preceding the twelfth century and relate to lay interference. It is made clear the property was considered necessary for the purposes of the Church. Therefore, rigorous restrictions were placed against alienation and lay interference.

The right to control its own affairs and the capacity to make laws concerning those affairs were immediately recognized. In effect, the Church was regarded as a sovereign juridic personality that had existed as such even before the Empire deigned to give recognition to the fact.[10]

This legal capacity of the Church to acquire, hold and administer property has been elucidated in the concept of moral personality. A moral person is a juridic entity constituted by an act of a competent authority, existing independently of other persons and endowed with capacity of acquiring and exercising rights as well as of contracting obligations, by the means and to the extent determined by the competent authority.[11] The concept of moral personality had begun to evolve in the classical law of the Roman empire together with the rights and specific types of such moral personalities.

The municipalities had attained a degree of juridical status that had been exclusively held by private persons in private law. The method by which this juridical recognition of municipalities was attained consisted in an application of those principles that regulated the acts and duties of the individual physical person to the municipality, with appropriate variations. Further development of this concept was made when the christian religion became the state religion and the Church itself was recognized as a moral person. The recognition of a species of moral personality in physical entities, distinct from individual persons, such as churches, property, and funds which were the subjects of rights and obligations assumed importance. These physical entities came to be called non-collegiate moral persons; whereas groups of persons that were the subjects of rights and obligations, distinct from the individual persons, came to be called collegiate moral persons.[12]

---

[10]Brendan Brown, *The Canonical Juristic Personality with Special Reference to Its Status in the United States of America,* The Catholic University of America Canon Law Studies, n. 39 (Washington, D.C.: The Catholic University of America, 1927), pp. 10-33. (Hereafter cited as Brown.)

[11]Abbo-Hannan, I, 143-144.

[12]Brown, pp. 10-32.

It is not to be denied that where the State recognizes these rights of the Church, the faithful will more generously contribute to the needs of the Church. For that reason, during the centuries of this freedom to acquire and hold property, the Church acquired vast holdings which it did not readily relinquish. With the acquisition of property, the Church assumed many obligations according to the intentions of the donors or because of charitable obligations to be met in society. In the 13th century a reaction set in against this tendency of the Church to accumulate property. *Mortmain* statutes were enacted that prevented the conveyance of lands to the Church.[13]

Numerous heresies arose at this time to increase the popular sentiment against the rights of the Church to hold property. These heresies attempted to give a philosophic or dogmatic bases for the actions of the State against church property. The errors of Arnold of Brescia (1090-1155), of the Waldenses (1210), of Marsilius of Padua (1327), and of Wycliffe of England (1328-1384) were the objects of condemnations. These errors denied the right of the Church to any property. Marsilius of Padua was especially adept at falsely interpreting scriptures. His contention was that the Pope had usurped powers of government and the Church possessed no rights to property without authorization from the civil power.[14] Wycliffe went so far as to assert that Christ Himself forbid the acquisition of temporal goods.[15] Ultimately, the contest between the State and the Church on this right of the Church to acquire property was decided in favor of the State by force of the Protestant revolt that culminated the movement of the heresies. During this period, wholesale expropriations of church property was made in practically every country, so that the Church not only lost

---

[13]Abbo-Hannan, II, 705.

[14]Mathaeus Conte a Coronata, *Institutiones Iuris Canonici ad usum utriusque cleri et scholarum* (5 vols., 3. ed., Taurini-Romae: Marietti, 1947-1951) Vol. II, *De Rebus*, 4 ed., 1951, n. 41, p. 50. (Hereafter cited as Coronata.)

[15]J. E. Mundy, *Ecclesiastical Property in Australia and New Zealand*, Catholic University Canon Law Studies, n. 387 (Washington, D.C.: The Catholic University of America Press, 1957), p. 3.

the unimpeded right to acquire property, but also the right to hold and administer property for those needs proper to itself.[16]

It has been said that prior to the Protestant Revolt, the ideal position of the church in respect to its own legal personality and the ownership of property arose. This position has been described as follows:

> The Church Universal is a moral person by Divine Right. She has the inalienable right to establish inferior moral personalities as efficient mediums for the fulfillment of her divine mission, as effective instruments, therefore, for the accomplishment of all those ends, whether spiritual or temporal, which contribute to the accomplishment of the purpose divinely ordained. . . . The Bishops as successors of the Apostles represented the Church Universal in their respective dioceses. With the spread of the Church, therefore, and the erection of bishropics, there arose immediately dioceses whose jurisdictional essence from the very beginning consisted in this: that the territory and the faithful living in that territory were subject to the Bishop. But the geographical division of the ecclesiastical territory was merely a matter of feasibility and had nothing to do with the juridical character of the bishopric, which sprang, rather from the fact that it constituted the domain where the Bishop exercised his episcopal duties. Nor did the existence of the faithful constitute the material element of the juristic personality of the diocese. . . . The diocese was the first instance of the ecclesiastical juristic person. There followed other forms, as the parish, the cathedral chapter, the *mensa episcopalis,* but these derived their personality from the position which they occupied toward the Bishop. The system of ecclesiastical juristic personality was, therefore, greatly extended with the further growth of Christianity. Parishes arose and these, too, became complete juristic entities with capacity to exercise all necessary corporate rights. They were actually legal personalities in the strict sense, distinct from the Cathedral Church, yet obtaining their person-

[16]Abbo-Hannan, II, 705

ality by virtue of the ecclesiastical relation to the Cathedral Church.[17]

The recognition of the Church as a moral person and the evolution of this concept continued through the 14th and 15th centuries. The rights of the Church before the Protestant revolt were at times threatened but political recognition of the moral personality of the Church perdured. However, in the era that followed the Protestant Revolt, the prohibition to acquire property became more rigorous. Finally, every religious corporation and establishment required the approval and authorization of the civil powers in order to be recognized as possessing juridical personality.[18]

The doctrines of Richerianism and Febronianism led to the logical conclusion that the Church had no right to any legal capacity independently of the authorization of the civil power. Hence it has been said that:

> The legal basis for this teaching was the concept that the Church received its juridical personality from the civil law of the land. As this doctrine spread and as its effects became apparent it was met by the insistent teaching of the ecclesiastical authorities that the Catholic Church by its very nature was a perfect society and thus possessed a legitimate and natural right to property. Local councils and concordats between the Holy See and various governments clarified and made more effective the Catholic doctrine, emphatically insisting upon the inherent character of the right to acquire and its complete independence from the State.[19]

The effect of the erroneous doctrines promulgated since the 13th century have greatly affected the Church-State relations of continental Europe. A study of the many concordats made

---

[17]*Mode of Tenure, Roman Catholic Church Property in the United States,* A Survey by the Legal Department, National Catholic Welfare Conference (Washington, D.C.: National Catholic Welfare Conference, 1941; Supplement, 1954) Supplement, p. 4. (Hereafter cited as *Mode of Tenure,* Survey or *Mode of Tenure,* Supplement.)

[18]Goodwine, p. 80.

[19]*Ibidem,* p. 81.

between the Church and the respective European countries in the last two centuries has shown that in general, the nations would enter into contractual relations to respect certain rights of the Church in exchange for a relinquishment of certain privileges by the Church. At times, the Church conceded long established rights. However, these concordats generally failed because of a breach of trust by the nations. It seems that the condition of the Church is more stable today than it has been for the past few centuries in the non-Communist European countries.[20]

No concordats have been entered into with Anglo-American governments and the common law is the source for determining the legal status of the Church. The doctrines concerning the legal status, the moral personality, of the Church that has been prevalent on the continent, were also found in England. The doctrine that there can be no moral personality that is not the creation of the State and that all tenure of property requires civil authority was also a part of the English common law.[21] The English common law had conceived of the corporation sole whereby the bishop, pastor or other ecclesiastical dignity was the juridical personality with his rights and liabilities passing to his successors in office, rather than to his heirs, executors or administrators. The purpose was to give them some legal capacities and advantages, particularly that of perpetuity, which in their natural persons they could not have had.[22]

Therefore, today it can be said that the Church's claim to temporalities in order to fulfill the purposes for which it is established is accorded recognition in non-Communist countries. The theory that is the basis for non-recognition of any juridical person not created by the State has been a restrictive force on the rights of the Church.

---

[20]Goodwine, pp. 82-98: E.g., France entered concordats often, the last being made in 1906, but soon broken, so that in 1906, Pope St. Pius X spoke out vehemently against the actions of the French. No new concordat has been made.

[21]Dignan, p. 50.

[22]*Black's Law Dictionary*, p. 440, "corporation."

Article II. Church Law on Moral Persons

From the foregoing section, it is clear that the Catholic Church has considered itself a juridical entity apart from any action of the State. In canon 100, it is stated that there are two moral persons that exist by divine institution. They are the Catholic Church, established on earth by Jesus Christ, true God, and the Apostolic See, established by the same divine authority. Subordinate moral persons are constituted by ecclesiastical law for religious or charitable purposes in two ways: by provision of law and by special decree.

Section 1. Nature of Moral Persons

What is called a moral person in church law is termed a corporation in the law of the State. A moral person has been defined as a juridic entity constituted by an act of a competent authority, existing independently of other persons and endowed with the capacity of acquiring and exercising rights as well as of contracting obligations, by the means and to the extent determined by competent authority.[23]

This definition of moral personality is identifiable with the following definition of a corporation except in so far as the determination of the subject that can be incorporated and the competent power to incorporate:

> A corporation is an artificial person or legal entity created by or under the authority of the laws of a state or nation, composed, in some rare instances, of a single person and his successors, being the incumbents of a particular office, but ordinarily consisting of an association of numerous individuals, who subsist as a body politic under a special denomination, which is regarded in law as having a personality and existence distinct from that of its several members, and which is, by the same authority, vested with the capacity of continuous succession, irrespective of changes in its membership, either in perpetuity or for a limited term of years, and of acting as a unit or single

[23]Abbo-Hannan, I, 144; T. Bouscaren and Adam Ellis, *Canon Law, A Text and Commentary,* 3 ed. (Milwaukee: The Bruce Publishing Co., 1957), pp. 86-87. (Hereafter cited as Bouscaren.)

> individual in matters relating to the common purpose of the association, within the scope of the powers and authorities conferred upon such bodies by law.[24]

The ecclesiastical juridical entity can be either a group of natural physical persons or of property and resources, which are separated from the ownership and control of other persons and dedicated to some religious or charitable purpose. The corporation concept does not admit of the non-collegiate juridical entity.[25]

The nature of the moral person or corporation is made clear when the material and formal elements, as well as the purpose and the means, are evident. The material element is the plurality of persons or the endowment of goods, although in the latter case there is an implication of the cooperation of physical persons to administer and benefit from the same. The formal element constituting the moral person is the act of the public authority which gives it existence before the law which may be either a divine, ecclesiastical, or civil act. The purpose of a moral person in the Church must always be either religious or charitable in order that the moral person may participate in some way in the very reason for which the Church was founded and exists. The purpose of a corporation at civil law may be any purpose within the competence of the civil power. The means to accomplish the purpose of the moral person may not exist in fact, but must be in potential existence.[26]

The capacity for ownership of property, and the capacity to sue and to be sued are two distinctive characteristics of moral personalities. Whenever the law attributes either of these attributes to a class of ecclesiastical entities, it implicitly declares the entities of that class to be moral personalities.[27] How-

---

[24]*Black's Law Dictionary,* p. 438, "corporation." Cf. Sovereign Camp v. Fraley, 94 Tex. 200, 59 S.W. 905, 51 L.R.A. 898, (1898).

[25]Cf. Canon 99 as commented on by Bouscaren, p. 86.

[26]Abbo-Hannan, I, 144; cf. *Black's Law Dictionary,* p. 438, "corporation."

[27]J. P. Murphy, *The Laws of the State of New York Affecting Church Property,* Catholic University of America Canon Law Studies, n. 388,

ever, moral personalities do exist which possess only one of the characteristics mentioned. Certain religious communities by force of their constitutions deny themselves the capacity to own property.[28] The universal Church actually possess no property. Canon 1495 declares that the Catholic Church, the universal church is meant, has full capacity for ownership of property. Canon 1499 states that "Under the supreme authority of the Apostolic See, the ownership of property belongs to that moral person which has legitimately acquired it." These words cannot be construed to mean that the universal Church owns property only through subordinate moral persons by necessity. The fact is that the universal Church has placed few acts concerning property independently of the Apostolic See or another subordinated moral person in the Church.[29]

As to the power to sue and to be sued, this is exercised only through physical persons, either individuals or a group authorized to act for the moral person, since by nature, moral persons are incapable of acting for themselves.[30] At least one moral personality is not subject to suit since there is no competent judge before whom it can be sued. This is the Apostolic See.[31]

These essential elements of a moral person are to be found in every juridical personality. The State is a perfect society, that has its own distinct end, temporal beatitude, and the means within itself to attain its end. Therefore, the material element is the union of families, the purpose is the attainment of temporal happiness for its members, the means are the systems of control set up by the legislature, the executive and the judicial branches of the government. The origin of the State is to be found in the natural law by which man is of necessity ordained to live in a society.[32]

(Washington, D.C.: Catholic University of America Press, 1957) p. 22. (Hereafter cited as Murphy.)

[28]Canons 531 and 582.

[29]Coronata, II, n. 1034, p. 450.

[30]Canon 100, §3, states that all moral persons are considered as "minors" before the law; Cf. Bouscaren, p. 87.

[31]Canon 1556.

[32]Coronata, II, n. 27, p. 32.

Section 2 Origin of Moral Persons in the Church

There are positive and definitive proofs to sustain the assertion that the Church was established by Christ. These proofs rest upon revelation as presented in Sacred Scripture and Tradition, wherein it is evident that Christ founded His Church upon Peter, the Prince of the Apostles. These proofs demonstrate that the Church is a visible society with all the means, both spiritual and temporal, to attain its end.[33]

Because of the rejection of the Church as a juridic person by some who reject the supernatural or the proofs adduced from revelation, Catholic authors have developed an argument from the natural law by considering the Church as a human society. It is clear that the Church is a human society but it is not true to consider the Church as a mere human society, both in origin and in composition of members. Consequently, this argument limps from incompleteness in the beginning. Yet, there is some validity and the argument is worth repeating.[34]

Fundamentally, the argument proceeds from the principle that the natural law gives men the right to form associations or societies whose purpose it is to obtain a legitimate end by honest means. This right of men flows from individual liberty and from the necessities of human nature. What are the particular necessities that compel the individual to form these societies, and how far they induce men to live his life in the company of his fellowmen can be determined from the various existing societies into which men have entered. Among these societies, the most evident are the State and the Church. Therefore, both the State and the Church have the right to exist by force of the natural law. This argument will not lead to the conclusion that the religious society is independent of the control of the State, but the right to existence and to an exercise of those rights necessary for its sustenance can be sustained.[35] Thus, Pope Leo XIII said:

---

[33]Cf. Goodwine, pp. 6-27.

[34]*Ibidem*, pp. 28-38.

[35]*Loc. cit.*

> Particular societies, although they exist within the State, nevertheless cannot be prohibited by the State, absolutely and as such. For to enter into a society of this kind is the natural right of man; and the State must protect natural rights, not destroy them; and if it forbids its citizens to form associations it contradicts the very principle of its own existence; for they and it exist in virtue of the same principle, viz., the natural propensity of man to live in society.[36]

However, not only does the Church assert that it has the power to establish subordinate moral personalities which are effective instruments of the Church, but this establishment is to be made independently of the power of the State. These subordinate moral personalities are necessary to the Church for the attainment of those ends for which God has established the Church.[37]

These subordinate moral personalities are imperfect juridical persons in that they depend upon the juridically perfect society in which they exist and by which they are established.[38] These moral personalities are founded for both spiritual and temporal purposes that contribute to the ultimate end of the Church, the sanctification and the salvation of souls. The Church provides for the constitution of these entities for religious or charitable purpose in two ways: by provision of law, and by special decree.[39] The significant words of the canon are *"ceterae inferiores personae morales in Ecclesia eam sortiuntur."* By these words the Church is asserting that the subordinate moral persons are dependent upon the Church and must be supported by it in the fulfillment of their particular end. Similarly, they

---

[36]Five Great Encyclicals (New York: Paulist Press, 1939), n. 37-38; litt. encycl. *Rerum Novarum,* May 15, 1891—*Codicis Iuris Canonici Fontes, cura Emi. Petri Card. Gasparri editi,* (9 vols., Romae postea Civitate Vaticana: Typis Polyglottis Vaticanis 1923-1939), III, n. 611, p. 373. (Hereafter cited as *Fontes.*)

[37]Canon 100, §1; Brown, p. 24.

[38]M. Conte a Coronata, *Institutiones Iuris Canonici, Introductio: Ius Publicum Ecclesiasticum* (Romae: Marietti, 1948), n. 22, p. 25. (Hereafter cited Coronata, *Ius Publicum.*)

[39]Canon 100.

are supported in the choice of and exercise of means to obtain that end. These subordinate moral persons have a share in the divine commission, and this implies absolute incompetency of the civil power in the creation of any ecclesiastical moral personality; therefore, these words demand the authority of the Church in order that an ecclesiastical moral person might exist.[40]

Section 3. Creation of Moral Persons

It has been shown that there are two moral persons that exist by divine institution, namely, the Catholic Church and the Apostolic See. The Apostolic See, in the canon declaring it a moral person, does not include the departments of the Roman Curia. Subordinate moral persons are established by Church law in two ways: by provision of law and by special decree.[41] By provision of law, in either express words or equivalently so, certain moral persons exist: the College of Cardinals,[42] the diocesan Curia,[43] the Roman Curia,[44] parishes,[45] dioceses,[46] churches,[47] ecclesiastical benefices,[48] seminaries,[49] universities of study,[50] and many others. It is important to remember that where ecclesiastical moral personalities exist other than by virtue of the law itself, they exist only by virtue of a positive act on the part of the proper authority. This is absolutely necessary so that an association in the Church that exists without this authority is not an ecclesiastical moral person. Associations are approved that are not established as ecclesiastical moral persons. The existence of these moral persons come by

[40]Brown, p. 91; Murphy, p. 18.

[41]Canon 100, §1.

[42]Canons 231 and 241.

[43]Canon 363.

[44]Canon 242.

[45]Canons 1208, §3 and 1209.

[46]Canon 215.

[47]Canons 99; 1423; 1495.

[48]Canons 99 and 1409.

[49]Canons 99 and 1354.

[50]Canon 1376.

force of the formal decree of establishment from the competent superior.[51]

Section 4. Termination of Moral Persons

A moral person is by nature perpetual but it expires if it is suppressed by lawful authority, or if it has been out of existence for one hundred years. If one member of a collegiate moral person survives, the rights of all are united in him.[52] The lawful authorities who can suppress the various moral persons are carefully enumerated in the law of the Church and in no case can a non-ecclesiastical power, such as a lay or civil power, effectively suppress an ecclesiastical moral person. Generally, the suppression of moral persons is reserved to the Holy See except for certain moral persons that were established by the local ordinary or one of his predecessor.[53]

The cessation of a moral person by force of the juridical fact that the personality's substratum has ceased to exist for one hundred years, takes effect at the completion of the time designated. It must be noted that the time begins to run for the non-collegiate moral person when the substratum of goods ceases to exist. This might occur when the property is entirely destroyed or is irrevocably removed from the owner's possession or the fund of money is totally expended. The time begins to run for the collegiate moral person only after the resignation or death of every member or by the voluntary act of dissolving itself.[54]

Article III. Religious Societies in the United States

The courts in the United States did not give general acceptance to the English device of the corporation sole. The tendency in this country was to regard all religious denominations as mere associations of individuals grouped together for the purpose of worship.[55] Subsequently, the legislatures of the constitutions of the several states enacted corporation statutes in

[51]Murphy, pp. 24-27.

[52]Canon 102.

[53]Murphy, pp. 28-30.

[54]*Ibidem,* pp. 31-32.

[55]Dignan, p. 51.

order that the various denominations would have juridic personality.

The predomination of the congregational form of church organization in which the control of church property was vested in the lay trustees or held by associations dominated by laymen, caused the corporation statutes to be limited in scope. The statutes permitted the formation of trustee corporations only. Therefore, many religious societies did not benefit from the statutes.[56] The Catholic Church attempted to adapt itself to this corporation concept in order to receive legal recognition. The adaption was not successful because the conscientious lay trustees did not adequately distinguish between their duties before the civil law and those before the church law. The lay trustees assumed powers over ecclesiastical matters that were not intended by reason of their civil trusteeship. As a result, the abuses led the Church to put strict prohibitions upon the interference by laymen in the administration of church property.[57]

Section 1. Types of Religious Corporations Developed

The early practice of the several States to concede legal status to religious societies by the formation of corporations was not accepted by all states. Some states adopted a trust system; some few gave no recognition to the peculiar needs of religious societies. Zollman enumerates five distinct forms of corporations that have existed in the several States. In the beginning, there was the territorial parish which was a governmental instrumentality in those colonies that had established churches. These territorial parishes disappeared when the established churches were abolished.

With the passing of the territorial parish, three types of corporations were introduced. The membership corporation was

---

[56]Zollman, p. 103.

[57]Cf. *Concilii Plenarii Baltimorensis II, In Ecclesia Metropolitana Baltimoriensi Habiti, Acts et Decreta* (Baltimorae: Joaness Murphy, 1868), Decrees nn. 182-188, pp. 111-113, where a clear and complete statement of the Church's rights and privileges regarding tenure and administration of property is made. (Hereafter cited as II Plenary Council.)

the most common. This is a corporation aggregate with the members as incorporators. The corporation is to provide for the election, government and removal of trustees created to fill the needs of a congregational type of religious body. The next type was the trustee corporation. In this type, the body of trustees were the corporation so that the religious society had legal status in that body. The final type was the corporation sole. In this corporation, one person becomes the corporation and assumes the rights and obligations of the religious society. The corporation does not cease with the death of the office holder in whom the corporation exists but his successor in the particular office becomes the corporation.

The final form of corporation that has arisen in the territory of the United States is the Roman Catholic Church, according to Zollman. In fact, the United States merely abided by its treaty with Spain after the war of 1898. In that treaty, recognition was to be accorded to the Catholic Church in the same manner that it was recognized juridically while subject to Spain.[58]

The development of these corporation statutes covered many years and in some instances, many judicial and legislative struggles. After the States came to understand more of the organization of the Catholic Church and the requisites of that organization, appropriate legislation was passed to permit the proper functioning of the organization of the Catholic Church. Therefore, after the Catholic Church had conquered the evils of lay trusteeism both in the civil and ecclesiastical courts, certain jurisdictions began to pass favorable legislation for the benefit of the Catholic Church. This has led to the present methods by which the Church exercises its rights.

Section 2. Present Modes of Tenure in the United States

A recent study of the methods by which the many dioceses

---

[58]Zollman, pp. 102-129; Santos v. Holy Roman Catholic And Apostolic Church (1908), 212 U.S. 463, 29 S.Ct. 338, 53 L. Ed. 599; Ponce v. Roman Catholic Apostolic Church in Puerto Rico, 210 U.S. 296, 28 S.Ct. 737, 52 L. Ed. 1068, (1908); Barlin v. Ramirez, 7 Philippines 41, (1906).

in the United States have legal capacity to acquire, hold and administer property has enumerated four methods. These are:

> 1) The parochial or diocesan corporation that exists by virtue of statute, originated in New York and is now found, with some variations in at least sixteen jurisdictions.
>
> 2) The corporation sole, which exists by statute and also by common law and in general follows the common law concept, is found in about twenty jurisdictions.
>
> 3) The Ordinary as trustee holding the property in trust for religious uses is found where incorporation is not possible or is inadvisable. This exists by judicial construction.
>
> 4) The Ordinary as owner in fee simple without a trust exists in Virginia, West Virginia and Kansas, which states recognize none of the above as permissible to religious societies.[59]

A. Corporation Sole

In those jurisdictions upholding the corporation sole, the Ordinary is declared to be a corporation in himself, and holds property in that capacity for himself and his successors in office. The Church is considered as such a corporation by statute or by the courts which follow the common law of England. Statutes may designate the Church as a corporation in the person of the Ordinary, or the bishop or a similar chief officer in other religious societies, may be permitted to become a corporation sole. This method is preferred to the mere fee simple method and is at present generally adequate in those jurisdictions where it exists. The vesting of title in some jurisdictions is a source of difficulty. When the church officer that constitutes the corporation sole dies, the title to church property vests in no one until his successor is appointed. Therefore, proper ad-

[59]*Mode of Tenure,* Supplement, p. 6; Cf. *Canon Law Digest, The* ed., by T. Lincoln Bouscaren, 4 vols. (Milwaukee: Bruce Publishing Co., 1934-1957), II, canon 1499, p. 443. The Sacred Congregation of the Council in a decree dated July 29, 1911 expressed a preference for the first method, a toleration of the second method, and abolition of the fourth. The third method was not considered. (Hereafter cited as Digest.)

ministration is gravely hindered. Other jurisdictions permit the vesting of title to church property in the administrator of the diocese or a comparable official immediately after the death, resignation or removal of the church officer who constitutes the corporation sole.[60]

B. The Corporation Aggregate

The corporation aggregate is composed of a number of individuals vested with corporate powers. When general and popular legal speech treats of a corporation, the corporation aggregate is usually intended.[61]

In 1911 the Sacred Congregation of the Council was petitioned by the American bishops to give directions for the holding of church goods in this country. After obtaining the opinions of the archbishops in the country through the apostolic delegate, the congregation laid down the following norms on July 29:

> 1. Among the methods which are now in use in the United States for holding and administering church property, the one known as *Parish Corporations* is preferable to the others, but with the conditions and safeguards which are now in use in the State of New York. The bishops therefore should immediately take steps to introduce this method for the handling of property in their dioceses, if the civil law allows it. If the civil law does not allow it, they should exert their influence with the civil authorities that it may be made legal as soon as possible.
>
> 2. Only in those places where the civil law does not recognize *Parish Corporations,* and until such recognition is obtained, the method commonly called *Corporation Sole* is allowed, but with the understanding that in the administration of ecclesiastical property the Bishop is to act with the advice, and in more important matters with the consent, of those who have an interest in the premises and of the diocesan consultors, this being a conscientious obligation for the Bishop in person.

---

[60] *Ibidem,* p. 9.

[61] *Black's Law Dictionary,* p. 438, "corporation."

3. The method called *in fee simple* is to be entirely abandoned[62]

1. The Corporation Aggregate: The New York Plan

There is no method of holding property in United States law which is in perfect conformity with all the regulations of canon law. However, of the various modes available to the Church in this country, that called the *Parish Corporation* has been officially declared to be the most preferable. This method is a type of aggregate corporation. An aggregate corporation is defined by Brown as "a juridical person incorporating the members of a parish or a congregation."[63] Various aggregate corporations, however, will differ in the manner established for the management of the corporation. The aggregate incorporation of a parish or congregation makes each individual of the parish or corporation a member of the corporation, even though the names of only a very few members are included in the articles of incorporation. Thus, *de iure,* "the sovereignty of the legal personality is referable to the members themselves."[64] However the *de facto* exercise of this sovereignty depends upon the method established for the appointment of the directors or trustees of the corporation. If all these directors are elected by a majority of the members of the parish, the laity will have actual control of the church property. If the directors or trustees are ecclesiastics, by reason of their official position, and if the naming of all directors is controlled by the church authorities, the danger of lay control of church goods is removed, and the demands of canon law are more nearly met. Without this important feature in a corporation aggregate, the lay members of the parish could control the goods of the parish, even if these

---

[62]Digest, II, 444-445.

[63]Brown, p. 137; this section on the New York Plan has been taken from Welsh, Maurice L. *The Laws of the State of Nevada Affecting Church Property,* The Catholic University of America Canon Law Studies, n. 409 (Washington, D. C.: The Catholic University of America, —) unpublished at this time.

[64]*Ibidem,* p. 138.

fell into heresy or recusancy.[65] It is because the New York law for parish corporations keeps the *de facto* control of the management of the church property in the hands of the church authorities, that the sacred congregation favored that method of incorporation for all American dioceses.[66]

The New York plan provides that the archbishop or bishop, the vicar general, the pastor of the parish being incorporated, and two laymen selected by these three, may incorporate the parish by filing articles of incorporation with the Secretary of State. The New York courts have interpreted this statute as having the effect of incorporating all the members of the parish, not just the five trustees who file the incorporating document with the secretary of state. The trustees have the office of managing the corporation, and the method established for their appointment insures that the incorporated parish will remain under ecclesiastical control.[67]

The New York corporation law was named as preferable by the sacred congregation because of the special "conditions and safeguards" which it contains. These concern the manner of selecting the five trustees, and filling their offices when they become vacant, the requirements for the validity of the acts of these trustees, and the rules for the disposition of property in the event of the division of a parish.

With regard to the naming of the five trustees, filling vacancies in their offices, and validity of their acts, the New York statute decrees:

> The Archbishop or Bishop, and the Vicar General of the diocese to which any incorporated Roman Catholic church belongs, the rector of such church, and their successors in office, shall, by virtue of their offices, be trustees of such church. Two laymen, members of such incorporated church, selected by such officers or a majority of them, shall also be trustees of such incorporated church, and such officers

[65]Klix vs. Polish Roman Catholic St. Stanislaus, 137 Mo. App. 347, 118 S.W. 1171 (1909).

[66]Cf. Brown, pp. 137-140.

[67]People's Bank vs. St. Anthony's Roman Catholic Church, 109 N.Y. 512, 17 N.E. 408 (1888).

> and such laymen trustees shall together constitute the board of trustees thereof. The two laymen signing the certificate of incorporation of an incorporated Roman Catholic church shall be the two laymen trustees thereof during the first year of its corporate existence. The term of office of the two laymen trustees of an incorporated Roman Catholic church shall be one year. Whenever the office of any such layman trustee shall become vacant by expiration of term of office or otherwise, his successor shall be appointed from the members of the church, by such officers or a majority of them. No act or proceeding of the trustees of any such incorporated church shall be valid without the sanction of the Archbishop or Bishop of the diocese to which such church belongs, or in their absence or inability to act, without the sanction of the Vicar General or of the administrator of such diocese.[68]

Thus the archbishop or bishop, the vicar general, and the pastor of each parish so incorporated, are ipso facto members of the five-man board of trustees, giving ecclesiastics a majority of the board membership. Their successors in office become trustees as soon as they succeed to the office. Furthermore, these three board members have the power of naming the two laymen who will serve on the board of trustees with them. The laymen hold office for only one year, so that the ecclesiastics could easily replace a layman who became a heretic or in any way fell away from the church. Finally, the bishop's authority, as supervisor of the church property in his diocese, is protected by the regulation invalidating acts of the trustees which do not have the bishop's sanction.

With regard to the division of parishes, the New York statute also gives the archbishop or bishop powers to act, which are quite consonant with the powers granted him in the Code.[69] The New York Statute regarding the division of parishes states:

> Wherever a Roman Catholic parish has been heretofore

[68]Digest, II, 444-445 cites the text of §91 of the *New York Religious Corporations Law.*

[69]Cf. canon 1427.

or shall hereafter be duly divided by the Roman Catholic bishop having jurisdiction over said parish and the original Roman Catholic church corporation is given one part of the old parish, and a new or second Roman Catholic church corporation is given the remaining part of the old parish, and it further appears that by reason of the said division the original Roman Catholic church corporation holds title to real property situated within the part of the old parish that was given to the new or second Roman Catholic church corporation, then the said Roman Catholic bishop or his successor shall have the right and power, of himself, independently of any action or consent on the part of the trustees of the original Roman Catholic church corporation to transfer the title of the said real property, with or without valuable consideration, to the new or second Roman Catholic church corporation. Said transfer shall be made by the said Roman Catholic bishop or his successor after having complied with the requirements of the code of civil procedure in the same manner as the trustees of any religious corporation are compelled to do before making a transfer of church property. If a valuable consideration is paid for the transfer the same shall be received by the said . . . original Roman Catholic church corporation and the new or second Roman Catholic corporation in such proportions as in the discretion of the said bishop or his successor may deem proper.[70]

This power gives the bishop independent power in the matter of the division of parishes. The Code likewise gives the bishop independence in dividing parishes, so long as he acts with a just and canonical cause. The Code remarks that he may divide the parish even against the will of its rector and without the consent of the people, although recourse may be had to the Holy See in order to revoke the action. The Code also calls for the division of the goods between the new and old parishes to be done by the bishop in proper proportion and in all fairness.[71] Thus the concord between the New York Statute and the canons

[70]Brown, pp. 142-143 citing § 92 of the *New York Religious Corporations Law.*

[71]Canons 1427, 1428, and 1500.

of the Code is remarkable in this matter of the division of parishes.

2. *Other Aspects of the New York Law*

In the state of New York, a general statute permits the incorporation of the different forms of religious societies and particular provisions are made for some, such as the Episcopal and Lutheran religions, but no particular provision is made for the Catholic diocese. On the other hand, provision is made for the parish. The diocese is incorporated by a special enactment for each diocese in New York. The result has been that New York has a parish and diocesan corporation arrangement that is a corporation aggregate. This is the system that was preferred by the Sacred Congregation of the Council in 1911.

The acts incorporating the diocese in New York unite the Bishop, the vicar-general, and the chancellor of the diocese into the corporation. They are the only members and their successors in office are *ex officio* members without need of appointment by another.[72] The parish corporation requires a certificate of incorporation to be filed. The members of the corporation are to be the Archbishop or Bishop, and the vicar-general of the diocese within which the parish to be incorporated is located, the rector of the church and two laymen, members of the church to be incorporated. The laymen are selected by the three church officials who are *ex officio* members of the corporation.[73]

The advantage of the corporation aggregate method is that the church property is vested in a body corporate that holds the property under their control, but their possession is the possession of the artificial person whose agents they are. The body corporate has a voice in the management of the property, but this voice amounts to authoritative power only, not an estate or title in the property. The rights of the clergy and the power of the bishop is not jeopardized, and at the same time the laity can be represented. There is no danger that the life of the corporation will be affected by the death of a trustee nor that the prop-

---

[72]Murphy, p. 54.

[73]*Loc. cit.*

erty will be attached as in the corporation sole and the fee simple methods.[74]

The corporation aggregate is in this way peculiarly adapted to the demands or needs of the Catholic Church. The participation of the laity is not present in the diocesan corporation, although that has been effected in some jurisdictions. The parish corporation of New York makes proper provision for the participation of the laity while at the same time safeguarding the hierarchical system of the Church.[75]

C. The Fee Simple

The few jurisdictions that do not have adequate corporation laws to meet the needs of the hierarchical system of the Catholic Church necessitates the holding of church property in fee simple by the bishop.[76] There is great danger that the property of the church will be diverted from the uses for which it was originally obtained. Judicial decisions in all but a few jurisdictions would construe a trust relationship to exist when the Bishop holds in this fashion. However, because of the precariousness of this manner of holding, it is best to avoid it if possible. In all events, canonical safeguards must be strictly adhered to so that the Bishop will make a proper will that conforms to the formalities set up by civil law for validity.[77]

D. The Ordinary as Trustee

The trust relationship exists in many jurisdictions. Since this is the present manner in which the diocesan and archdiosecan church property is held in Texas, more extensive treatment will be given subsequently. It is important to note that when the

---

[74]Doheny, *Church Property: Modes of Acquisition,* The Catholic University of America Canon Law Studies, n. 41 (Washington, D.C.: The Catholic University of America, 1927) p. 40. (Hereafter cited Doheny.)

[75]Murphy, p. 55; Cf. Dignan, p. 120.

[76]Cf. *Black's Law Dictionary,* p. 761, "fee simple." Fee simple title designates that the one with such a title has unconditional power of disposition during his life and the entire property descends to his heirs and legal representatives upon his death intestate. Cf. Veselka v. Flores, 283 S.W. 303, (Civ. App., 1926).

[77]Cf. Zollman, pp. 221, ff; II Plenary Council, n. 191; Canon 1301.

Church in Ohio was threatened with loss of property by the personal creditors of a deceased Ordinary, the court permitted evidence to show that the property was in fact held in trust for the use of the Church.[78]

In summary, it can be said that even though the laws of the majority of the States create no great difficulties relating to church property, the Church has not been recognized as a juridical person independently of the State. This formality of becoming a civil creature of the State, such as a corporation, or by a construed trust relation, is undoubtedly necessary with the existence of such a vast number of religious societies. The Hierarchy in the II Plenary Council stated that:

> While cheerfully recognizing the fact, that hitherto the General and State governments of our country, except in some brief intervals of excitement and delusion, have not interfered with our ecclesiastical organization or civil rights, we still have to lament that in many of the States we are not as yet permitted legally to make those arrangements for the security of Church property, which are in accordance with the canons and discipline of the Catholic Church. In some of the States, we gratefully acknowledge that all is granted in this regard that we could reasonably ask for. The right of the Church to possess property, whether churches, residence for the clergy, cemeteries, or school houses, asylums, etc., cannot be denied without depriving her of a necessary means of promoting the end for which she has been established. We are aware of the alleged grounds for this refusal to recognize the Church, in her corporate capacity, unless on the condition, that, in the matter of the tenure of ecclesiastical property, she conform to the general laws providing for this object. . . . These laws however, . . . are the expression of a distrust of ecclesiastical power as such. . . .[79]

These words still ring true, but the whole complex situation of the State and almost three hundred religious societies that would seek the privileges of the law must be given consideration.

[78] 46 Ohio State 102 (1888).

[79] nn. 182-204.

Article IV. Religious Societies in Texas

The legal status of the Catholic Church in the legal system of the State of Texas is by no means crystal clear. There is recognition given to the existence of both unincorporated and incorporated religious associations. However, the unincorporated religious society does not receive legal capacity to acquire, hold and administer property, or to sue and be sued independently of trustees. The unincorporated religious societies can perform no legal act in its own name.[80] On the other hand, the incorporated society acts in its own name both as to the exercise of its rights and in the defense of the same.[81] This does not deny that the unincorporated associations receive recognition of their rights, and even liabilities that might accrue. It is merely asserting that the unincorporated association is incapable of pursuing these rights or of defending itself when under liabilities without the intervention of a third party.[82]

In the Catholic Church in Texas, property is held by two separate types of ecclesiastical moral persons. They are the archdiocesan/diocesan moral person and the religious community. The property which belongs to the archdiocese or the dioceses in the State, or to one of the subordinate moral persons in the diocese, such as the parish, are held by an unincorporated religious society under Texas Law. The property which belongs to the many religious communities in Texas, are held by the religious communities as a corporation. Some religious communities have incorporated and by virtue of the corporation charter, they hold title to all the hospitals, colleges, or other institutions which they operate. Other religious communities hold property that is destined for the particular community use under one corporation charter. Other corporation charters are obtained for each hospital, college or other institution which they operate and the property for these institutions is held under the proper charter of the institution.

---

[80]Humphries v. Wilie, 76 S.W. 2d 793, (Civ. App., 1935); Magnolia Petroleum Co. v. Jackson, 82 S.W. 2d 1011 (Civ. App., 1935).

[81]Mood v. Methodist Episcopal Church South, 289 S.W. 461, 296 S.W. 506, modified opinion on other grounds in 300 S.W. 30 (1928).

[82]*Loc. cit.*

The subsequent sections will clarify the law of Texas concerning religious societies. After an understanding is had of the unincorporated and incorporated religious society in Texas, the present status of the Catholic Church will be more evident.

Section 1. General Conspectus of Religious Societies

The courts in Texas have recognized three distinct forms of religious societies: the congregational, the presbyterian and the hierarchical.[83] Membership in these religious societies is not unilateral but the church has the right to decide for itself whom it wishes to admit into its number or who shall be excluded or expelled without question from the courts.[84] By the higher plane theory, the membership recognizes the superior authority of the church to which it pertains whereas the membership in other voluntary societies does not submit itself to such extensive authority. This theory is harmonious with the teachings of the Catholic Church whereby the Church claims that because of divine intervention in her founding, she has authority from God Himself, independently of human authority, and that the members owe the Church that obedience and service due to God's representative.[85]

Therefore, the courts adopt the policy that where the rules and regulations are made by proper church functionaries, and they are authorized by the rules of the society, they will be enforced by the courts, if not in conflict with some civil law on the subject.[86]

Various definitions have been enunciated by the courts that concern religious societies. In general, these definitions are *obiter dicta,* that is, the concepts are defined in order that an

---

[83]Kelly v. Curry, 15 S.W. 2d 109, (1930); Brown v. Clark, 108 S.W. 421 (Civ. App.) reversed in 102 Tex. 323, 116 S.W. 360, 29 L.R.A. (N.S.) 670 (1909); Blanc v. Asbury, 63 Tex. 489, 51 Am. Rep. 666 (1872).

[84]Minton v. Leavell, 297 S.W. 615, (Civ. App., 1927).

[85]McGrath, p. 278.

[86]Schumann v. Dally, 29 S.W. 2d 422 (Civ. App., 1931); Alexander v. Bowers, 79 S.W. 2d 342 (1935).

explanation of the sentence might be given. Important amongst these definitions are:

1) A religious society is a voluntary association of individuals or families united for the purpose of having a common place of worship and to provide a proper teacher to instruct them in religious doctrine and duties and to administer the various ordinances of religion.[87]

2) Theological or religious seminaries are places for the preparation for the ministry of persons who are destined to teach religious doctrine.[88]

3) A place of worship is a place at which the worship might be indulged in so continuously and in such a manner as to be characterized as a place set apart for worship.[89]

4) A minister is one in whom the ministerial functions are vested.[90]

Christianity has a favored place in our legal system in Texas and is considered to be interwoven in the "web and woof" of the system so that some have justifiably stated that "christianity is a part of the law of the land."[91] However, the courts will not be deceived by any fraudulent schemes that are broached under the veneer of religion. The fact that one's religious convictions sanction actions that disrupt public good order will not mean that the law recognizes such convictions as sanctioned; on the contrary, the law will take measures to guard against such fraud and ill-ordered convictions.[92] It can be said that the law must envision the vast number of religious societies that arise and have arisen with a presumption that they are not

[87]Church v. Bullock, 104 Tex. 1, 109 S.W. 115, 16 L.R.A. (N.S.) 860 (1909).

[88]*Loc. cit.*

[89]*Loc. cit.*

[90]Olcott v. Gabert, 86 Tex. 121, 23 S.W. 985 (1893). The court stated that in the Catholic Church this minister is a priest subject to the control of the bishop.

[91]Church v. Bullock, 104 Tex. 1, 109 S.W. 115, 16 L.R.A. (N.S.) 860 (1908); Cf. Zollman, p. 26, citing Thomas Jefferson to the contrary.

[92]Scott v. Thompson, 21 Iowa 599 (1866); cf. Zollman, p. 23.

frauds. For that reason, the courts should seek wherein the respective religious society fits in the law of the State.

Section 2. Incorporated Religious Societies

The Constitution of 1876 has set the stage, so to speak, for the legislation that permits religious associations to incorporate. Article 1, Section 6 states:

> All men have a natural and indefeasible right to worship Almighty God according to the dictates of their own consciences. No man shall be compelled to attend, erect or support any place of worship, or to maintain any ministry against his consent. No human authority ought, in any case whatever to control or interfere with the rights of conscience in matters of religion and no preference shall ever be given by law to any religious society or mode of worship. But it shall be the duty of the Legislature to pass such laws as may be necessary to protect equally every religious denomination in the peaceful enjoyment of its own mode of public worship.

In following this authorization and exhortation of the Constitution, the Legislature passed a corporation statute particularly adapted to the congregational and assembly form of religious societies:

> Any religious society . . . may, by the consent of a majority of its members become a body corporate under this title, electing directors or trustees, and performing such other things as are directed in the case of other corporations; when so organized shall have all the powers and privileges, and be subject to all the restrictions in this title contained, for the objects named in the charter, and shall have the same power to make by-laws for the regulation of their affairs as other corporations.[93]

The act permitting the incorporation of private associations enunciates the following purposes for which such associations may incorporate:

[93]*Vernon's Texas Statutes*, 1948 (Kansas City, Mo.: Vernon Law Book Co., 1948), Article 1396. (Hereafter cited as Revised Statutes Article 1396.)

1. The support of public worship.

2. The support of any benevolent, charitable, educational or missionary undertaking.

3. Charitable corporations may be created for the purpose, or purposes of owning and operating non-profit co-operative hospitals, and for the purpose of providing a suitable place in the immediate locality where members and families and members of such corporation may obtain medical, dental, health, surgical, nursing, hospitalization, and related services and benefits.

4. Corporations may be created as charitable, benevolent and non-profit corporations to furnish hospital services to its members.

5. Corporations may be created for one or more of the following purposes, namely: religion, charitable, literary, scientific or educational.[94]

A. Creation of Religious Corporations

Religious associations may make use of the private corporation law to incorporate. Three or more persons may enter a voluntary association for the purposes authorized by law and in the manner described by the law.[95] The law requires that a charter be prepared setting forth: 1) the name of the corporation; 2) the purpose for which it is formed; 3) the place or places where its business is to be transacted; 4) the term for which it is to exist; 5) the number of directors or trustees and the names and residences of those who are appointees for the 1st year; 6) the amount of its capital stock, if any, and the number of shares into which it is divided.[96]

This charter must be subscribed to by three or more persons, two of whom must be citizens of the State, and the charter must

---

[94]Revised Statute Article 1302, sec. 1, 2, 2A, 104, 105.

[95]Revised Statute Article 1303.

[96]Revised Statute Article 1304; the constitutional and statutory laws of the State that are in force when the charter is granted are parts of the charter although the law may not be expressly incorporated therein and they generally are not so incorporated. Shaw v. Lone Star Bldg. and Loan Ass'n., 123 Tex. 373, 71 S.W. 2d 863 (1934).

be acknowledged by them, before an officer duly authorized to take acknowledgment of deeds.[97] At one time, married women were unable to be subscribers to a charter, but the legislature removed this lack of capacity and at the same time, declared that there should be no limit to the number of persons who may subscribe to the corporation.[98]

Although the corporations that are treated of here do not have capital stock since they are not operated for profit, these corporations must submit an estimation of the value of the goods, chattels, lands and all rights and credits owned by the corporation.[99] The charter is to be filed with the Secretary of State, and a copy is to be given to the corporation, while the original is left in the office of the Secretary of State. Both copies are to bear the seal of the office of the Secretary of State and the date, which date of filing indicates the beginning of the existence of the corporation.[100]

It may happen that a corporation will not comply with the full requisites of the law. If there has been a bona fide effort to incorporate and an actual use of the rights claimed to be conferred by such a law has been made, a "de facto" corporation will come into existence. However, there must be a law permitting a corporation with the powers this association has assumed.[101]

B. Continuance and Termination

The charter is simply amended by filing the amendment with the Secretary of State; however, this may not be done contrary to the general laws of the association or of the State.[102] The amendment is effective upon filing, therefore, the date of filing is of paramount importance.[103]

---

[97]Revised Statute Article 1305.

[98]Revised Statute Article 1306.

[99]Revised Statute Article 1308.

[100]Revised Statute 1313.

[101]Roaring Springs Townsite Co. v. Paducah Telephone Co., 164 S.W. 50 (Civ. App., 1914).

[102]Articles 1314; 1396; Wallace v. Wells, 228 S.W. 111 (Civ. App., 1924).

[103]Davis v. Turner, 148 S.W. 2d 256 (Civ. App., 1941).

The renewal of a charter given to a corporation created for the support of benevolent, charitable, educational or missionary undertakings is privileged. When such charter expires by limitation, the members need only file a new charter, according to the provisions of the law. That requires a majority consent and a recital of the privileges and immunities and the rights of property. A certified copy of the original expired charter must be filed with the Secretary of State with the new charter. This new charter revives the old charter with all the privileges, immunities and rights of property, real and personal, exercised and held by it at the date of the expiration.[104]

The extension of a charter for a private corporation can be made for fifty years by filing with the Secretary of State at any time within ten years prior to the expiration date set for the old charter for a profit corporation and twelve years for a non-profit corporation.[105]

By general provision of the law, the corporation thus created or extended will not succeed to itself longer than fifty years. During this period, they may perform all the actions permitted to a juridical person.[106] At the end of this period, the corporation ceases to exist by operation of the law. Further, the corporation ceases to exist when a court of competent jurisdiction issues a judgment decreeing the termination of the corporation. The members may voluntarily dissolve the corporation by a majority vote within a meeting according to the by-laws of the corporation or by a unanimous vote of the members outside the meeting. The results are to be submitted to the Secretary of State before the corporation is dissolved.[107] Further, if the corporation does not act within three years of the filing of its charter, it forfeits the charter by operation of law without a judicial act. In all these cases, the court is to appoint a receiver to extend the corporation in order that it may settle its affairs. This extension may be up to three years.[108]

---

[104]Revised Statute Article 1315.

[105]Revised Statute Article 1315 (a).

[106]Revised Statute Articles 1320, 1321.

[107]Revised Statute Article 1387.

[108]Revised Statute Article 1389.

Section 3. Unincorporated Religious Societies

It has been stated that the unincorporated religious society is incapable of pursuing its rights or of defending itself when under liabilities without the intervention of a third party. It can perform no legal act in its own name independently of trustees.[109] In order to understand the legal capacity of such associations, which include the Catholic Church, a summary review of the status of trusts in Texas Law must be considered.

The trust concept in the law of Texas has developed from the trust relationship that arose in English common law and was adopted in the various States of the United States. The Crown sought to eliminate restraints on alienation. Because of this, gifts to the Church were hindered and the mortmain statutes were passed to prevent conveyances to religions. The people sought to avoid the limitations placed by the Crown upon their power to bestow their property to the uses they favored. The practice arose of giving the legal title to one individual with the stipulation that the property so conveyed be used for some other individual or purpose. In 1553, the Crown passed the Statute of Uses to forbid uses that defeated creditors and feudal obligations so that all uses were converted into estates at law. Again the courts permitted the purpose of the Statute to be voided in Tyrrel's case in 1557. This permitted the conveyance of land to A to the use of B in trust for C so that the first use was destroyed and absolute title was placed in B, who held in trust. In this way the present-day trust relationship came into being. There is no need for such devious conveyance to create a trust relationship today. The conveyance is made to one person in trust for a certain person or use as expressly declared or implied.[110]

The trust has been defined as a "fiduciary relationship in which one person is the holder of the title to property, subject to an equitable obligation to keep or use the property for the

---

[109]Cf. *supra* pp. 84-85.

[110]*Texas Jurisprudence* (43 vols., San Francisco: Bancroft-Whitney Co., 1935), Vol. 42, p. 598. (Hereafter cited in this manner: 42 Tex. Jur. 598).

benefit of another."[111] In general, States have limited the use of a trust relationship because they fear that perpetuities will arise in which properties will be withdrawn from the general uses of society.[112] Thus, the States have restricted trusts so that indefinite trusts, often irrational or absurd, will not be valid. However, in so doing, the States have at the same time prevented the creation of many works greatly beneficial for society. In those instances, subsequent legislation or judicial interpretation have generally altered the situation for the better.[113]

A. Legislation Governing Express Trusts

In 1943, the State of Texas passed special legislation governing express trusts and provided that express trusts can be created for the following purposes:

> A trust in relation to, or consisting of, real, personal or mixed property may be created or established for any use or purpose which is not illegal. A person has the same capacity to create a trust by declaration, transfer inter vivos, devise, bequest or appointment, that he has to transfer, devise, bequeath or appoint free of trust. A person has the capacity to create a trust by making a promise to another person whose rights against the promisor are to be held in trust for a third person, to the same extent that he has the capacity to make a contract.[114]

The requisites for the creation of an express trust under this act are the following:

> A. A declaration in writing by the owner of the property that he holds it as a trustee for another person, or persons, or for himself and another person or persons; or
>
> B. A written transfer inter vivos by the owner of the

---

[111]Restatement of the Law of Trusts (2 vols., St. Paul: American Law Institute, 1935), Vol. I, p. 6. (Hereafter cited *Restatement.*)

[112]Levy v. Levy, 33 N.Y. 97 (1865).

[113]E.g., New York, Cf. Murphy, pp. 137-142.

[114]Revised Statutes, Article 7425b, 3: this act concerns an express trust only, not a constructive or resulting trust, nor any type of business trust. Passive trusts are not included in this act.

property to another person as trustee for the transferor or for a third person or persons; or

C. A transfer by will by the owner of property to another person or persons as trustee for a third person; provided that a natural person as trustee may be a beneficiary of any such trust; or

D. An appointment by a person having a power of appointment to another person as trustee for the donee of the power or for a third person; or

E. A promise by a person to another person whose rights are thereunder to be held in trust for a third person; or

F. A beneficiary may be a co-trustee and the legal and equitable title of the estate will not merge by reason thereof.[115]

B. Constructive or Resulting Trusts

The statute does not prevent the creation of charitable, religious or educational trusts that are not expressed in unequivocal terms in an instrument. In general, the elements of a trust will be:

1) a designated beneficiary;

2) a designated trustee;

3) a fund or other property, sufficiently designated or identified to enable title to pass to the trustee; and

4) the actual delivery of the fund or other property, or a legal assignment thereof, to the trustee, with the intention of passing legal title thereto to him as trustee.[116]

Thus, in Texas law, it is considered essential to the creation of a trust that the legal and equitable estate be separated. The legal estate is to be vested in the trustee and the equitable title in the beneficiary. The authorities all agree that when both of these titles unite in the same person, the trust terminates.[117]

---

[115] *Ibidem*, 7.

[116] Murphy, p. 147, citing Hodgmann v. Cobb, 202 App. Div. 259, 195 N.Y.S. 428 (1922).

[117] McCamey v. Hollister Oil Co., 241 S.W. 689, affirmed in 115 Tex. 49, 274 S.W. 562 (1926).

1. Trusts for Unincorporated Religious Societies

Where there is a conveyance to the trustees of an unincorporated religious society which by itself is incapable of taking and holding real property in the associate name, the conveyance must take place through the intervention of trustees.[118] When there is a deed that conveys fee simple title to the trustees of a church, it is a deed in trust for the use and benefit of the church.[119] Thus, the courts hold that the trustees of a religious association hold the title to church property for the benefit of the members of the church according to the discipline for that particular church.[120]

Where the trust is for the benefit of a particular church, parish, denomination or religious association, the court will ascertain the exact nature of the religious body by reference to its constitution and rules of government in force when the grant was made, and define the trust in such terms.[121] Thus, when the church, parish, denomination or religious association was affiliated with a central body at the time a trust existed, the rules of the central body bound the subordinate church. In this case, the central body promulgated the established doctrine and rules of discipline binding upon its associated members by virtue of recognized authority.[122]

An anomaly seems to arise between the doctrine that schisms

---

[118] Humphries v. Wiley 76 S.W. 2d 793 (Civ. App., 1934).

[119] Magnolia Petroleum Co. v. Jackson, 82 S.W. 2d 1011 (Civ. App., 1935); Smallwood v. Midfield Oil Co., 89 S.W. 2d 1086 (Civ. App., 1935); Parrish v. Looney, 194 S.W. 2d 419 (Civ. App., 1946).

[120] Olcott v. Gabert, 86 Tex. 121, 23 S.W. 985 (1893); Macedonia Baptist Church v. Farm and Home Savings and Loan Ass'n, 110 S.W. 2d 1013 (Civ. App., 1941).

[121] Clark v. Brown, 108 S.W. 421; modified in 116 S.W. 90, 102 Tex. 323 (1909).

[122] This case upheld the right of the union of the Cumberland Presbyterians and the Presbyterian Church of the United States to take control of those properties belonging to individual churches which did not accept the union. The individual church in this case had objected to the union on doctrinal grounds. The union was held to bind the individual church because the central assembly had the power to change doctrine and to unite with other bodies.

will not permit property dedicated to the use of a particular church to be diverted to other uses and the doctrine that the majority faction controls. It has been held by force of the first doctrine, that property impliedly dedicated to the use of a determined religious society and for the promulgation of its doctrine, will not be diverted to the use of schismatics, who are promoters of different doctrine. The size of the schism was declared to be of no importance in the decision of the court.[123] Another court has declared that the will of the majority controls.[124] However, the majority rule doctrine is commonly held to apply only for those churches and religious bodies, which although a part of a larger religious group, are completely independent in character. In these religious bodies, the doctrines and teachings are not fixed and congealed by the discipline of any central body, but are left to the majority faction who may also control the disposition of the property for the persual of those christian uses which the majority approve.[125]

The majority rule doctrine should never have application to the properties of the Catholic Church if the court follows the constant interpretation given to the powers of the Bishop according to the well-known discipline of the Church.[126] Therefore, according to this law of Texas on trusts for unincorporated religious societies, it can be seen that a conveyance to the

[123]Peace v. First Christian Church, 48 S.W. 534, 20 Civ. App. 85 (1898).

[124]First Baptist Church of Paris v. Fort, 93 Tex. 215, 54 S.W. 892 (1898).

[125] *Loc. cit.;* Cf. also Gibson v. Morris, 31 Tex. Civ. App. 645, 73 S.W. 85 (1903); First Baptist Church of Redland v. Ward 290 S.W. 828 (Civ. App., 1927); Jarrell v. Sproles, 20 Civ. App. 387, 49 S.W. 904 (1899); Paul Martin, "Property Rights among Factions in Independent Churches," 7 *Baylor Law Review* 425.

[126]Blanc v. Asbury, 63 Tex. 490 (1885). The court observed that the form of government in the Roman Catholic Church is an episcopacy, and the diocesan bishops possess enlarged powers, respecting the temporal as well as the spiritual affairs of the Church in their respective dioceses. Cf. Olcott v. Gabert, 23 S.W. 985, 86 Tex. 121 (1893); Cussen v. Lynch, 245 S.W. 932 (1922); Community of St. Basil v. Byrene, 236 S.W. 1016 (1922).

Ordinary, as Bishop of the diocese, and to his successors in office and assigns forever, will indicate a charitable trust. This trust is interpreted because of the nature and functions of the respective bishops as ecclesiastical administrators according to the precepts of Canon Law. The presumed religious intention of the grantor, if any, does not create the trust. However, this does not mean that the donor or testator or grantee should not exercise caution and spell out the exact nature of the use with great exactness by stipulating that the property is granted for the use of the Roman Catholic Church.[127]

2. *The* Cy Pres *Doctrine Affecting Implied Trusts*

In Texas law, charitable trusts are favored and the courts apply the *cy pres* doctrine to provide that the trusts will be effective.[128] The courts have upheld charitable trusts without regard to the extent of the charitable purpose, the uncertainty of the beneficiary, so that the *cy pres* doctrine is applied to all grants and conveyances in which a trust is either implied or can be construed for a religious use.[129]

The *cy pres* doctrine is a rule for the construction of instruments by which the intention of the party is carried out as near as may be, when it would be impossible or illegal to give it literal effect. Thus, in the case of charitable uses, where the language used may be so vague or uncertain that the intent of the party must be sought out by the court, this will be done in order that the true intention of the party may be put into effect.[130] A limitation to the use of the doctrine was stated in one case. The doctrine was not applied for a particular object

[127] *Mode of Tenure, Survey,* p. 160.

[128] Boyles v. Gresham 260 S.W. 2d 155 (Civ. App., 1953) reversed on other grounds in 263 S.W. 2d 935 (1954).

[129] Laird v. Bass, 50 Tex. 412 (1878); Community of St. Basil v. Byrne, 236 S.W. 1016 (1922); Magnolia Petroleum Co. v. Jackson, 82 S.W. 2d 1011 (1935); Clark v. Brown, 108 S.W. 421, 116 S.W. 90, 102 Tex. 323 (1909); Olcott v. Gabert, 23 S.W. 985, 86 Tex. 121 (1893); Peace v. First Christian Church, 48 S.W. 534, 20 Civ. App. 85 (1898).

[130] *Black's Law Dictionary,* p. 497, *"cy pres"*; Cf. Ft. Worth Bank v. Gerking, 284 S.W. 2d 791 (Civ. App., 1955).

or institution but the court declared that the doctrine would apply only for public charity according to a general intention.[131] However, this limitation is seldom imposed, except in those cases wherein it is evident that the intention is for private purposes. This is evident from the many cases in which the doctrine is upheld.[132]

When applying this doctrine, the courts have held that they are to adhere as closely as possible to the general intention of the testator or donor even to the exact designation of the control and administration of the trust. Consequently, when keeping up a school for females was impracticable, the court held that the trust should be applied to some use in close approximity to that cause.[133] The doctrine has been applied to make charities perpetual for the basic reason that charities benefit the State and discharge those duties which are the duties of the community towards its citizens.[134] Therefore, it can be truly said that the doctrine will apply whenever the purpose can be interpreted as charitable, or for any purpose which will be beneficial to the community. These purposes will include projects to help the poor, blind, sick, to relieve any distress, to advance religion or to promote health, and also projects that advance governmental purposes.[135]

Charitable or religious trusts can be imposed by any manner in which the legal title can be transferred to the trustee, for example, by a gift, conveyance *inter vivos,* bequest or will. However, the conveyance must take place during the life of

---

[131]Women's Christian Temperance Union v. Cooley, 25 S.W. 2d 171 (Civ. App., 1932) where it is indicated that the true test is not the motive of the donor, but the purpose to which the money or property is to be applied. Thus, generally speaking, uncertainty of the individual object is required in order that there be no personal, private use. Cf. Davis v. Gulf Ry. Co., 196 S.W. 603 (1920); Pascal v. Acklin, 27 Tex. 173 (1863).

[132]42 Tex. Jur. 600 ff.

[133]Inglish v. Johnson, 95 S.W. 558, 42 Civ. App., 118 (1900); Ryan v. Porter, 61 Tex. 106 (1885).

[134]Scott v. Sterrett, 234 S.W. 2d 917 (Civ. App. 1950); Scott v. All Saints Hospital, 203 S.W. 146 (Civ. App., 1920).

[135]9 Tex. Jur. Supplement 55.

the settlor unless made by will.[136] The conveyance must conform to all the requirements of the law so that the conveyance will be valid. Thus, in the case of realty, the conveyance must take place by deed or testamentary writing. Delivery is required. However, in the case of personalty, the requisites are more lenient so that any legal transfer that is legally effective, even if by parol, will be upheld.[137]

Once the courts construe that the documents uphold a trust relationship, the trustee and beneficiary must be determined. If there is no designated trustee, the court must appoint a trustee to execute the trust.[138] The attorney general has the particular duty and the authority to use the court to enforce these trusts for public charities.[139] Although the administration of the trust is the function of the trustees,[140] a supervisory power remains in the courts.[141]

Section 4. The Catholic Church in Texas

The Catholic Church in Texas consists of an archdiocese and six dioceses. Each diocese and the archdiocese are moral persons. Within the territories of these respective moral persons are other moral persons. These include parishes, religious institutes, and charitable projects. The property of these moral persons is held in diverse manner according to the legal status of the moral person in civil law. Religious institutes and those projects administered by them in the State are held by corpo-

[136]Samuell v. Brooks, 207 S.W. 626, (Civ. App., 1920), Powe v. Powe, 268 S.W. 2d 558, (1954).

[137]42 Tex. Jur. 615, n. 13 citing Ballard v. Ballard, 296 S.W. 2d 811 (1956).

[138]Lightfoot v. Poindexter, 199 S.W. 1152 (Civ. App., 1920); Lake v. Hood, 79 S.W. 323, 35 Civ. App. 32, (1894); Tunstall v. Wormley, 54 Tex. 476 (1878).

[139]Miller v. Davis, 136 Tex. 299, 150 S.W. 2d 973, 136 A.L.R. 177 (1941); cf. Revised Statutes Article 4412a effective April 29, 1959.

[140]Hopkins v. Upshur, 20 Tex. 89, 112 S.W. 433 (1904).

[141]Revised Statutes Articles 690-695: but for religious purposes the supervisory power of the court would seem definitely limited. Cf. Olcott v. Gabert, 23 S.W. 985 (1893) and Clark v. Brown, 116 S.W. 360 (1909).

rations. The properties that belong to the diocese or to parishes of the diocese are held by the bishops in trust for the Roman Catholic Church.

The religious institute in the Catholic Church is a society approved by legitimate ecclesiastical authority, the members of which strive after evangelical perfection according to the laws proper to their society, by the profession of public vows.[142] Similar to these religious societies are those societies that do not take public vows, yet, they strive after evangelical perfection.[143] There are also associations of the laity, which when established according to the norms of canon 100, have moral personality in the Church. These ecclesiastical moral persons have incorporated according to the laws of Texas. It can be seen that these are more homogeneous moral persons than the diocesan or parish moral person.

This section will indicate the origin and development of the present manner of holding diocesan properties. After that, it will be possible to make some observations upon the feasibility and advisability of incorporating the dioceses and parishes in Texas.

A. Origin of the Trust Relationship

The legislative grant of those church properties formerly held under the pre-Republic of Texas governments, began the practice of the Catholic Church of holding property in the bishop and his successors in office, for the use of the Roman Catholic Church. This is a trust relationship. The exact nature of this trust and the consequences that have come into effect will be examined. It does not seem that a definitive answer can be given as to the exact nature of this trust relationship, but a better view can be obtained.

A historic decision held that the right of church property in Spanish America was in the crown of Spain, as the head of both the temporal and spiritual jurisdictions, and that this right, after the Mexican revolution, vested in the government of Mexico as the successor of the former sovereign power. The

[142]Canon 488.

[143]Canon 673.

reason for this interpretation is to be found in the misunderstanding of historical works of the era of Judge Lipscomb who said:

> The Spanish monarchs became in effect, the heads of the Catholic Church in their American possessions.[144]

Judge Lipscomb came to this conclusion from the fact that the King administered the revenues of church properties and distributed the benefices to those he wished by virtue of the donations of Alexander VI and Julius II granting the privilege of Royal patronage to Spain.[145] Of great influence in the decision were the actions of the Mexican and Spanish governments to regulate religious ceremonies and feasts. These actions, together with the Mortmain Statute that forbade the church to own property, indicated that the title to the property was in the Crown and Republic of Mexico.[146]

An Alabama case is cited wherein the sale of church property by the Spanish Crown was upheld. The court concluded that this indicated a holding of all church property in the Spanish dominions by the Crown. The counsel of Bishop Odin pointed out that in the Alabama case, the original conveyance gave the Crown the power to sell the property to meet repairs and that the property was sold for that purpose. But it seems that the court was not incorrect in its conclusion for another reason. The reason is that the Crown had usurped the title to church property as indicated in Chapter I. Therefore, although

---

[144]Blair v. Odin, 3 Tex. 288 (1848).

[145]*Loc. cit.*

[146]Decree n. 263, art. 7, of the Mexican Republic and the State of Coahuila, is quoted:

> The Churches, monasteries, convents, and all other ecclesiastical communities, as well secular as regular, charity houses, hospitals, poor houses, schools, confraternities, brotherhoods, commandancies, and every other establishment, whether ecclesiastical or lay, known by the name of mortmains, cannot, from this time, in the future, acquire any real or immovable property, in any province of the monarchy, by testament, donation, purchase, rentcharges, infeudation, adjudication of rents, in payment of rents due, nor by any title whatsoever, either lucrative or onerous.

unjustly acquired, the right and dominion by absolute title to church properties rested in the Mexican government before the revolution. The right to the use or usufruct, according to the civil law, was in the pastors of the respective Catholic churches in Texas, which right was exercised at the will of the government.[147]

A later case upheld the legislative grant of 1841 against the claim of the City of San Antonio in 1855. The City attempted to sell the Alamo, which had been granted to the Bishop in 1841. The court upheld the trust relationship that had been created by the grant.[148] The City objected that the legislative grant was too vague and uncertain as to the persons to whom the trust was confided and the objects it had in view. The court replied that it could be said that the act conferred on the persons designated as trustee, the capacity to hold, and made him a corporation sole quoad the object of the act. However, the court denied that there was uncertainty as to who were to be the trustees, nor was there any doubt as to his capacity to take. Further, those who were to continue to execute the trust were sufficiently determined. As to the objects of the trust, the court denied that there was any ambiguity in stating that the property was for the use of the Roman Catholic Church. Therefore, the court held that the Bishop and his successors held the property in trust for the use of the Catholic Church as designated.[149]

Hence, the origin of the trust relationship was the legislative grant of 1841 as interpreted by the courts. The courts rejected the contention that the bishop was to be considered as a corporation sole.

B. Trusts Construed from Deeds of Conveyances

The extent of this trust relationship has been clarified somewhat in subsequent cases. In the case of Blanc v. Asbury, the

[147] *Loc. cit.*

[148] City of San Antonio v. Odin, 15 Tex. 539 (1855). The city had been authorized to sell public lands by a prior grant, which it had not used, thus the legislative grant prevailed.

[149] *Loc. cit.*

Bishop had been given land in the town of Hempstead by a deed of conveyance that stated:

> To have and to hold unto him, the said Claudius M. Dubuis, for the use of aforesaid, and his successors and his or their assigns, forever. It is hereby declared that the premises herein described are granted the said Claudius M. Dubuis for the purpose of erecting thereon a Roman Catholic Church, and other buildings pertaining thereto, or to be exchanged or used in the purchase of other property in the town of Hempstead for said purpose.[150]

By force of this conveyance, the Bishop held as a trustee and in securing the object of the trust, he had to sell a portion of the land in order that the church building might be constructed. The parishioners entered this suit against the grantee but the court held that by the conveyance, much was left to the discretion of the Bishop, who, as head of the Church in the diocese, had the necessary power as supplemented by the conveyance, to manage the property as his judgment might approve as the best in securing the object.[151]

It cannot be concluded that Blanc v. Asbury permitted the Bishop to subject the property held in trust for one parish, to a debt or obligation for the betterment of another part of the diocese. Nor can it be concluded that the court in this case would prohibit such use of the property.

However, in the case of Olcott v. Gabert, property conveyed to a Bishop for the use of the Roman Catholic Church made the Bishop a trustee with the power to dispose of the property for any cause that he might deem necessary.[152] In that case, the Bishop had received property from a railroad for the purpose of constructing a Catholic Church in the town of Nacogdoches. This purpose was not expressed in the conveyance but

[150]63 Tex. 489, 51 Am. Rep. 666 (Com. App., 1885).

[151]The court noted that "the form of government in the Roman Catholic Church is an episcopacy, and the diocesan bishops possess enlarged powers, respecting the temporal as well as the spiritual affairs of the Church, in their respective diocese."

[152]86 Tex. 121, 23 S.W. 985 (1893).

it was understood. When the railroad went bankrupt, the Bishop returned the land because he did not foresee how the church could use the land in the absence of the railroad. The court held that the presumption that everything is rightfully done by officers or trustees of an association has especial force in the case of the actions of a Bishop of the Roman Catholic Church.

Subsequent cases construed the trust relationship by virtue of the fact that the land was conveyed to the Bishop and his successors in office. A Dallas case reached the civil court when a disobedient priest refused to leave a parish and the Bishop claimed possession of the property by virtue of the legal title. The court did not state that the Bishop held the property as a trustee for the Roman Catholic Church. The action of the court in reviewing the canonical jurisprudence on the powers of the Bishop to suspend a priest and remove a pastor indicated that the Bishop was considered a trustee with determined powers. The powers were determined by the law of the Church.[153]

In a Galveston case, the Bishop entered a suit against the Basilian Fathers to clear the title to church property in Waco. The Bishop had originally conveyed land held in his name as Bishop of the diocese to theBasilian Fathers. The court stated that the Bishop held the property in trust. Evidence was permitted that showed the pastor and parishioners agreed with the Bishop's action in conveying the property to the community for school purposes. It must not be assumed that this evidence indicated that the Bishop had the pastor and parishioners joined to him as trustees. On the contrary, the action of the Bishop alone in making the conveyance was sufficient.[154]

C. *Final Observations*

The question commonly proposed is this: should the diocese/archdiocese and parishes of the Catholic Church seek to incorporate under the present law of incorporation in the State of Texas? It seems that the creation of several separate corpora-

[153]Cussen v. Lynch, 245 S.W. 932 (1922).

[154]Community of Priests of St. Basil v. Byrne, 255 S.W. 601 (Com. App., 1923).

tions, one for the diocese, one for each individual parish might be formed. Fundamentally, the Statute requires the existence of an unincorporated religious association,[155] which legally exists in the State. This legal existence of a voluntary unincorporated religious association is had by the Catholic Church.[156]

The Statute favors the incorporation of the congregational and presbyterian or assembly type of religious society and is not readily adaptable to the incorporation of an hierarchical form. The members of the religious association are to determine by a majority vote as to the act of incorporation. The members of the religious association are to elect the directors or trustees. A question was raised in the work of the National Catholic Welfare Conference as to the advisability of such incorporation. Such stipulations could be destructive of necessary discipline. However, the National Catholic Welfare Conference presented the following observations on the possibility of incorporating:

> This association may, by the consent of the majority of its members, become a body corporate, electing directors or trustees, and performing such other things as are directed in the case of other corporations; and when so organized shall have all the powers and privileges conferred, subject to restrictions of law for the objects named in the charter, and shall have the same power to make by-laws for the regulation of their affairs as other corporations. Though the statute appears primarily designed to give corporate status to religious denominations organized on an independent or congregational basis, with the initial source of authority residing in the lay members, it does not for this reason appear unadaptable to Catholic Church use. The only question is whether the Bishop may join with himself, the Vicar-General of the diocese, the Pastor of the given parish and two laymen selected from within the parish precincts, and, calling this association a religious society, file

---

[155]Revised Statutes Articles 1320, 1396.

[156]Jung v. Neraz, 71 Tex. 396, 9 S.W. 344 (1881); Olcott v. Gabert, 86 Tex. 121, 23 S.W. 985 reversing 22 S.W. 286 (Civ. App., 1893).

> with the proper authority articles of incorporation in the desired form. There is nothing in the statute forbidding such an organization. Nor is there any element in the present tenure of church property preventing its transfer to the trustees of such a religious body once they have been elected by its members, provided the property is held to be subject to the same uses theretofore imposed. Since the articles and by-laws may lay down conditions precedent to membership, there is no conceivable objection to providing therein that the Bishop, or his diocesan administrator, the Vicar-General and the Pastor of the given parish shall be ex officio member of the religious society, and that the remaining two members are to be selected by these three from among the parish members at prescribed intervals. Then the corporate structure may be built in a manner carefully reserving, in practical effect, ultimate control in the Bishop. Reference may be had to similar corporate forms in use in the New York, Iowa, Wisconsin and other States for information on the preferable system to be pursued. Much may be said for such an arrangement since it gives the lay members of the parish a helpful and cooperative voice in parish administration. Diocesan corporations may likewise be established in a similar manner, with those existing in other States being used as precedents.
>
> A corporation so formed has the power of succession by its corporate name for not longer than fifty years, may purchase, hold, sell, mortgage or otherwise convey such real estate and personal estate as the purposes of the corporation shall require, or as the security for payment of indebtedness to the corporation may demand; and may enter into any obligation or contract essential to the transaction of its authorized business.[157]

Hence, incorporation under the present statute is not definitely impossible nor impractical. If it were found that the present method of holding diocesan/archdiocesan properties according to a trust relation is not satisfactory, an attempt to incorporate according to these suggestions would be advisable.

However, the Constitution explicitly states that:

---

[157] *Mode of Tenure,* Survey, p. 161-162, citing various Revised Statute Articles from 1320-1396.

> . . . it shall be the duty of the legislature to pass such laws as may be necessary to protect equally every religious denomination in the peaceful enjoyment of its own mode of public worship.[158]

Therefore, the legislature should seek to pass those laws which would permit the incorporation of such a large body as that which comprises the Catholic Church. Similar difficulties probably face other hierarchical religious societies, such as the Episcopalian and Orthodox religions. In the course of this study, it will be evident that the policy of the State has been to favor religious societies. When religious societies have suffered by adverse judicial decisions, the legislature has acted to pass Constitutional amendments and subsequent legislation to remove the burdens.[159]

---

[158] Article 1, Section 6.

[159] Trinity Methodist Episcopal Church v. City of San Antonio, 201 S.W. 669 (1918) pastor's residence taxed but exempted by Constitutional amendment of 1928 and legislation of 1931, Revised Statute Article 7105b.

CHAPTER III

ACQUISITION

The Church states that it has an inherent right to acquire property for the attainment of its proper end. Since this is a native right, the Church is careful to declare that it holds that right freely and independently of any civil authority. That is, the Church, in obtaining and owning its property, is not subject to the imposition of burdens by the civil law. The independence claimed by the Church denies the necessity of legal recognition by the civil power and the need of any legal permission on the part of the State.[1] In laying claim to this right, the Church merely repeats what it has stated from the time of its divine institution by Christ.

This same right to acquire, hold and administer property is extended by the law of the Church to individual churches and other moral persons which have been duly established by church authority as juridical persons according to the norms established by the Code of Canon Law.[2] By "individual churches" is meant groups of the faithful determined by territorial limits under the government of an ecclesiastical superior. By "other moral persons" is meant those societies which have been given juridical personality by the proper ecclesiastical authority through a formal decree of erection. The moment that these individual churches or other moral persons separate themselves from the unity of the Church, they lose all the rights which they possessed.[3] This principle is recognized by the civil law.[4]

---

[1]Canon 1495; Cf. Cappello, *Summa Iuris Canonici* (3 vols., Vol. II, 4. ed., Romae: Apud Aedes Universitatis Gregorianae, 1945), II, 546, n. 572.

[2]Canon 1495, §2; cf. also canons 100, 531, 676.

[3]Bouscaren, pp. 797-798; cf. canon 100, §1.

[4]Zollman, p. 260.

Article I. Church Law on Acquisition

The property to which the Church claims a native right includes all those revenues that are placed at her disposal and are destined either immediately or mediately to serve the end of the Church which is the worship of God and the salvation and sanctification of men. Churches, chapels, cemeteries, benefices and the lands belonging to them, first fruits, tithes, offerings of money and property (both real and personal) are church property in the strict sense.[5]

According to the Code of Canon Law, church property comprises the temporal goods that belong to the universal Church, the Apostolic See, or to any other moral person within the Church. However, the property of the clergy and the laity that is held as a personal possession is not church property.[6] Some of the pre-Code canonists indicated a division that placed the income received by a cleric from a benefice within the scope of defined church property. The limitations indicated in canon 1497 do not permit this division. The present notion of church property includes only the property of the ecclesiastical moral persons, not the property of individual physical persons, even though they are ecclesiastics.[7]

The Code declares that all temporal goods, whether corporeal, both movable and immovable, or incorporeal which belong to the universal Church and the Apostolic See or to any other moral person in the Church, are church property. Corporeal property is that property which is perceivable to the sense in some manner, whereas, the incorporeal is that property which is not perceivable by the senses but by the mind only, such as legal rights and obligations regarding property.[8] Immovable property is that which cannot be moved from place to place

[5]Goodwine, p. 3.

[6]Canon 1497.

[7]Goodwine, p. 4.

[8]U. C. Wiggins, *Property Laws of the State of Ohio Affecting the Church,* The Catholic University of America Canon Law Studies, n. 367 (Washington, D.C.: Catholic University of America Press, 1956), p. 57. (Hereafter cited as Wiggins.)

either naturally or legally, while movable property can be so moved.[9]

Church property is further divided into sacred things, *res sacra,* and precious property, *res pretiosa.* Church property is said to be precious, not by reason of its quantity nor by reason of the large income it produces, but only by reason of one or more of the three titles mentioned: art, such as a painting; history, such as ancient codices; material, such as precious stones. Sacred things are those which are destined for divine worship by reason of their consecration or blessing, such as a church, a chalice or the like.[10]

Canon 1498 defines the word "church" for the purpose of determining the exact meaning of the canons on church property. "Church" is defined to be not only the universal Church or the Apostolic See, but also any moral person in the Church unless the canon as taken in its context and nature would not permit such an interpretation so that the law indicates another meaning. The word is to be taken in the broad sense. The strict sense would limit the meaning to places of divine worship only. However, the canon includes every ecclesiastical moral person constituted as such by church authority for the purpose of religious and charitable activity as permitted by canon 100. This broad sense of the word "church" includes hospitals, schools, religious houses and institutes, chapters of religious persons and other moral persons. The canon excludes associations that are merely approved and that are not moral persons according to canon 100. Thus, the Society of St. Vincent de Paul, the Knights of Columbus and similar societies that have been established by private persons without ecclesiastical approval as required in canon 100 do not own "church" property. These pious and charitable societies are not ecclesiastical moral persons but they may be incorporated by the civil law and thus exercise their rights. Canon 1498 intends to make definite those moral persons included under the broad sense of the word "church." The canon does not intend to prohibit such

[9]Bouscaren, p. 799.

[10]Canon 1497, §2; cf. Bouscaren, p. 799.

associations from incorporating according to the prescripts of civil law.[11]

Section 1. Means of Acquisition

The Church, like all other physical or moral persons, can acquire temporal property by every just means allowed by the natural or the positive law.[12] The purpose of Canon 1499 is to reject all the unjust limitations sometimes imposed upon the Church by the laws of the State. These limitations sometimes regard the object, such as bequests. The Canon makes clear that the Church acquires property not only by collections of tithes or free-will offerings, but by every just means common to all.[13]

The just means of acquiring property by natural law are occupation, accession and labor which may bring property into one's possession by nature or industry.[14] The civil law permits transferal of property from one person to another so that after one has originally acquired property, that propety may go into the hands of another. The common means of transfer is by contract, conveyances, last will or testament, gifts, legal succession, and prescription. The Church has particular legislation on the acquisition of property by moral persons. The property of a moral person devolves to another upon the dissolution of a moral person. The transfer is also effected by appropriate division of the property to another moral person. Acquisition of church property is commonly had in the exaction of tithes and first fruits, collections, taxes of various types, stole fees, prescriptions, wills and gifts *inter vivos* or *causa mortis*.

A. Division and Dissolution of Moral Persons

When the territory of an ecclesiastical moral person is divided in such a way that either a part of it is given another moral person or a distinct moral person is created for the separated

[11] Bouscaren, p. 800.

[12] Canon 1499, §1.

[13] Abbo-Hannan, II, 710; Cf. Murphy, p. 103; Bouscaren 801.

[14] Bouscaren, p. 801.

part of the territory, an equitable and proportionate division shall be made. This division is made by appropriate ecclesiastical authority. The division is to give a proportionate share of the property which was held for the benefit of the whole territory. The debts which were contracted for the entire territory are also to be divided. There is a provision that the intentions of pious donors and founders must be respected. Legally vested rights and special laws governing the moral persons involved must be observed.[15]

When the moral person is extinguished, the ownership of its property devolves upon the immediately superior moral person to the extinguished moral person, provided, however, that there be always respected the intentions of founders or donors, legally vested rights and special laws governing the moral person which has ceased to be.[16]

B. Tithes, First-fruits, Collections

Tithes are the tenth part of all fruits and sacrifices justly acquired. These were held to be due to God in recognition of His supreme dominion over men so that for the Jews of the Old Testament, tithes and first-fruits were of strict precept.[17] Canon law states that the special statutes and the laudable customs of individual regions shall be observed in regard to the payments of tithes and first fruits. This is a recognition of the oldest and best known means of acquiring those temporal things required by the Church. The canon does not insist upon the establishment of tithes. However, where the practice exists of tithing and giving first fruits, such a practice is to be retained.[18]

In the United States, the most common means of support for ecclesiastical moral persons are collections. Voluntary offerings generally suffice and strictly defined laws requiring a

---

[15]Canon 1500.

[16]Canon 1501; Cf. Abbo-Hannan, II, 711, note that the property of a dissolved association of the laity seems to devolve upon the diocese while observing that some hold it to devolve upon the religious community, if established by religious, e.g. third orders, sodalities.

[17]Exodus XXIII, 16.

[18]Canon 1502.

certain tribute have been unnecessary. Since there is a danger of abuse of the practice of making collections, the Church has seen fit to place definite limitations upon the use of this means. These limitations are placed to restrain zealous persons desiring to promote a worthy cause as much as to restrain unscrupulous persons. Therefore, private persons, whether clerics or lay persons, are forbidden to solicit funds for any pious or ecclesiastical institution or purpose without proper permission. This permission is to be written. The proper authority to give this permission is either the Apostolic See or the ordinary of the person collecting and the local ordinary of the place in which they wish to collect.[19] This canon is not meant to be a restriction of the privileges of strictly mendicant orders when they collect within the diocese in which their monastery is located according to canons 621-624.

The third Plenary Council of Baltimore expressly forbade such solicitation by private persons as a means to forestall the indiscreet solicitation of alms which are impositions upon the faithful and interference with the right of pastors.[20] Pastors are not private persons within their own parishes and they can make collections for those causes they deem necessary but they cannot give permission to others to make such collections without permission of the local ordinary.[21] However, pastors must permit those who have the proper permissions to make collections in their parish to do so. Oriental clerics cannot obtain such permission from the local ordinaries but they must approach the local ordinary by proceeding through the Sacred Congregation for the Oriental Church or through the Apostolic Delegate.[22]

Generally speaking, the canonists have agreed upon those collections which are strictly forbidden without permission and those which are permitted. The canon intends to forbid begging in the strict sense, that is, proceeding from door to door to

---

[19]Canon 1503. The ordinary is determined by Canon 198, cf. p. 39 *infra.*

[20]*Acta et Decreta Councilii Plenarii Baltimorensis III, A.D. MDCCCLXXXIV* (Baltimorae: John Murphy, 1886), n. 295.

[21]Abbo-Hannan, II, 712.

[22]Digest, I, 719.

ask for alms. Visiting the most generous persons of a community for the purposes of such a collection is also forbidden. However, the following actions are definitely permitted:

1) asking help of those who are personally known to one when done with discretion;
2) collecting alms in a church or at the meeting of some society, since such gifts are considered voluntary offerings;
3) going to certain homes at the invitation of the occupants; and
4) visiting benefactors to thank them and so forth.[23]

C. *Taxes and Stole Fees*

It is evident that the property treated of in the preceding section is church property in the sense of canon 1497. Tithes, first-fruits and collections are received for the moral persons of the Church. Certain taxes and stole fees are not received for moral persons of the Church and so they are not church property. The *cathedraticum* is a moderate tax paid annually to the Bishop in token of subjection by all churches and benefices subject to his jurisdiction and also by the various confraternities in the diocese.[24] If this tax is meant to be personal income for the bishop as a physical person, then it is not ecclesiastical property. If it were to accrue to the Episcopal See, then it would be ecclesiastical property. Since the tax is not to be paid when the diocese is vacant, it seems to be personal income and is not ecclesiastical property. Similar reasoning excludes stole fees from the strict meaning of ecclesiastical property. Stole fees are gratuities and remunerations given by the faithful recipients on the occasion of the administrations of sacraments and sacramentals and are the property of the minister.[25]

The other taxes mentioned in the Code accrue to the moral person for which the tax is assessed. The bishop is permitted

---

[23]Bouscaren, p. 805.

[24]Canon 1504: the amount is determined by custom or in line with the ruling contained in canon 1507, §1.

[25]Canon 1507; cf. canon 463 which states that the stole fees go to the pastor, and canon 824, §1, which states that the celebrant is the recipient of the mass stipend.

to tax all the parishes and ecclesiastical moral persons, even if exempt for the support of the seminary. This tax cannot exceed 5% of the taxable income.[26] This tax must be a general tax and imposed at the same rate for all the moral persons in the diocese.

The ordinary is permitted to impose taxes for special diocesan necessities on all beneficiaries, secular or religious. The canon indicates that the sum is to be taken from the physical person or moral person who holds the benefice, and the sum is to be moderate and proportioned to the income of the beneficiary.[27] The ordinary can exact contributions from churches, benefices, and other ecclesiastical institutions only in the act of foundation or consecration. The purpose of this tax must be the good of the diocese as determined by the ordinary. However, the exaction of the tax is restricted to a precise time. This act of foundation means the act of consent given by the ordinary, as required by law, to build a church or institution on a certain piece of ground; the act of consecration is the actual consecration of the church, not the simple or the solemn blessing of the church.[28]

The prevailing method of supporting the bishop and the diocesan curia is by means of a tax imposed upon each parish in proportion to its income as based upon the legislation of the Second Plenary Council of Baltimore:

> Since it is equitable and just that all the faithful of each diocese should contribute to the proper support of the Bishop who bears the burden and care of all, the Fathers assembled judged that this matter was to be treated in the Diocesan Synods in which the priests having the care of souls were to take counsel among themselves and agree on a certain pension to be given annually to their Ordinary, to be made up of a definite portion of the income of each church. Such an assignment and division, after being

[26]Canons 1355, 1356.

[27]Canon 1505.

[28]Canon 1506; cf. Bouscaren, p. 808.

examined and approved by the Ordinary, shall be published as a diocesan law to be observed by all.[29]

It has been said that this tax has been abrogated by the Code although it is the common practice in the United States. There are authors who contend that this tax is still permissible, which opinion seems in accord with the conditions in the United States.[30] This tax cannot be said to be included in the special diocesan necessities of canon 1505 for two reasons. First, canon 1505 permits a tax to be placed upon the beneficiaries, whereas this tax is placed upon the parish. Second, the special diocesan necessities has been interpreted to mean special needs such as: the expenses incurred in the consecration of a bishop, unusual diocesan debts, necessary and extraordinary repairs of the cathedral church, the expenses for the *ad limina,* and so forth. The broader term used in canon 1506, "for the good of the diocese" would certainly include such support of the bishop and the diocesan curia. However, in this canon, the tax is imposed only at the time of the act of foundation or consecration. Consequently, since the canons do not include this tax, the present practice can only be sustained by virtue of the legislation of the Second Plenary Council.[31]

D. Prescription

Prescription is a mode of acquisition by which a person who has been in possession of a thing for a long time so that he is generally regarded as its owner, is accepted as the owner by legitimate authority. Property is acquired by this mode of acquisition when the following five conditions are fulfilled: First, the object must be subject to prescription; second, good faith must be present when the time of prescription begins and must continue for the entire time; third, the possessor must have a just title, even though it is a color of title; fourth, the pos-

[29]Decree n. 100; Cf. Bouscaren, p. 808 citing a reply of the Sacred Congregation for the Oriental Church approving a similar method for the Greek-Ruthenian Church in the United States in 1929.

[30]Abbo-Hannan, II, 713, footnote 16.

[31]Cf. Bouscaren, p. 808; Doheny, p. 59.

session must be just; and fifth, the time required by law must be fulfilled.

The reasons for accepting this mode of acquisition are that men are naturally careful not to give up whatever belongs to them and the stability of society demands that a possessor not be regarded as an usurper. Therefore, these apparently arbitrary rules have been devised to assist owners in reclaiming their rights or to permit the one prescribing to preclude attack of his apparent rights by making them actual rights.[32]

The Church accepts the legislation of the respective nations on prescription with certain limitations. Certain objects are not subject to prescription.

1) whatever pertains to the divine law, whether natural or positive,

2) what can be obtained by Apostolic privilege alone,

3) spiritual rights which lay persons are not capable of receiving, if there is a question of prescription in favor of lay persons,

4) certain and undoubted boundaries of ecclesiastical provinces, dioceses, parishes, vicariates, and prefectures apostolic, prelatures and abbacies nullius,

5) mass stipends and their obligations,

6) a benefice without a title, that is, without even a color of title to form a basis for the right to the benefice,

7) the right of visitation and of obedience if the consequence would be that subjects can be visited by no prelate and are no longer subject to any prelate,

8) payment of the *cathedraticum*.[33]

The reason for the restrictions imposed by this canon is that the Church as a perfect society established by God, not only has the right, but also the duty, according to her divine mission, to insure respect for spiritual things, and to make provisions that the divine and the natural law will be observed.[34]

---

[32]Doheny, p. 66.

[33]Canon 1508.

[34]Doheny, p. 70; Cf. Thomas O. Martin, *Adverse Possession, Prescription and Limitation of Actions, the Canonical "Praescriptio,"* A commentary on canon 1508, Catholic University of America Canon Law

Other precautions are required by the Code so that sacred things will be respected. Sacred things that are property of private persons, may be prescribed by private persons. If they are not owned by a private person but by an ecclesiastical moral person, they are not subject to prescription by a private person but are, however, subject to prescription by another ecclesiastical moral person. Sacred things cannot be prescribed for profane uses.[35] Sacred things are those things destined for divine worship by consecration or benediction. They lose the consecration or blessing when they are so badly damaged or changed as to lose their original form. Thus, they become useless for their purpose. This loss of consecration or blessing occurs when they are used for unbecoming purposes, are offered for public sale, or are placed on auction. When the consecration or benediction is lost, these sacred things can be freely acquired and given to profane uses. However, they may never be given to sordid uses.[36]

The Church requires that the element of good faith be present at all times when one is acquiring an object by prescription. The element of good faith is the judgment by which one prudently concludes that he justly possesses a thing as his own without any violation of the rights of another. One sins if he keeps a thing belonging to another without good faith and with the conscious obligation that he must restore the thing to its owner. The Church will not permit sin to be rewarded by the law.[37]

The Church requires a definite time limit for the prescription of certain objects. Immovable things and movable precious things, rights and actions, real or personal, that are the property of the Holy See must be held for the space of one hundred years. If these things are the property of some other ecclesiastical moral person, they must be held for thirty years. All

---

Studies, n. 202, (Washington, D.C.: The Catholic University of America Press, 1944).

[35]Canon 1510, §1, 2.

[36]Canons 1510, 1497, §2, and 1305.

[37]Canon 1512; Bouscaren, p. 812.

other property would be prescribed once it is held according to the time prescribed by the civil law, providing all the other requisites of law are observed.[38]

E. Donations and Bequests

Five canons of the Code set forth the church law concerning gifts and bequests that are made to the Church. The obligation is imposed upon those concerned to see that these gifts and bequests are carried out according to the intention of the donors.[39] Anyone who is capable of disposing of his property, both according to the natural and ecclesiastical law, may give his property to pious causes either by gifts *inter vivos* or by gifts *mortis causa.* Gifts can also be made by wills or bequests. The solemnities of the civil law are to be observed in making these gifts. However, if these solemnities are not observed, the intention of the testator is to be observed by the executors and heirs.[40]

The practice of the faithful to leave their property to the Church in some manner can be traced back to Apostolic times. The Church was permitted to be an heir at Roman law before A.D. 321. The faithful have always been anxious to have Masses said for the repose of their souls, to spread the faith, to help the poor and afflicted and for other pious or charitable causes. Bequests and wills have been recognized as a sure means of fulfilling this desire of the faithful. Therefore, a universal custom developed of leaving property to the Church. This property became the subject of much legislation concerning the conscientious attestation and execution of wills, with special penalties being arranged for those who violated the rights of the Church in this matter.

The errors that denied individuals the right to bequeath their property to the Church have been condemned in the interest of justice and truth. The Council of Constance condemned Wycliffe who held it sinful to found convents or to bequeath

---

[38]Canon 1511.

[39]Canons 1513-1517.

[40]Canon 1513.

money to clergy. Pius IX similarly condemned the errors of the Nineteenth century. These condemnations were to insure that the inherent rights of individuals to dispose of his goods in whatever way they desire would be preserved. If the public good is to be jeopardized, this inherent right might be limited. The Church also asserted that it has the right to acquire property by all just means of the natural and positive law that are permitted to other persons, either moral or physical. Therefore, the Church has the right to acquire property by means of bequeaths and legacies which are universally acknowledged as a legitimate means of acquisition.[41]

Pious causes have been defined in connection with canon law as anything that is done principally in consideration of God and for a supernatural end, either to merit grace or glory with God or in satisfaction for one's own or another's sins. If the donor is a Catholic, there is a presumption in favor of a pious cause. However, a motive of mere philanthrophy does not suffice. This motive often moves donors to support hospitals and recreation works of various types.[42]

Gifts are effective either during the life of the donor or upon his death. Heirs should be admonished to carry out the intention of the donor.[43] The intention of the donor, as expressed, is to be fulfilled both in the manner of administration and in the spending of the gifts while the rights of the ordinary are to be respected.[44] The property must not be diverted to other good works even though they may seem more useful than that designated by the donor.

The ordinary is the executor of all pious wills, bequeaths,

---

[41]Doheny, pp. 87 ff., gives a historical basis of great length for these canons.

[42]Bouscaren, p. 814.

[43]Canon 1513; Abbo-Hannan, II, 720 note that the unbaptized also are held notwithstanding the contrary legislation of secular authorities. Cf. Doheny, p. 90 who states that a confessor of an unwilling heir must act prudently so that, if the heir is in good faith or unwilling and the testator's wishes are invalid at civil law, then recourse should be made to the Sacred Penitentiary for composition or condonation.

[44]Canon 1514.

donations, whether *inter vivos* or *inter mortuos,* so that he is able to exercise vigilance, and should do so, even by visitation if necessary, to see that the will of the donor is being diligently fulfilled. Other executors must, after fulfilling their duties, render an accounting to the ordinary. This obliges the executor even though there is a clause in the gift that is contrary to the rights of the ordinary. Such clauses are to be considered as not present.[45] Clerics or religious who receive property in trust for a pious cause, whether by donation *inter vivos* or *mortis causa,* must inform the ordinary of the trust. The report must indicate the nature and the extent of the property involved, whether movable or immovable. The cleric or the religious may not accept the trust when the donor expressly forbids this report to the ordinary.[46]

As executor and one exercising vigilance, the ordinary must oblige the trustee to deposit the trust in a safe place and to invest it if necessary. He must also see that it is carried out according to the above norms of canons 1515. Trust funds given to a religious that are intended for the benefit of churches, or of the inhabitants, or of pious causes of the place or of the diocese, are under the jurisdiction of the local ordinary. In all other cases, such trust funds are under the jurisdiction of the proper ordinary of the religious.[47]

Only the Holy See is recognized as having the power of eminent domain in these matters and the ordinary may not act to make reductions, restrictions, condonations nor commutations in absence of such delegation by the Holy See, and then

---

[45]Canon 1515.

[46]Canon 1516. Bouscaren, p. 819, states that before the Code in 1918 lay trustees were forbidden to take such trusts. By the present law, the lay trustee may accept such trusts but they must submit to the visitation of the ordinary and give him an accounting of the administration of these pious trusts according to the ruling of canon 1515.

[47]Canon 1516. Cf. canon 198, the ordinary of non-exempt religious is the local ordinary. Bouscaren, p. 819, notes that the exemption of religious orders from the jurisdiction of the ordinary of the place extends generally to their churchs, houses of studies, but not to parochial churches, schools, orphanages, and hosptials. This statement must be taken with certain reservations.

only for a just cause. However, the person who makes the will may expressly grant this power to the local ordinary so that with sufficient reason, such changes might be made. It would be destructive of the trust that is had in the testamentary system if refusal of reasonable change or commutation for just and necessary reasons would work untold hardships upon individuals and militate against the public good.[48]

Article II. Texas Law on Acquisition

It is to be remembered that the State of Texas adopted the common law as practiced by the several States in the United States after the Revolution in 1836, when the State was still a Republic. However, the Republic did not seek a complete transformation from the civil law that had been known under the regime of the Mexican Republic, but rather a more easily understandable law. For that reason, some of the elements that prevailed in the complex common law system were not adopted.[49] Consequently, the State of Texas is under the common law in so far as it is applicable to the situation of the State and in so far as it is not inconsistent with the constitution.[50]

In 1840, the act to adopt the common law expressly excluded the laws of Spain and Mexico that related exclusively to grants and the colonization of lands. Excluded also were those laws that concerned the reservation of islands and other lands on the coasts.[51] Subsequently, the courts stated the principle that those land holdings which were acquired under prior governments would be given full recognition by the State of Texas. The maxim adopted stated that the least possible injury to the rights of persons and communities should be caused by the revolution and consequent change in government.[52] Later, a

[48]Canon 1517. Doheny, p. 102, says that just causes are decreased revenues in consequence of inflation, wars, national or international crises, and similar causes. When such cause is present, the ordinary might use canon 81.

[49]Markham, p. 904 ff.

[50]1 Gammel 1077.

[51]1 Gammel 262.

[52]Blair v. Odin, 3 Tex. 288 (1848).

court was to express the maxim in this manner: "the people change their allegiance; their relation to their ancient sovereign is dissolved, but their relation to each other and their right of property remain undisturbed."[53]

The source of title in the State of Texas is held to be the will of the people, whereas in England, the source of title was the King, so that if he were dethroned, the source of title would be lost. But the sovereign will of the people as the source of title was declared to be defined and expressed by well regulated laws of their own making.[54]

Section 1. Kinds of Property

In the common law that has been adopted by the State of Texas, property is generally classified as either:

> 1) immovable, or real property, which is composed of land and those things that are permanently attached to it, and
>
> 2) movable, or personal property, which is composed of those things not so attached to land, and is also denominated chattels.

Certain types of property may be held to be real for one purpose and personal for another: such as, growing timber or crops.[55] All property may be owned, except certain physical things, which by their nature are incapable of being owned, such as air, light and running water.[56]

Immovable, or real, property includes land, things growing on land until severed, fixtures, personal interests in land, and incorporeal hereditaments.[57] Personal, or movable property, comprises those movable and tangible things such as animals, ships, furniture, merchandise, besides incorporeal or intangible things such as personal annuities, stocks, shares, copyrights and such

---

[53] McMullen v. Hodge, 5 Tex. 34 (1853).

[54] *Loc. cit.*

[55] 33 Tex. Jur. 938.

[56] 33 Tex. Jur. 942.

[57] *Black's Law Dictionary,* p. 1447, "property."

things. The distinction between the two lies in mobility.[58] The word, property, as used in this book, is always used to denote everything which is the subject of ownership, corporeal or incorporeal, tangible or intangible, visible or invisible, real or personal. Or as it has been said, everything that goes to make up wealth or an estate is property.[59]

The ownership of property is acquired by many methods that can be considered, generally, under the concept of original acquisition and derivative acquisition. Original acquisition is that by which a man secures a property in a thing which is not at the time he acquires it, and in its then existing condition, the property of any other individual. Derivative acquisition is that which is had when property is procured from others.[60]

Section 2. Acquisition of Personal Property

A. Original Acquisition

The State of Texas has in general followed the norms of the common law for the acquisition of personal property. As a consequence, there has been no limitation upon religious corporations as to acquiring this type of property.[61] At times, due to particular situations, statutes indicate variations from the common law as to manner of acquisition. Thus the acquisition of domestic animals is controlled by Statute,[62] whereas the common law rules the acquisition of wild animals.[63]

Acquisition of abandoned property is had by the first person to take possession with the intention to make it his own. Abandonment occurs when there is a voluntary giving up and relin-

---

[58]*Loc. cit.*

[59]*Loc. cit.*

[60]*Ibidem*, p. 33, "acquisition."

[61]Zollman, p. 164; Alden v. St. Peter's Parish in City of Sycamore 158 Ill. 631, 42 N.E. 392, 30 L.R.A. 232. (1895).

[62]Revised Statutes, Article 6911, requires that the possessor have the animal for at least a year and publicize the fact of possession.

[63]Jones v. State, 45 S.W. 2d 612 (1936) held the first to take possession or complete control with the intent to own acquires title.

quishing of all ownership and rights in a thing.[64] The question of abandonment is a question of fact which is to be determined by all the facts in the record. An essential element is the intention to abandon and such intention must be shown by clear and satisfactory evidence. The mere non-use of a right is not sufficient of itself to show abandonment, but if the failure to use is long, continued and unexplained, it gives rise to an inference of intention to abandon.[65]

Lost or misplaced personal property is acquired by finding. The Supreme Court has asserted that the "treasure trove" doctrine is not recognized in the law of Texas. This doctrine was founded in the common law that arose after the departure of the Romans. Hidden treasures left by the Romans were to be kept by the finder since the owner was unknown.[66] Lost property is that property which is involuntarily parted with through neglect, carelessness or inadvertence. The general rule is that the finder is to retain the property as against the owner or possessor of the premises where it is found. On the other hand, mislaid property is that property which is intentionally placed in a certain place but the owner forgets where he placed it. The general rule gives a presumption that the property is to be left in the custody of the owner or occupier and the right of possession is in the owner or occupant of the premises as against all except the owner of the property that has been mislaid.[67]

Property may become the property of another by the doctrine of accession. By this doctrine, labor, new material or objects are added to an article. When one wilfully converts and enhances the value, the owner receives the enhanced value regardless of the proportion to the actual value, or the owner may have

---

[64] 1 Tex. Jur. 9.

[65] City of Anson v. Arnett, 250 S.W. 2d 450 (1953); Sikes v. State, 28 S.W. 688 (1893).

[66] A. Mitchell, *Personal Property,* Law Review Series (Austin: Hemphill's Book Store, 1956), p. 4. (Hereafter cited as Mitchell, *Personal Property.*)

[67] Schley v. Couch, 284 S.W. 2d 333 (1955) gives all the doctrine in a case where D found money buried in a jar while working for P. The money was awarded to P.

a return of the chattel, if it can be identified.[68] But if the converter is innocent, the owner is entitled to the value of the property at the time of the conversion, and is not entitled to the enhanced value or to a return of the finished product.[69] When the property of two or more different owners is incorporated together, the title goes to the owner of the principal good if the articles cannot be detached without injury to the principal.[70]

The doctrine of confusion is to rule when there is an intermixture of property by different persons, to the degree that the property of each cannot be distinguished. This occurs only when goods of a similar nature, such as wheat, oil and the like, are involved. The question is: can the goods be separated and can a reasonably certain estimate of the amount be made?[71] The owners are tenants in common when confusion is had by consent or by an act of God or by an act of a third party.[72] The one who wilfully causes confusion is held to the burden of proving that part of the property which is his.[73] But when one deliberately so mingles articles with the intent to defraud, "all things are presumed against the spoliator."[74]

B. Acquisition by Operation of Law

Acquisition by operation of law gives personal property to a possessor who holds adversely to the real owner under determined conditions. This is called acquisition by adverse possession. Acquisition may be had by satisfaction of judgment which is also by operation of law. When an owner sues for conversion of his chattel and receives the value of the chattel in judgment, instead of the chattel itself, the title is conveyed to the convertor by the judgment.[75] If the judgment is not satisfied, title does not pass but part payment is an estoppel on the

[68]Ochoa v. Rogers, 234 S.W. 693 (1926).

[69]Werner Stave Co. v. Pickering, 119 S.W. 333 (1911).

[70]Firestone Service Stores v. Darden, 96 S.W. 2d 316 (1938).

[71]Ortiz Oil v. Luttes, 141 S.W. 2d 1050 (1940); 9 Tex. Jur. 371.

[72]Belcher v. Cassidy, 62 S.W. 924 (1897); 9 Tex. Jur. 370.

[73]Johnson v. Hocker, 39 S.W. 406 (1894); 9 Tex. Jur. 475.

[74]Holloway Seed Co. v. City Bank, 47 S.W. 95 (1895).

[75]Greer v. Lafayette County Bank, 47 S.W. 737 (1895).

owner from attacking the claim of the buyer from such a convertor. Similarly, purchase at a judicial sale makes the purchaser an innocent purchaser, and when he complies with the terms of the sale, he is to receive title that the court is authorized to convey.[76]

Acquisition of title to personal property may be had by adverse possession when the conditions required by law are fulfilled. These conditions are that the property be held for two years with a claim to title. Further, actual possession is adverse only when there is an element of claim to the title by the possessor. Where one has original possession by permission, a disclaimer of the original permissive title and a subsequent hostile possession of which the true owner had notice, or is presumed to know, arises. The possessor must have the property in good faith.[77]

Where an article is originally stolen and sold to another, the purchaser who holds in good faith and open use for two years perfects the title. The good faith and open use for two years are necessary.[78] Where one party loans chattels to another, the passage of two years time without demand does not convey the chattel to the possessor. However, the owner might suffer loss of the title as against creditors and purchaser of the persons in possession. To prevent such loss of title, the owner must make demand for repossession of the chattel, by due process of law in writing, duly acknowledged or proved and recorded.[79]

The law requires that actions for detaining of personal property be instituted within two years after the cause of action has accrued, and not afterwards, in order that ownership might be evident to the public. This requirement applies to convertor's also.[80] The time that the cause of action accrues varies with the time that the adverse possession begins. The statute is applicable even when the purchaser is aware of the claim of the owner so

[76]Revised Statutes, Articles 3813, 3816; 26 Tex. Jur. 545.

[77]2 Tex. Jur. 68; Revised Statutes Article 5526.

[78]Woodward v. San Antonio Traction, 95 S.W. 76 (1899).

[79]Mitchell, *Personal Property*, p. 9.

[80]Revised Statutes Article 5526.

that the purchaser is not in good faith.[81] The law favors the transfer of title against a delinquent owner.

C. *Acquisition by Transfer*

The most frequently used means of acquisition is by transfer from one party to another through contracts, sales, gifts, and bequests or wills. For a transfer by contract, the essential elements of a contract must be present. A contract may be defined as an agreement, upon sufficient consideration, to do or not to do a particular thing. The transfer of personal property by such a contract is not limited by special legislation.[82]

1. *Sales*

A credit sale transfers title and possession but the payment is postponed whereas a cash sale transfers title and possession when payment is made. At times, a sale permits the purchaser to return the article even though the title passed on delivery. Such a privilege to return is construed to remain for a reasonable time. Other sales are on approval so that the title passes when approved. In general, when articles are shipped, title passes to the purchaser upon delivery to the shipping point if the purchaser pays the shipping. However, if the seller pays the shipping title passes when the destination is reached. The risk of loss of the goods sold is upon the person holding legal title.[83]

All the requirements of a valid contract must exist before a valid sale may occur because a sale of personal property is based upon a contract. Therefore, there must be two parties capable at law of contracting, a good consideration, a legal subject matter and in the absence of an estoppel, a mutuality of assent.[84] But it must be remembered that sales are generally informal contracts and for particular articles that are objects of sales, the contract may not be too evident.

---

[81]Williams v. Davenport, 212 S.W. 675 (1920). The case concerned a specific creditor of the possessor.

[82]Cf. Black's Law Dictionary, p. 421, "contract"; Mitchell, *Real Property*, p. 22.

[83]37 Tex. Jur. 193; Mitchell, *Personal Property*, p. 23.

[84]37 Tex. Jur. 101.

2. *Gifts*

Acquisition by gift is had both by gifts *inter vivos* and *causa mortis*. A gift is a transfer of property without any consideration or compensation in exchange being given.[85] The basic requirement of a valid *inter vivos* gift is present donative intent coupled with the delivery of the subject matter of the gift. This delivery may be actual, symbolic or constructive. A statute states that no gift of any goods or chattels is valid unless by deed or will duly acknowledged or proven and recorded. The gift is also considered valid when actual possession comes to, and remains with, the donee or someone claiming under him.[86] If a chattel is capable of manual delivery, actual delivery is required unless the gift is by deed or will according to Article 3998. A chattel that is not capable of manual delivery is considered delivered when constructive delivery is had. Constructive delivery is a general term, comprehending all those acts which, although not truly conferring a real possession of the thing, have been held, by construction of law, equivalent to acts of real delivery.[87]

Gifts *causa mortis* take place when a gift is made in the expectation of death then imminent so that the property belongs to the donee if the donor dies as anticipated and leaves the donee surviving him without having expressly revoked the gift.[88] This gift is revokable by the donor or by operation of law if the donor does not die as anticipated, whereas a gift *inter vivos* is immediate and irrevocable when made.[89] Delivery is required for gifts *causa mortis* as it is required for gifts *inter vivos*. The anticipation of death must be present, even though it is a groundless apprehension of death. The death must come from the anticipated cause. If death proceeds from another cause than that anticipated, the gift is revoked by oper-

[85] *Black's Law Dictionary,* p. 843, "gift."

[86] Revised Statutes, Article 3998; Mitchell, *Personal Property,* p. 18.

[87] Wells v. Sansing, 245 S.W. 2d 964 (1949); Hillebrand v. Brewer, 6 Tex. 45 (1853); 20B Tex. Jur. 460, 463; *Black's Law Dictionary,* p. 549, "delivery."

[88] Chevallier v. Wilson, 1 Tex. 161, (1846).

[89] 20B Tex. Jur. 445, 501.

ation of law. This was the decision in a case where the donor died from an illness instead of an anticipated operation although death came at the approximate time anticipated.[90]

3. *Wills*

A gift by will, also called a bequest or a legacy, takes effect upon the occurrence of death on the part of the donor but no delivery is required before death. A will is the legal expression or declaration of a person's mind, or wishes as to the disposition of his property, to be performed or to take effect after his death.[91]

The laws of the State of Texas require that wills bequeathing personal property be set forth in writing, attested to by two or more credible witnesses above the age of fourteen years, subscribing their names thereto in their own handwriting and in the presence of the testator. However, the writing is valid if wholly in the handwriting of the testator.[92] The validity of a will concerning personal property is the law of the domicile of the decedent at the time of his death in common law. This rule is followed in the State of Texas.[93] In this matter, movable and immovable properties are not always held to be convertible terms with real and personal properties.[94]

Section 3. Acquisition of Real Property

Real property is that property which has the characteristic of immobility or permanency in location. This concept includes land, things growing on land until severed, fixtures, personal interests in land and incorporeal hereditaments or proprietary

[90]Brind v. International Trust Co., 179 Pac. 148; Mitchell, *Personal Property*, p. 22.

[91]*Black's Law Dictionary*, p. 210, "bequests"; p. 1846, "will."

[92]*Texas Probate Code, Vernon's Texas Statutes, 1956 Supplement*, (Kansas City, Mo.: Vernon Law Book Co., 1956) p. 613, sections 58-60. (Hereafter cited as *Probate Code*, sections 58-60.)

[93]Holman v. Hopkins, 27 Tex. 38 (1863); Stumberg, G. W., "Testamentary Dispositions and the Conflict of Laws," 34 Texas Law Review 28 (1955).

[94]Toledo Society for Crippled Children v. Hickok, 152 Tex. 578, 261 S.W. 2d 692 (1953).

rights in the land of another.[95] The importance of the distinction between real and personal property lies in the formalities required for transfer. Whereas much personal property is acquired by original acquisition, real property is acquired by transfer, which original transfer is had from the sovereign. In Texas, the source of title is said to be from the sovereign will of the people in contrast to the English system where the source was the sovereign will of the Crown.[96]

The transfer of real property is effected by intestate or testate succession, by deed of conveyance, adverse possession, and estoppel. Specific formalities are required in the transfer of real property that are generally not required for the transfer of personal property. The specific formalities will be indicated in the following sections.

A. Inter Vivos *Transfer*

Transfer of title to real property by deed, adverse possession, and estoppel are the present modes of transfer *inter vivos*. The title to this property must have passed out of the sovereign power before transfer can be made by individual owners. That it, the political power, having *de jure* jurisdiction, must have parted title to individual owners. The property law of Texas must be studied with respect to the respective jurisdictions of Spain, Mexico, the Republic of Texas and the United States. This complex problem will not be treated here. It is only to be noted that there is a presumption which favors the imperfect title given by a former sovereign in order to foster peace of mind among those persons who owned under grants by those sovereigns.[97] Texas as an independent republic, first established a General Land Office in 1837. This office was to have custody and control of all books, records, papers, land documents, and to act as the issuing agent of titles to Texas lands granted after 1837. Subsequently, the State has transferred out of the sovereign will of the people, almost all the land in the territory.

---

[95]Mitchell, *Real Property*, p. 1.

[96]McMullen v. Hodge, 5 Tex. 34 (1853).

[97]McMullen v. Hodge, 5 Tex. 34 (1853); San Antonio v. Odin, 15 Tex. 539 (1855).

What has not been definitely transferred out of the sovereign is at least appropriated and set apart for various purposes, such as the public school fund, eleemosynary institutions, and so forth.[98]

1. Deed

The most common method of transferring property *inter vivos* is by the use of the deed. Contracts to convey land and the actual conveyance thereof must be in writing according to the provisions of the law.[99] The following deed has been declared to be sufficient as a conveyance of the fee simple estate in any real estate, with an express covenant of general warranty:

> The State of Texas
> County of........................(where the land lies)
> Know all men by these presents: That I .... (name of grantor) of........................, ..., County, ..., for and in consideration of ....dollars (this clause is known as the consideration clause), to me in hand paid by..............................., having granted, sold and conveyed, and by these presents do grant, sell and convey unto .... (this clause is known as the granting clause) of the city of ...., ...County, ..., all that certain tract (then follows the description)........... ....
>
> To have and to hold the above described premises (this is the habendum clause) together with all and singular rights and appurtenances thereto in any wise belonging, unto the said .... (the grantee), his heirs or assigns forever. And I do hereby bind myself, my heirs, executors and administrators to warrant and forever defend all and singular the said premises unto the said................, his heirs and assigns, against every person whomsoever, lawfully claiming or to claim the same, or any part thereof (this is the clause of general warranty, which may be omitted or replaced by a clause of special contractual warranty, or any other agreement, depending upon the desire and intent of the parties).

[98]Cf. Mitchell, *Real Property*, pp. 61-67.

[99]Revised Statutes, Articles 1288, 3995.

Witness my hand this the..........day of................., 19........
Signed in the presence of .... and ..../.[100]

....

Grantor's Signature

Certain parts of this deed are required for validity. The statement of the county and the state are not necessary as placed at the beginning but the complete description of the property must include the county and the state within the body of the deed so that the land can be identified. The grantor clause should set forth the name and capacity of the grantor. That is, if the grantor is an individual selling in his own right or an agent or administrator selling for another, this should be in evidence. The granting clause and/or habendum clause grants the estate and creates certain implied warranties. If the clause purports to grant a greater estate than is in fact conveyed, all the estate owned by the grantor will pass in order that the deed will not fail.[101] Words such as "grant" or "convey" imply a warranty that the grantor has not conveyed the estate or an interest therein to others and that the estate is free from incumbrances.[102]

The consideration clause is immaterial if the fact that consideration passed can be proven by other legal evidence.[103] The description must be sufficient or the deed is void. The description is either complete within itself or by reference to data which will enable a complete description of the property to be made.[104] Delivery is essential to constitute a conveyance of the property so that until delivery, even though the deed is properly subscribed, sealed, recorded, and complete in every detail, there is no basis for the title. The recordation of the deed gives rise to the presumption of delivery but in the absence of delivery, the deed is inoperative as a basis of title.[105] The

[100]Revised Statutes Article 1292; parenthesis remarks in Mitchell, *Real Property*, pp. 69-70.

[101]Cf. Revised Statutes Articles 1290-1291.

[102]Revised Statutes, Articles 1297-1298.

[103]Mitchell, *Real Property*, p. 72.

[104]*Ibidem*, pp. 72-73.

[105]*Ibidem*, p. 74.

grantee of the deed must accept the conveyance, which acceptance is usually presumed in the absence of proof to the contrary.[106]

Texas requires that certain conveyances of real property be recorded and authorizes the recordation of other conveyances. In order that the following be valid, recordation is required:

> All bargains, sales and other conveyances whatever, of any land, tenements and hereditaments, whether they may be made for passing any estate or freehold or inheritance or for a term of years; and deeds of settlement upon marriage, whether land, money or other personal things; and all deeds of trust and mortgages . . .[107]

The following instruments of writing which shall have been acknowledged or proved according to law are authorized to be recorded, viz:

> All deeds, mortgages, conveyances, deeds of trust, bonds for title, covenants, defeasances or other instruments of writing concerning any description; provided, however, and in cases of subdivisions of real property no map (shall be recorded until approved by the proper city official or board).[108]

Article 6626 permits the recordation of certain instruments whereas article 6627 requires the recordation of certain instruments for validity of the instrument against creditors and purchasers without notice. The recordation statutes serve notice on prospective purchasers, but not such that it destroys a conveyance of a better title. The effects of the recordation is not destructive of rights that exist in the land for others who have those rights by a prior and better title.[109]

As it has been noted, all contracts to convey realty and the actual conveyance of the interest in realty must be written as required by articles 1288 and 3995 of the Revised Statutes.

---

[106]*Ibidem,* p. 75.

[107]Revised Statutes Article 6627. However this article is to protect creditors and purchasers without notice. The deed is valid with respect to heirs and purchasers with notice.

[108]Revised Statutes Article 6626.

[109]Mitchell, *Real Property,* pp. 76-77.

The conveyances effected by these conveyances should be recorded with the county clerk as required by article 1289. The county clerk is to keep an index of these conveyances by deed according to the name of the grantee in alphabetical order, the type of the instrument, the land affected by the instrument, and the volume and page number upon which the instrument is recorded.[110]

2. *Adverse Possession*

Adverse possession is the term usually applied to lands whereas prescription is the term usually applied to incorporeal hereditaments.[111] It can be defined as a manner of acquiring the ownership of property, or discharging debts, by the effect of time, and under the conditions regulated by law. The prescription by which the ownership of property is acquired, is a right by which a mere possessor acquires the ownership of a thing which he possesses by the continuance of his possession during the time fixed by law. The prescription by which debts are released is a peremptory and perpetual bar to every species of action, real or personal, when the creditor has been silent for a certain time without urging his claim. This is commonly expressed by a similar term, the "bar of the statute of limitations."[112]

The following elements must be present in acquiring real property by adverse possession:

1) the actual, open notorious possession and enjoyment of real property or of any estate lying in grant,

2) continued for a certain length of time,

3) held adversely and in denial and opposition to the title of other claimants. Or it may be held under circumstances which indicate an assertion or color of right or title on the part of the person maintaining it, as against another person, who is out of possession.[113]

Texas has three types of statutes by which a claimant will

---

[110]Revised Statutes Articles 6591-6597.

[111]*Black's Law Dictionary,* p. 1405, "prescription."

[112]*Loc. cit.*

[113]*Ibidem,* p. 1383, "possession."

acquire property by adverse possession. The length of time required by these statutes varies from three to twenty-five years. The statutes are called curative, prescriptive and tolling statutes.

There are two curative statutes enacted to insure a claimant's title against others when the title is not regular, due to some defect that does not extend to the want of intrinsic fairness and honesty. The three year statute arose to cure titles that had been issued by the State. At least a color of a title issued was required. A void deed or one executed by an agent did not give color of title so the statute in effect required nearly perfect title. The five year statute extended to a void deed, but not to forged deed or one executed under a power of attorney that is forged. The statute was to cure those titles excluded by the strict requirements of the former statute.[114]

The possession required by these statutes must be open and notorious without recognition of any superior right of others. The five year statute envisions peaceable and adverse possession such as cultivating, using or enjoying the land, paying taxes thereon and claiming under a deed that is duly registered. Neither of these statutes will operate unless there is some inceptive legal right existing in a claimant according to the norm mentioned for peaceable and adverse possession.[115]

The ten year statute is called a prescriptive statute and operates to give a claimant with no enforceable inceptive right, either equitable or legal, title, which when required, relates back to the time a cause of action arose in favor of the true owner to evict him.[116] The possession required is that the claimant hold by adverse, continued, visible, notorious distinct and hostile possession, considering the nature, situation, and the use of the land. The statute embraces only 160 acres of land including the improvements. When the land is actually inclosed, the statute will extend to more than 160 acres. If the possession is interrupted by an adverse suit, it is not peaceable possession.

[114]Revised Statutes Articles 5507-5509.

[115]Mitchell, *Real Property*, p. 82.

[116]*Ibidem*, p. 80.

However, the possession can be by an actual, constructive, or even a recorded instrument asserting possession. The ten year possession need not rest in one individual alone. The possession of any number of claimants may be added together as long as there is privity of estate between the claimants which is had when a transfer of property occurs.[117]

The twenty-five year statute is a combination tolling statute and a cure-all statute. There are two statutes: one covering the naked trespasser without initial deed or deeds under which he claims, and the other covering those claiming by force of a deed or deeds, or any instrument or instruments, which have been recorded in the records of the county in which the real estate is located.[118] Article 5518 gives title by adverse possession to the naked trespasser. This statute does not operate for that time in which the true owner of the land is a minor, until the minor is 21 years of age, nor in time of war against military personnel until the owner is released from the military. Nor does the statute begin to toll when a person is of unsound mind or imprisoned until released. Further, when a person is absent from the state, the statute does not toll. The time ceases to toll for a period of twelve months in the case of the death of the person with a cause of action unless the executor is qualified by law before that time.[119] The claimant under article 5519 acquires title after the twenty-five year period without the time ceasing to toll because of minority, and so forth.[120] The twenty-five year statutes grant title to the claimant regardless of the size of the estate claimed.[121]

B. *Acquisition by Will*

The present law of Texas for the transfer of property by will is stated in the Probate Code of 1955. According to the common law, property passed immediately upon the death of

---

[117]Revised Statutes Articles 5510, 5514, 5516.

[118]Revised Statutes Articles 5518, 5519.

[119]Revised Statutes Articles 5537, 5538.

[120]*Loc. cit.;* also Republic v. Lee, 121 S.W. 2d 973 (1938).

[121]*Loc. cit.*

the owner. The personal property passed to his executor or administrator, to be distributed, after the payment of debts, to his legatees or his next of kin. The real property passed to his heirs or devisees, subject to the payment of his debts, according to the Texas Statutes of Descent and Distribution.[122] However, the present law passes all the property immediately to the heir or devisee.

Every person who is 19 years or over or that has been lawfully married, if of sound mind, has the power to make a last will as prescribed by law.[123] Such a person may devise and bequeath all the estate, right, title and interest in possession, reversion or remainder, which he has, or at the time of death shall have, of, in or to any lands, tenements, hereditaments, or rents charged upon or issuing out of them, or shall have of, in or to any personal property whatever, subject to the limitation prescribed by law.[124] The requisites of such wills are that they be in writing and signed by the testator or some other person by his direction and in his presence. If they are not wholly in the handwriting of the testator, they must be attested to by two or more credible witnesses above the age of fourteen years, subscribing their names to the document in their own handwriting and in the presence of the testator.[125] Where the will is in the writing of the testator in its entirety, the attestation of the subscribing witnesses may be dispensed with. The will is made self-proved, by the acknowledgment of the testator and by affidavits of attesting witnesses before an officer authorized to so acknowledge these acts. The will must have evidence of this by a seal or certificate.[126] It is important that a legatee or devisee not be a subscribing witness if the will cannot otherwise be proven. In that case, the bequest will be void.[127]

The common law rule is that a will for the passing of movable

---

[122]Mitchell, *Real Property*, p. 2.

[123]*Probate Code*, section 57.

[124]*Ibidem*, section 58.

[125]*Ibidem*, section 59.

[126]*Ibidem*, section 60.

[127]*Ibidem*, section 61.

property must be valid in the state in which the testator has his domicile. The will for the passing of immovable property must be valid in the state in which the immovable property is located. The validity of the will must be determined by the law of the state in which the immovable property is located. For that reason, the use of a holographic will, which is valid in Texas or the use of only two witnesses, when certain States require three, would be dangerous if the testator were to own property in another jurisdiction.[128]

These fundamental safeguards for the common good have been included in the Probate Code. The testator is permitted to revoke his will by any subsequent will that complies with the formalities required by this Code.[129] However, the law will give recognition to wills that are made at the time of a last sickness only with restrictions. The Probate Code states that wills made during one's last sickness must be made at home or where the party had resided for more than ten days preceding the date of the will, except when taken away from home sick and dying before returning.[130]

As to the interpretation of the will: Texas law holds that the intent of the testator will control. The courts should never adopt any rule of construction which has the effect of destroying the manifest intention of the testator.[131]

---

[128]Holman v. Hopkins, 27 Tex. 38 (1863); Crossland v. Dunham, 135 Tex. 301, 140 S.W. 2d 1095 (1940).

[129]*Probate Code,* section 63.

[130]*Ibidem,* section 65.

[131]McDow v. Lund, 250 S.W. 2d 247 (Civ. App., 1950); Bristol v. Mazza, 288 S.W. 2d 564 (Civ. App., 1956).

CHAPTER IV

ADMINISTRATION

ARTICLE I. CHURCH LAW ON ADMINISTRATION

With the divine right of the Church to acquire and to hold temporal goods firmly established, it follows that the Church has a similar right and duty to conserve and to use temporal goods in furtherance of the salvation of souls. The administration of church goods, in so far as it differs from their acquisition and alienation, includes the control and the care of the temporal goods of the Church with a view to having them fully serve the purpose for which they were acquired. Therefore, administration includes all those acts that are necessary or useful to keep the property in good repair and condition, to make it productive, to derive profit from it, and, in general, to apply, disburse and to use its return for charitable and legitimate purposes.[1]

Section 1. Administrators

The ownership of church property is vested in the individual moral person in the Church, but such property is administered by physical persons. The reason is that moral or legal persons in the Church are regarded as being equivalent to minors.[2] The relation of this physical person to the moral person is similar in effect to the trust relationship in common law. The similarity lies in this: the physical person who administers the property is not free to use or to dispose of the property as he would his own. The goods are acquired for the specific purposes of the

---

[1]James McManus, *The Administration of Temporal Goods in Religious Institutes*, The Catholic University of America Canon Law Studies, n. 109 (Washington, D.C.: The Catholic University of America Press, 1937), p. 12.

[2]Canon 100.

moral person to which it belongs. The manner of use is determined by the instrument of conveyance, the rules of the society for which the property is destined and the civil law. The basic distinction lies in the fact that the dominion or title to church property is in a moral person. The title of the trust at civil law is two-fold: legal and equitable. The legal title is in the trustee and the equitable title is in the beneficiary. These concepts will receive more detailed treatment in their proper places.

A. The Roman Pontiff, Supreme Administrator

The Roman Pontiff is not the owner of church property, but as the Head of the Church, he is declared to be the supreme administrator and dispenser of all ecclesiastical goods.[3]

The supreme power of the Roman Pontiff to administer the property of the Church means that he had administrative power both immediately and mediately over all property of the Church. Immediate administration is the direct management of the property. Mediate administration signifies the indirect management of the property through subordinate administrators.[4] As supreme administrator, the Roman Pontiff is not subject to the rules concerning the ordinary and extraordinary acts and their validity.[5]

By virtue of this power, the Roman Pontiff can dispose of all church property if an urgent reason exists and the welfare or tranquillity of the universal Church demands such disposal.[6] If the church property of subordinate moral persons were disposed of by this power, adequate compensation should be made. At times this will be impossible. Therefore, condonation by

---

[3]Canon 1518; Joseph J. Comyns, *Papal and Episcopal Administration of Church Property,* Catholic University of America Canon Law Studies, n. 147 (Washington, D.C.: The Catholic University of America Press, 1942), pp. 57 ff. (Hereafter cited as Comyns.)

[4]Comyns, p. 57.

[5]Mundy, p. 76.

[6]Wiggins, p. 98. Hence, the Pope could not take the property of any ecclesiastical moral person for his private possession or that of his family. The urgent reason and welfare of the universal Church are conditions for the validity of the act.

the Holy See of usurpation of church goods by the secular authority, which is done for the cause of peace, will not be compensated.[7]

The administration of the property of the Holy See is immediately administered by the Roman Pontiff through the offices and officials of the Roman Curia.[8] Local ordinaries have the duty to watch carefully over the administration of all ecclesiastical property in their territories. The law of the Church indicates the powers that the Roman Pontiff has communicated to intermediate or subordinate ordinaries, such as residential bishops and pastors.

B. The Local Ordinary as Administrator

The local ordinary is defined as the residential Bishop, an Abbot or Prelate *nullius,* a Vicar General, an Apostolic Administrator, a Vicar Apostolic and Prefect Apostolic. Included also in the definition would be any who, in default of the above, temporarily succeed to the government, either by law or by virtue of approved religious constitutions, or the territory.[9]

The duty of the local ordinary in his territory is to carefully watch over the administration of all ecclesiastical property which has not been withdrawn from his jurisdiction, with due regard for the more extensive rights which he may enjoy through legitimate prescriptions.[10] The bishop has the right and obligation of making visitation to all persons, things and pious places not exempt, for those things concerning the good of religion. Many of these things subject to the bishop's inspection are acts of administration, such as the keeping of books for an auditor's report.[11] By this power of supervision, the bishop can compel the administrators of church property to comply with the requirements of the civil law for the purpose of safeguarding the property.[12] The Code exhorts local ordi-

[7]*Loc. cit.*

[8]Abbo-Hannan, II, 724, footnote 1.

[9]Canon 198; Abbo-Hannan, I, 254-255.

[10]Canon 1519.

[11]Canons 343-346.

[12]Mundy, p. 77.

naries to regulate everything that pertains to the administration of church property by enacting special statutes or instructions as the occasion demands. In doing this, they must keep within the bounds of the Code and take into account the rights of others, legitimate customs, and circumstances.[13]

The rights of others that must be considered are those pertaining to individual moral persons, such as parishes and other institutions. Each individual moral person in the present organization of the Church has the administration of its own property. The ordinary cannot dispose of such property but all administrative acts must be made in the name of the moral person. The administrators of the respective moral persons are subject to the vigilance of the local ordinary and must obey the regulations that he may make.[14]

The local ordinary is the direct administrator of certain property. The *mensa episcopalis* is that property which constitutes the episcopal benefice, as such.[15] The local ordinary is to be the administrator of this *mensa episcopalis* as well as of all property that is specifically diocesan property.[16] The law states that the local ordinary is to administer the funds of the seminary and the cathedral.[17]

The ordinary has the responsibility of superintending the administration of the property of the entire diocese as well as the responsibility to directly administer those properties above mentioned. In order that the administration may be properly performed, every ordinary is to establish in his episcopal city a board of administrators. The members of this board of administrators are to be the president, who is the bishop himself, and two or more qualified men who are, if possible, experts in civil law. The selection of these men is to be made after hearing the consultors of the diocese. However, if custom has provided

[13]Canon 1519, §2.

[14]Canon 1495, §2; canon 485 (rectors); canon 1182 (funds for repairs); canon 1476 (beneficiaries); canon 1491 (non-collegiate institutions).

[15]Bouscaren, p. 823.

[16]*Loc. cit.;* Abbo-Hannan, II, 725.

[17]Canons 1357-1359; 1182.

an equally effective mode of administration, there is no need to change.[18]

This board of administrators is to be consulted in more important administrative matters. Their vote is only consultative, unless the common law requires their consent.[19] At all times when consent is required by the law of the church, acts made without such consent are invalid. However, when consultation is required, such consultation is not required for the validity of the acts.[20]

C. *Subordinate Administrators*

Funds that are destined for the maintenance of a moral person are considered the property of that moral person and are to be administered by the duly appointed administrators of that moral person. The administrator must administer the funds of the Church according to the sacred canons. When the administrator is a pastor, whether a secular or religious priest, an account of the administration must be given to the ordinary of the place.[21] In those instances where no administrator of church goods has been appointed, the local ordinary must appoint administrators. The appointees shall be suitable men of good reputation and proven foresight, who shall be replaced at the end of a three-year term, unless local circumstances urge otherwise.[22]

In certain places, laymen have shared in the administration of ecclesiastical property. The administration of the Church in these instances must be carried on in the name of the Church and without prejudice to the rights of the ordinary to make an inspection, to demand an accounting, and to prescribe the method of administration[23] The canon is not prescribing the

[18]Canon 1520, §1-2, forbids the selection of relatives within the 1st or 2nd degree of consanguinity or of affinity.

[19]Canon 1520, §3.

[20]Canon 105. There is a *dubium iuris* as to the validity of acts done without consultation. Cf. Bouscaren, p. 91.

[21]Canon 1182.

[22]Canon 1521, §1.

[23]Canon 1521, §. Cf. *Concilium Plenarium Totius Americae Septen-*

participation of the laity in the administrative actions of the pastor. In fact, laymen cannot be placed in sole control of the administration of ecclesiastical property. At least one cleric must be designated.[24]

However, the Church is concerned that the laity realize their position in the Mystical Body. There is a recognition of the possible greater financial and legal acumen, in civil matters, on the part of many laymen. This can often furnish a reason for the appointment of laymen to help in the administration of church property.[25] At the same time, the natural solicitude of the Church for the security and improvement of its property, gives a natural preference for clerics as administrators. By virtue of their state in life, clerics seek at all times to promote those things necessary to further the cause of Christ. Clerics with this state of mind will also seek to use those capable laymen at the disposal of the Church in order to enhance the value of church property.

Before the board of administrators take office, they are obliged to perform the following:

> 1) they must take an oath, in the presence of the local ordinary or the rural dean, that they will efficiently and faithfully attend to their work of administration;
>
> 2) they must prepare an accurate itemized inventory of immovable property and of precious and other movable property with a description of it and an estimate of its value; or a previously made inventory must be accepted with an account of the property which has been acquired or lost since it was made. This inventory must be signed by the administrators; and
>
> 3) they must file one copy of this inventory in the archives of the council of administration, and another in the archives of the diocesan curia. In both copies there must be noted whatever change may have occurred in the status of the property.[26]

---

trionalis Foederatae, Baltimori Habitum (Baltimori: Joannes Murphy, 1852), p. 47 n. 16.

[24]Abbo-Hannan, II, 726; III Plenary Council, nn. 284-287.

[25]Canon 1183.

[26]Canon 1522.

Similar legislation has bound all holders of benefices in the United States since the Third Plenary Council. Therefore, pastors are bound to make an inventory of their own property and of that of the ecclesiastical property and to send a copy to the chancery while retaining a copy on the files of the parish.[27] Bishops must draw up an authentic inventory accurately stating which sacred furnishings are personal property if the bishop wishes to keep these separate from the sacred furnishings of the diocese.[28]

For the security of church property, all holders of ecclesiastical benefices are required to execute a last will in such a form that it will be valid before the civil law. This law binds cardinals,, bishops in residence, and all clerics who have a benefice, such as pastors. The will should designate an executor who will fittingly administer the estate. This person will have the duty of taking possession of the sacred furnishings, books, documents and other things belonging to the church, and of delivering them to their rightful claimants.[29]

Administrators are expected to show the same degree of responsibility for church property which they administer as a good householder, and therefore they must:

> 1) be on guard that the property entrusted to their care shall not be destroyed or damaged;
>
> 2) observe the requirements of both canon law and secular law, as well as those specified by the founder or the donor or imposed by legitimate authority;
>
> 3) collect promptly and in full all income and profits, safeguard them, and distribute them in accordance with the intention of the founder or with established laws or norms;
>
> 4) invest for the benefit of the church itself the money of the church which is left over and above expenses and which can be thus profitably employed;
>
> 5) keep well posted books of receipts and expenditures;
>
> 6) put in proper order and file in the archives or in a

[27] III Plenary Council, n. 276; canons 1476; 1483.

[28] Canon 1299.

[29] Canon 1301.

> suitable and adequate safe belonging to the church the documents and deeds on which the rights of the church are based; and, where it can readily be done, deposit authentic copies of them in the archive or the safe of the curia.[30]

The third Plenary Council of Baltimore required that adequate fire insurance be carried and that the deeds to parish property be drawn up under the supervision of experts.[31] The pastor or the church committeemen must send an annual revision of the inventory to the chancellor as required by the same Plenary Council.[32]

The Church is concerned lest the fundamental principles of social justice be forgotten by zealous administrators of church property. Therefore, all contracts of hire must provide the employees with an honorable and just wage. The administrator must arrange the schedule of employees so that they can devote a suitable time to piety. On no account shall the employees be withdrawn from the care of their family or be burdened with such a work load that transcends their physical capacity. Nor should they be burdened with work to which their age or sex is not suited.

It seems that at times those working for the church are considered the recipients of charity. In fact, they are, in general, persons of responsibility and highly trusted because of their faithfulness. Because of the paternal relations that exist with the administrators, the pastors of churches in particular, these employees do not join labor organizations. For all the more reason should the administrators feel a particular obligation to pay an honorable and just wage. This would be a wage that is sufficient for a family, not an individual worker. Commentators consider the payment of this wage an obligation of both the natural law as well as the positive law.[33]

---

[30]Canon 1523, nn. 1-6.

[31]nn. 270, 278.

[32]n. 282.

[33]Regatillo-Zalba, *Theologiae Moralis Summa* (3 vols., Madrid: Biblioteca de Autores Cristianos, 1952-1954) II, nn. 805 ff.

Section 2. Acts of Administrators

A. Ordinary and Extraordinary Acts

The division of acts of administration is based upon the frequency, necessity and importance of the acts. Ordinary administration includes whatever is necessary for the preservation of church property and whatever actions are required to collect the income from such property. Also, the payment of current bills and taxes, the making of ordinary repairs and keeping an ordinary bank account are acts of ordinary administration. Those acts which are necessary and done at fixed intervals for the customary transaction of business are also acts of ordinary administration.

Acts of extraordinary administration include such acts that are of greater importance and generally not as frequent. An Instruction of the Sacred Congregation for the Propagation of the Faith for the diocese of Holland has been cited as a directive norm for acts that exceed the limits of ordinary administration:

> 1. To accept or to renounce an inheritance, legacy, donation or foundation;
> 2. To purchase immovable property;
> 3. To sell, exchange, mortgage, or pawn immovable church property; or to subject it to other servitude or burden, or to lease it for a period of more than three years;
> 4. To sell, exchange, mortgage, or divert in any other way from the place for which they are destined, objects of art, historical documents, or other movable property of great importance;
> 5. To borrow large sums of money as a (temporary) loan, or to make agreements and other onerous contracts;
> 6. To build, pull down, or rebuild in a new form any church building or to make extraordinary repairs on them;
> 7. To establish a cemetery;
> 8. To start or to suppress parochial institutions which are parish property;
> 9. To impose a per capita tax, to put on a drive, or to give to others things belonging to the parish church;

10. To enter upon a lawsuit either as litigant or as defender.[34]

It has been said that acts of ordinary administration are those which the administrator may perform validly by reason of his office and without the permission of the local ordinary. If, however, the law states that an act is invalid apart from the required permission, or if it requires a special faculty in the administrator before his act will be considered valid, then the acts of administration that are so conditioned are to be considered as acts of extraordinary administration.[35] However, this approach is not materially different from the former that considers the difference to hinge upon the frequency, importance and necessity of the acts. The law requires further permission for the validity of the acts because it envisions that these actions are infrequent and of great importance.

B. Particular Acts of Administration

1. Litigation, Contracts

Litigation is considered an act of extraordinary administration. The written permission of the local ordinary is needed, but in the case of urgent necessity, the permission of the rural dean may be obtained. The rural dean will then inform the ordinary. This is an act of extraordinary administration because litigation must be entered with exceptional prudence and momentary impulses must be restrained.[36] An administrator who goes into court without this permission and suffers loss is bound to restitution. His act of entering into litigation is considered invalid by church law for the consent of the ordinary is needed.[37]

If an administrator abandons his office, which had been expressly or tacitly accepted, loss may result to the Church. Consequently, such abandonment without authority and with resulting injury to the Church will bind the administrator to

[34] Bouscaren, p. 828. Cf. *Fontes,* Vol. VIII, p. 346, n. 4841.

[35] McManus, p. 82.

[36] Canon 1526; Bouscaren, p. 827.

[37] Canon 1527, §1; Bouscaren, p. 828; Wiggins, p. 107.

restitution. This obligation to restitution binds those who are not held by any title of benefice or ecclesiastical office expressly, as well as those who do hold such benefices or offices.[38]

The administrator is also bound to restitution for any loss suffered by the Church for contracts made without the necessary permission. The Church is not bound by these contracts and is therefore not responsible. However, in equity, the Church recognizes a responsibility in so far as it has profited from the contract. In this act of administration the administrator needs the written permission of the local ordinary.[39] In addition to the consent of the local ordinary, the administrator must fulfill the prescriptions of the civil law. The Church has canonically adopted the civil law of the different countries for contracts concerning ecclesiastical property and the rights connected with property. Therefore, whatever the civil law of Texas provides regarding contracts must be observed by Church administrators in Texas in the same way that the law of the Church is observed. Unless this State law is contrary to the divine law or provisions of canon law, it is equally binding. Formalities or rules required by the State law for the validity of a contract must be fulfilled.[40]

2. *Alienation*

a. Terms Defined

The alienation of church property is subject to stringent rules. In view of the stringency of these regulations, it is necessary to determine exactly what is "alienation" and what "church goods" are affected by the canons restricting alienation.

Alienation implies the transfer of the direct ownership of an object to another, as in a sale, exchange, gift and so forth. A wide interpretation is applied to the meaning of the word by the Apostolic Delegate to the United States, when he said:

> The term alienation includes not only purchases or transfers of property, but includes as well any contract,

[38]Canon 1528.

[39]Canon 1527, §2.

[40]Canon 1529.

debt or obligation. The Canon Law regards all transactions, which may render the financial condition of the Institute, Province or religious house, less secure, as Alienations.[41]

An extensive work on alienation considers the following acts as alienation within the meaning of the canon:

1. mortgages which confer on another a conditional right and title to church property;
2. leases and rentals extending for a period of time longer than nine years, since complete ownership of property is thus hampered by another's legal right to its use;
3. loans that give a conditional right to a part of ecclesiastical property corresponding to the amount of the loan;
4. passive easements or servitudes or the renunciation of active easements and servitudes;
5. acting as surety for others;
6. contracting of debts;
7. compromise and yielding lawsuits;
8. pawning of ecclesiastical goods.

These are all acts which place the condition of the Church in legal jeopardy.[42]

Certain acts which dispose of property belonging to the Church are not to be classified as alienation.

1. Spending money which is free capital to pay debts or to make purchases. Also, spending money for the purpose for which it was given.
2. Loaning money at a moderate rate of interest.
3. Selling movable property in order to replace it with new property of at least equal value.
4. Assumption of mortgages on property purchased.
5. Selling or exchanging immovable property in lieu of money for payment of debts;
6. Refusing to accept a gain or gift.

---

[41]Digest, II, 162. Letter from the Apostolic Delegate at Washington to all religious Superiors in the United States, on Nov. 13, 1936. The letter was authorized by the Sacred Congregation of the Religious.

[42]E. L. Heston, *The Alienation of Church Property,* The Catholic University of America Canon Law Studies, n. 132 (Washington, D.C.: The Catholic University of America Press, 1941), p. 70.

These and similar acts are not to be considered as acts which worsen the condition of church property.[43]

Church goods that are governed by the restrictions of the law on alienation are to be interpreted strictly. Therefore, the strictest interpretation holds that church goods are the stable capital of the moral person concerned. This stable capital is not a convertible term with movable or immovable property. Stable capital includes all those permanent assets which are not in ordinary circulation, as mediums of barter or exchange, which constitute the permanent basis of a church's financial security.[44] In case of doubt, the presumption favors the act of alienation so that what is doubtfully stable capital is not to be restricted from alienation.[45]

It has been observed that a more correct description of church property within the meaning of this canon would be to call it fixed patrimony. This term has historical use whereas stable capital has a modern connotation that is not as evident. Fixed, means that the goods are not freely alienable and patrimony, means all types of property owned by the Church. On the other hand, capital is understood to be money in modern parlance, and stable, indicates not easily moved.[46]

Therefore, church goods which belong to a moral person in the Church and are thereby subject to ecclesiastical authority are further divided by this canon. The following church goods are stable capital or fixed patrimony:

1. all money explicitly incorporated into the stable capital of an ecclesiastical corporation;
2. money or investments withdrawn from such capital;
3. money or securities received under annuity agreements;
4. money or securities from bequests and pious foundations;

---

[43]*Loc. cit.;* Bouscaren, p. 832.

[44]Heston, p. 73.

[45]*Loc. cit.* citing the Rule of Law, "Odia restringi convenit."

[46]Cahill, "The Dedication of Property to the Fixed Patrimony of a Church," *The Jurist 194-........* (Washington, D. C.: Catholic University of America School of Canon Law, 1957), 133 ff.

5. money or securities set aside by legitimate authority for the construction of buildings or for the purchase of other immovable property.[47]

The following goods are not stable capital or fixed patrimony, but may be termed free patrimony:

1. money used in meeting current expenses;
2. money or securities borrowed without explicit contractual obligations, even though nominal interest is paid;
3. proceeds from the sale of old equipment for the purpose of buying new;
4. withdrawals from investments pertaining to stable capital if for the purpose of purchasing buildings or constructing them when they will yield income (schools, hospitals, etc.);
5. money used for the purchase or construction of buildings when this money is already available;
6. sums used for the construction of residences for ecclesiastics or religious, particularly if this will prevent renting;
7. sums used for the repair of buildings already constructed;
8. resources changed from securities to simple bank deposits at interest;
9. portions of capital transferred to safer investments, which are at least equally lucrative;
10. money given for specific purposes;
11. money obtained by mortgage to construct;
12. property bequeathed that is incapable of being possessed by the Church.

Further, a refusal to accept a legacy or a donation is not an act of alienation within the scope of canon 1532.[48]

b. Norms for Alienation

In order that ecclesiastical goods classified as stable capital or fixed patrimony may be alienated, the following must be present:

[47] Heston, pp. 75-76.

[48] *Ibidem*, pp. 76-78.

1. an appraisal must be made by two experts;
2. a just cause must be had; and
3. the authorization of the legitimate superior must be obtained.

The appraisal is to be made by at least two experts. Their opinion is to be given in writing and should concern the present commercial value of the property in question. It is doubtful if the value put on property by public officials for the purposes of taxation is an appraisal that would be made by experts.[49] The failure to have the property appraised would not invalidate the alienation, although it would be a violation of a grave precept. Therefore, it is forbidden for the administrator to alienate the property for less than the appraisal made by the experts. For this reason, it is advisable that the experts submit a maximum and minimum price as the appraisal. The Code requires that alienation take place at public auction, or at least be made public, unless circumstances should dictate otherwise. The property should be sold, all things considered, to the one who offers the highest price.[50]

No property may be alienated without a just cause, that is, an urgent need or evident usefulness for the Church or some pious work which cannot be reasonably provided for by some other means.[51] An urgent need might be to avoid financial loss, to pay a mortgage or to meet a note. Evident utility would be found in any work of a spiritual or corporal nature that helps the suffering of the poor, educates the ignorant, while at the same time compensating in some degree for the spoliation of the goods of the Church, if possible. The lack of a just cause must be evident to the superior for the permission given to have been insincere and thus sinful. The absence of such a cause would not invalidate the permission.[52]

The authorization of the legitimate Superior is explicitly required for the validity of the alienation.[53] This authoriza-

[49]Canon 1530; Bouscaren, p. 833.

[50]Canon 1531; Cf. Heston 83-84.

[51]Canon 1530, §2.

[52]Heston, pp. 84-86.

[53]Canon 1530, §3.

tion must be in writing for religious[54] and it is advisable that this practice be established by synodical law for all acts of alienation.[55] Superiors should take all those precautions that are necessary in order to insure the Church against unnecessary damage.[56]

The legitimate superior whose permission must be sought is the Holy See when the property concerned is:

1. a precious thing, that is, whatever has a notable value by reason of art, history, or the material out of which they are made as stated in canon 1497, §2; or
2. of a value of more than $5,000 in the United States.[57]

Property that is of notable material value has been estimated as $167. This opinion was sustained in a case decided by the Sacred Congregation of the Council in 1919.[58] Alienations are to be judged individually unless the property that is alienated is divisible and is subject to coalesce by intention, time or purpose. Property that has physical unity, such as land, or even a moral unity, such as a herd of cattle, are divisible.[59]

When the value of the property is more than $167 but not more than $5,000, the legitimate superior for granting permission is the local ordinary. The local ordinary must obtain the consent of the cathedral chapter (the diocesan consultors in the United States), or the diocesan council of administration, and of the parties concerned. The parties concerned are the founders or patrons according to church law, the beneficiaries or the moral persons concerned.[60] For property of lesser value,

---

[54]Canon 534.

[55]Heston, p. 89.

[56]Canon 1530, §2.

[57]Canon 1532, §1, nn. 1-2. Cf. Digest, IV, canon 1532 the Sacred Consistorial Congregation communicated this sum as the limit beyond which the Holy See must grant authorization as required by canon 1532 for the United States, after October 18, 1952. The Code states that the legitimate superior is the Holy See when the property value exceeds 30,000 gold francs or lire. However, the $5,000 limit is binding.

[58]Bouscaren, p. 834. Cf. Digest, I, 728.

[59]Bouscaren, p. 836.

[60]Canon 1532, §3. Cf. Abbo-Hannan II, 737; Bouscaren, p. 837 that

the local ordinary may give the necessary permission after hearing the council of administration and obtaining the consent of the interested parties.[61] It would seem that in such cases the matter is of such small moment, there would be no need to consult the council. Also, the necessity is undoubtedly obviated by a contrary custom.

The requisites of the Code for alienation are to be observed in any contract entered into by administrators when the condition of the church will become less favorable. These contracts have been mentioned as mortgages, annuity obligations, and similar obligations of a contractual nature.[62] The Church has a right to institute a personal action against anyone who has alienated church property without the required formalities, as well as against his heirs. If the alienation was invalid, it has a right to a real action against any possessor whatsoever, but the purchaser has the right to claim damages from the administrator.[63]

3. *Other Acts of Administration*

a. Gifts

Small and moderate gifts sanctioned by local custom, are permitted to be made from church property. Administrators are forbidden to presume to make any donations from the movable goods unless there is a just reason, such as remuneration. Otherwise, the donation may be revoked by their successors. Immovable property is in general forbidden to be the subject matter of a gift because it is a part of the fixed patrimony.[64] Particular legislation cannot forbid the giving of alms

---

cites the letter of the Sacred Consistorial Congregation of July 13, 1951 which reduced the 30,000 gold francs to 10,000 gold francs and the letter of October 18, 1952 reducing it to $5,000. The Sacred Consistorial Congregation stated that the 1,000 gold francs was to be regarded as one-thirtieth of $5,000 or $167. Cf. Digest, I, 66; III, 581; IV, 162.

[61]Canon 1532, §2.

[62]Canon 1533.

[63]Canon 1534.

[64]Canon 1535; Bouscaren, p. 838.

occasionally for the moral persons in the Church are obligated to make these gifts.

There is a presumption that all gifts made to churches, unless the contrary is proven, are church property. These gifts may not be refused without the permission of the ordinary. If they are refused, the administrator is subject to an action to make restitution although he has not alienated church property. The gift may not be revoked by the giver because of the ingratitude of the administrator, because the gift is to the moral person, not to the physical person.[65] Particular legislation for the United States for the alienation of church property was summarized in the Third Plenary Council of Baltimore affirming the Apostolic Constitution *Romanos Pontifices.* This Constitution of 1885 approving the Second Provincial Council of Westminster, indicated the norms for judging what is meant for the personal use of a priest and what is meant to go to the Church.[66]

Gifts intended for personal use or given as a special token of affection or gratitude, such as by family or close friends, or on the occasion of Christmas or jubilees, are presumed to be personal gifts. In large gifts, the donor should be clear as to his intent. It would be best for donors to submit the administration of all large gifts to the administrator of the Church.[67] Gifts may be repudiated by the administrator only when natural obligations of the donor demand repudiation. Therefore, when the donor becomes a parent or makes a gift against his personal duties of charity and justice or affection, the administrator may repudiate the gift.[68]

b. Mortgages, Loans, Sales

To mortgage or pledge church property or to contract debts

---

[65]Canon 1536.

[66]III Plenary Council, n. 276.

[67]Heston, p. 153. The requirements, however, of the Plenary councils that written proof of the intent of the donor be had and that it be clear and without doubt, would not seem to be obligatory in the case of small gifts or such gifts as those mentioned above.

[68]*Ibidem,* p. 158.

burdening church property, a legitimate reason is required. The lawful superior for such acts must demand a previous hearing in the favor of the interested parties. In order that the debt be paid quickly, the annual rate of payments shall be designated in advance by the same lawful superior. Pledges concern personal property whereas mortgages burden real property.[69] All legal acts that subject the Church to possible loss of property come under this canon. Promissory notes that are unsecured would not be included unless, as a contract in civil law, courts of equity would permit attaching church property.[70]

Annuity agreements are bilateral contracts whereby one party agrees to pay another a fixed sum at specific periods in return for a gross amount of money or equivalent property. These can entail serious inconveniences and the Apostolic Delegate has declared that such use of the fund while the annuitant lives is dangerous, therefore, forbidden.[71]

It is forbidden to loan sacred things for those things which are repugnant to their nature.[72] Nor should the fact that an article is blessed or consecrated have any consideration in the determination of the price for the sale or exchange of the article. Administrators may exchange so-called bearer securities for other securities that are more secure, or at least equally safe and productive, to the exclusion of all semblance of trading or profit-seeking, after they have obtained the consent of the ordinary, of the diocesan council and of other interested parties.[73]

A sale is a consensual bilateral contract whereby one transfers ownership in consideration of a price which the other obligates himself to pay. Exchange or barter is the exchange of goods

---

[69]Stenger, *The Mortgaging of Church Property,* The Catholic University of America Canon Law Studies, n. 169 (Washington, D.C.: The Catholic University of America Press, 1942), pp. 69-72; Cf. also canon 1538.

[70]Heston, p. 166.

[71]Digest, II, 161, under canon 534. The Apostolic Delegate is speaking with the authority of the Sacred Congregation for Religious.

[72]Canon 1537.

[73]Canon 1539.

for goods. In both of these acts, delivery is necessary.[74] Sacred articles will lose their consecration or blessing if put up for public sale, and indulgenced articles lose their indulgences by any sale.[75] The Church is desirous of avoiding even apparent simoniacal actions or commercial enterprises. Therefore, this canon is to forestall that inclination to permit apparent advantages by such sales to cast a shadow upon the actions of administrators of the Church.[76]

c. Leases

Contracts of lease for any church real estate or land must be made in conformance with canon 1531. Such leases are to include effective provisions for the protection of established boundaries, for the adequate maintenance of church property, for the due payment of annual rents and for appropriate safeguards regarding the fulfillment of the conditions. When the value of the lease is in excess of $5,000 and the lease runs for more than nine years, approval of the Holy See is required. If the lease runs for not more than nine years or for more than nine years and the value is less than $5,000 and more than $167, the permission of the local ordinary, with the consent of the diocesan consultors, the diocesan council and any interested parties, is required. If the lease runs for less than nine years at a value of less than $5,000 and more than $167 or for more than nine years at a value of less than $167, the permission of the local ordinary, who must consult the counsel of administration and obtain the consent of interested parties, is required. However, for a lease of nine years for less than $167, the competent administrator needs no permission but must notify the ordinary.[77]

In the case of a perpetual lease by which the property is

---

[74]J. Cleary, *Canonical Limitations on the Alienation of Church Property,* The Catholic University of America Canon Law Studies, n. 100 (Washington, D.C.: The Catholic University of America, 1936) pp. 88 ff.

[75]Canons 1305, 924, §2.

[76]Cf. canons 730, 732.

[77]Canon 1541.

under an annual rental, the permission of the lawful superior suffices to release the lessee from the lease. The lessee shall be required to pay the rental value or to give an adequate guarantee of its payment and the fulfillment of the conditions imposed. It seems that a more personal relationship is envisioned in a contract for a perpetual lease than in a short term lease and for that reason the designation of an ecclesiastical arbiter and of other conditions is required by the Code.[78]

In the making of loans, the temptation of an ecclesiastical organization to make a profit is lessened by the strict laws of the Church. It is not permitted for the administrator to charge undue interest. In fact, no profit may be made by a contract of loan. This does not forbid the reception of a legal profit from the use of fungible goods. However, a just and proportionate title must be present to permit a greater profit. This title would be the risk involved and therefore, the current interest rate might be asked. This is a restriction on usury, not on wise investment.[79]

A peculiarly ecclesiastical institution is the pious foundation. This institution has arisen by the acts whereby temporal goods are given to some moral person in the Church, which moral person assumes the obligation of celebrating Masses or of fulfilling other ecclesiastical functions. The temporal goods must give a return perpetually or annually for a long time; generally, at least ten years is required. The foundation, once accepted, creates a "do ut facias" contract.[80] This obligation can become detrimental to the Church and for that reason, the written permission of the ordinary of the place is required. Further obligations of the local ordinary are delineated in the Code.[81]

The reduction of such obligations is reserved to the Holy See. The reduction often becomes necessary because of the changed circumstances and economic condition of a country or

[78]Canon 1542; Heston, p. 182.

[79]Canon 1543; Mundy, p. 119.

[80]Canon 1544.

[81]Canon 1546.

even of an investment.[82] Whatever funds are obtained from such pious foundations or from alienation of church property must be invested in a safe place designated by the ordinary.[83]

In general, the principles of law governing property administration are to safeguard productive property against dissipation and loss, to apply this property to income producing uses, to prevent loss of future benefits for the sake of present advantage, and to encourage improvement of church property.[84] Investment and reinvestment of church property must take these principles into consideration. Investment has been defined as the conversion of money into income-producing property or into claims to income, regardless of the permanence of this disposition of the funds.[85] The danger of speculation is averted by church law. Investment for periodic income and not for profit after resale is not speculation. Intention creates speculation and it is not illicit to resell if this conforms to the norms of efficient administration and investment management. However, investment is generally an act of extraordinary administration, and for that reason, the permission of the ordinary is required.[86]

Article II. Administration in Texas Law

The administration of church property under the laws of Texas is determined by both the statutory law of the State and judicial decisions. That church property which is held by religious communities and other moral persons in the Church as corporations, must be administered by the statutory laws on corporations. The church property that is held by the archdiocesan/diocesan moral persons as unincorporated religious societies in the state, must be administered by the trust relationship law as interpreted by the courts.

---

[82]Canon 1551; Mundy, p. 124.

[83]Canons 1547, 1531.

[84]Harry J. Byrne, *Investment of Church Funds,* Catholic University of America Canon Law Studies, n. 309 (Washington, D.C.: Catholic University of America Press, 1951), p. 21.

[85]*Ibidem,* p. 26.

[86]*Ibidem,* pp. 34-36.

It has been shown that the bishops and archbishops hold the diocesan/archdiocesan properties in trust for the Church. The law of trust must therefore determine how this property must be administered. There are statutes that affect the administration of an express trust but the principal law of the State that governs the administration of a trust is to be found in judicial decisions. In particular, judicial decisions have declared that the Roman Catholic Church is unique in its organization and in the consequent power given to authority in the Church. These decisions and the effect they have upon the administration of church property according to the laws of the State of Texas will be given particular consideration.

Section 1. Incorporated Religious Societies

A. General Scope of Directors Powers

Both religious societies and charitable organizations are permitted to incorporate in Texas law. The manner of incorporation has been adequately presented in the preceding chapters. There remains to be presented the powers, duties and obligations of the directors or trustees of such corporations. It is asserted in the corporation law that:

> The secular affairs of a religious corporation shall be under the control of a board of trustees, to be elected by the members of such corporations; and the title to all property of any such corporation shall vest in such trustees.[87]

Therefore, the purpose of the directors or trustees of a religious corporation is made clear. The purpose is to administer the property of such corporation, which property includes both corporeal and incorporeal rights. The trustees are firbidden to interfere in spiritual affairs:

> The directors or trustees of any corporation under this title shall not usurp or exercise the functions of any officer in charge of the spiritual affairs of any society.[88]

[87]Revised Statutes, Article 1397.

[88]Revised Statutes, Article 1398; Cranfill v. Hayden, 22 Civ. App. 656, 55 S.W. 805 (1896).

B. Powers, Duties and Liabilities of Trustees

The powers, duties and liabilities of church officers are not materially different from those exercised by the managing directors of other private corporations.[89] The general powers of a corporation are:

1. to have succession to itself for fifty years,
2. to maintain and defend judicial proceedings,
3. to make and use a common seal,
4. to purchase, hold, sell, mortgage or otherwise convey real estate and personal estate as the purposes of the corporation requires or to obtain, or secure payment of debts or liabilities due to such corporation,
5. to appoint and remove subordinate officers and agents as business requires and to allow a suitable compensation to them,
6. to make all by-laws not inconsistent with existing laws, for the management of its property, and the regulation of its affairs,
7. to enter any contract or obligation essential to the transaction of its authorized business,
8. to increase or diminish by vote of its stockholders, as by-laws directs the number of its directors or trustees, such number, however, not to be less than three.[90]

The officers that are to make up the board of trustees shall be a president, secretary and treasurer at least. If more officers are needed, they may be created by the corporation.[91] It is not required that the members of the board be members of the Church. In fact, they need not be members of the State as long as two of the members are from the State.[92] This board

[89]Clark v. Brown, 108 S.W. 421 (Civ. App.) reversed on other grounds in 102 Tex. 323, 116 S.W. 360, 29 L.R.A. (N.S.) 670 (1909).

[90]Revised Statutes, Article 1320. Cf. Article 1303 requiring 3 members for a corporation.

[91]Revised Statutes, Article 1325.

[92]Revised Statute Article 1305. Cf. Fort v. First Baptist Church, 55 S.W. 402 modified 93 Tex. 215, 54 S.W. 892, 49 L.R.A. 617 (1898) wherein it is stated that only one of the members must be from the State.

of directors may enact by-laws for the corporation but this does not mean that the board has unlimited powers to make by-laws contrary to the spirit and the purposes of the corporation.[93] However, the general management of the affairs of the corporation is in their hands. This means that the trustees receive the powers from the charter and should manage the corporation according to the general laws of the association and of the State.[94]

The religious corporation has the power to borrow money and to execute bonds on promissory notes, as well as the power to pledge property and income when it is necessary according to the purpose of the corporation. These acts are to be done through the board of trustees or directors.[95] The members of the corporation cannot question the validity of liens merged into deeds of trust that secure the buildings of the corporations. This applies equally to church buildings or to any buildings owned by the corporation which are deemed necessary by their directors or trustees who have been legitimately appointed.[96] However, the board of directors is to keep the records of the corporation open at all reasonable times for an inspection by the members of the corporation. These records concern all business transactions of the corporation.[97]

Vacancies in the board of trustees will occur when one of the members dies, resigns, is removed or departs for other reasons. In order to fill these vacancies, a quorum of the trustees or directors present must cast a majority vote for the one whom they wish to fill the vacancy.[98] Otherwise, annual elections

[93]Revised Statute Article 1326; Clark v. Brown, 108 S.W. 421, (Civ. App.) reversed on other grounds in 102 Tex. 323, 116 S.W. 360, 29 L.R.A. (N.S.) 670 (1908).

[94]Wallace v. Wells, 228 S.W. 111 (Civ. App., 1922).

[95]Revised Statutes Article 1321.

[96]Macedonia Baptist Church v. Farm and Home Savings and Loan Association, 110 S.W. 2d 1013 (Civ. App., 1938).

[97]Revised Statutes Article 1328: "stockholders" are mentioned in the Article, but by analogy this statute would permit members of a religious corporation to have the same right.

[98]Revised Statutes Article 1323.

must be made in accordance with the by-laws of the corporation.[99] The court will take the corporation into receivership if and when there are resignations that reduce the membership to less than a quorum. This could also happen because of deaths that deplete the membership of the boards. At least three members are required at all times.[100]

The law attempts to give religious societies and other private corporations rights and obligations before the civil law that are not available to such associations as long as they remain unincorporated. A voluntary association has real existence even before the act of legitimate authority giving it juridical rights. Therefore, it cannot be asserted that the corporations, as unincorporated associations or religious societies, do not exist before entering such corporative actions.[101] Texas law holds that religious associations owe their existence to the compact between the members and that the written constitutions are the terms of the compact in the eyes of the courts.[102] Yet, the religious society as a corporation is considered as an entity created at law, so that it may sue and be sued in its own name.[103]

The board of directors can transact business only when a quorum is present and the business transaction is approved by a majority of the board.[104] The general powers of this board are not materially different from those exercised by the managing directors of a private profit corporation. Religious associations having rights of property and contract come before the courts as private corporations and are equally under the pro-

---

[99]*Loc. cit.*

[100]*Loc. cit.* Cf. Haggset v. Dallas Mortgage Securities Co., 110 S.W. 2d 135 (Civ. App., 1938).

[101]Brown, pp. 52-58; the fiction theory, which holds that moral personalities do not exist without a creative act of legitimate authority, is rejected. Cf. Coronata, I, n. 135, pp. 155 ff.

[102]Clark v. Brown, 108 S.W. 421 (Civ. App.) reversed on other grounds in 102 Tex. 323, 116 S.W. 360, 29 L.R.A. (N.S.) 670 (1909).

[103]American Insurance Co. v. Edwards 78 S.W. 2d 1020 (Civ. App., 1935).

[104]Revised Statutes Article 1323.

tection of the law and the action of their members are subject to the same restraints.[105]

The corporation is bound by obligations entered into by the board of directors. In default of payments, stockholders are personally bound when the corporation is a profit corporation.[106] But in the case of a religious or charitable corporation, the execution of a court judgment may not extend to the individual member.[107]

C. Power of the State over Corporations

In the interest of the common welfare, the Attorney General of the State is given certain powers over corporations. The function of the Attorney General in State government is to safeguard the common welfare. In order to fulfill this obligation with respect to corporations, the statute has given investigative powers to the Attorney General. He, or his authorized assistant or representative has the authority to examine all the books, accounts, records, minutes, letters, memoranda, documents, and so forth of corporations as often as he deems necessary.[108] This examination is to be performed only after a written request for the inspection has been given to the board of directors.[109] If the board of directors refuses to submit to the inspection, the act of refusal will constitute a forfeiture of the charter and of all right to act (to do business) as a corporation.[110] Unless a judicial proceeding is held in which the inspection will be made public, the Attorney General is forbidden to make the results of the inspection public.[111]

The dissolution of the religious corporation was treated in the second chapter. It was observed that the court may appoint

---

[105]Clark v. Brown, 108 S.W. 421, reversed on other grounds 102 Tex. 323, 116 S.W. 360, 29 L.R.A. (N.S.) 670 (1909).

[106]Revised Statutes Article 1344.

[107]Revised Statutes Article 1345.

[108]Revised Statute Article 1366.

[109]Revised Statutes Article 1367.

[110]Revised Statutes Article 1370.

[111]Revised Statutes Article 1369.

receivers and extend the life of the corporation for three years.[112] In these cases, the board of trustees necessarily terminates its existence. The members of the church will be justified in removing those trustees who violate their trust. This removal must take place according to proper proceedings and others must be elected in their places. The court will give effect to such actions.[113]

When the Attorney General makes an inspection of the records of a religious corporation, this inspection must be limited to those acts of the board of trustees. These acts are limited to secular affairs and it is forbidden to the board to enter in any way into religious matters by usurping powers.[114] Similarly, the Attorney General is limited in his powers of inspection. Actions by the Attorney General that would amount to intervention into the spiritual affairs of a religious corporation would constitute a violation of the Constitution of the United States as well as that of the State of Texas.[115]

Section 2. Unincorporated Religious Societies

A. Powers of Unincorporated Associations

The State of Texas gives those religious societies that do incorporate a definite status in the law. Religious societies that do not choose to incorporate according to the present corporation statutes do not have a definite status in the law. In fact, those religious societies that do not incorporate are considered unincorporated voluntary associations and as such they are

[112]Revised Statutes Articles 1387, 1389.

[113]Fort v. First Baptist Church of Paris, 55 S.W. 402, modified 54 S.W. 892, 93 Tex. 215, 49 L.R.A. 617 (1899). It should be noted that this case concerned a congregational type of Church, as have most of the other cases cited in this section. It might be debated as to the effect of these decisions upon membership control upon the Catholic Church if it were incorporated.

[114]Revised Statutes Article 1398.

[115]United States Constitution, Amendments 1 and 14; Texas Constitution, Articles 1, Section 6: "No human authority ought, in any case whatever, to control or interfere with the rights of conscience in matters of religion."

legally incapable of placing legal acts. They may neither acquire, hold nor administer property in their own name. They lack the ability to sue and be sued in their own name.

The law on trust and judicial decisions has established certain principles that affect the legal acts and the legal status of these unincorporated associations. These principles seek to protect the members of the associations and society as well. Church organizations early realized their lack of capability to act as juridical persons in the absence of incorporation. The failure to organize and to file a charter as required by the corporation act of 1874 has made certain religious societies incapable of holding real estate or suing as an association.[116]

The courts have held that neither the unincorporated association nor an officer of such an organization are liable for its contracts. Although they are not liable as an organization, the officer is liable in his individual status.[117] This would preclude execution of the property of such an organization. However, the courts have held that a judgment establishing a debt and foreclosing a lien on church property must be executed when the church has profited. Otherwise churches would make inequitable gains which would be unseeming.[118] Therefore, a person who has furnished supplies and accepted a note may enforce an equitable lien on the property of the church.[119] Numerous cases forbid unincorporated religious associations from suing in their own names because these societies are not entities at law.[120]

---

[116]Tunstall v. Wormley, 54 Tex. 476 (1881); cf. African Methodist Episcopal Church v. Independent A.M.E. Church, 281 S.W. 2d 758 (Civ. App., 1955); Humphries v. Wiley, 76 S.W. 2d 793 (Civ. App., 1934); Methodist Episcopal Church v. Roach, 51 S.W. 2d 1100 (Civ. App., 1930).

[117]Summerhill v. Wilkes, 153 S.W. 492, 63 Civ. App. 456 (1910).

[118]Realty Trust Co. v. First Baptist Church of Haskell, 46 S.W. 2d 1009 (Civ. App., 1935).

[119]Slaughter v. American Baptist Publication Society, 150 S.W. 224 (Civ. App., 1910).

[120]American Insurance Co. v. Edwards, 78 S.W. 2d 1020 (Civ. App., 1935); Methodist Episcopal Church South v. Clifton, 34 Civ. App. 248, 78 S.W. 932 (1904); McCall v. Capers 105 S.W. 2d 323 (Civ. App.,

These are the principal limitations that fall upon an unincorporated religious association. In general, the courts favor supporting religious and charitable activities. Consequently, the rights of such associations, although not incorporated, are granted through the trustees that hold their property. On the other hand, the unincorporated religious or charitable society is held to the actions of their trustees.[121]

The courts seek to enforce trusts for charitable purposes according to the intention of the testators by force of the "cy pres" doctrine mentioned in chapter II. Therefore, when property is dedicated to the support of some specific form of religious doctrine, it is the duty of the courts to enforce the trust thereby created. The court must insure against diversion of the property dedicated to that trust to other purposes.[122] Thus, in one case, a resulting trust arose by declarations of a deceased grantee. The members of a religious club had paid for property and it was held that the property belonged to them even though they were unincorporated.[123]

When a person becomes a member of a voluntary religious association, he subscribes to all of its rules and regulations, and consents to the exercise of such powers as have been conferred on its managing officers. The member is thereby bound in the future by the acts of the managing officers who conduct the affairs of the religious association.[124] Therefore, it has been held that the members of such an unincorporated association are personally liable when they incur a debt or assent to the creation of a debt, although the association itself may be sued

---

1937); Wadlington v. Peoples Baptist Church, 296 S.W. 2d 784 (Civ. App., 1956).

[121]Brown v. Weir, 293 S.W. 916 (1927); Brown v. Warfield, 234 S.W. 2d 264, (Civ. App., 1950).

[122]Peace v. First Christian Church of McGregor, 20 Civ. App., 85, 48 S.W. 534, (1898); Jarrell v. Sproules, 20 Civ. App. 387, 49 S.W. 904, (1898): on changing doctrines.

[123]Brown v. Warfield, 234 S.W. 2d 264 (Civ. App., 1950).

[124]Clark v. Brown, 108 S.W. 421, reversed on other grounds in 102 Tex. 323, 116 S.W. 360, 29 L.R.A. (N.S.) 670 (1909).

through the trustees.[125] However, it has been held that such liability is enforceable only when the members sign or give express consent to the assumption of a debt by the trustees.[126]

These unincorporated religious associations are presumed to act through trustees. A deed signed by the trustees has been held to be effective against the association and not a *nudum pactum*.[127] The church is not precluded from repudiating the trustees' sale of church property where the action of certain trustees was without knowledge of the other trustees elected by the church.[128]

B. *Powers of Trustees, Their Duties and Liabilities*

As the directors and the board of trustees of the incorporated religious and charitable associations had particular duties, powers, liabilities defined by law, so the trustees of unincorporated religious associations have defined duties, powers and liabilities. Definite legislation indicates the power, duties and liabilities of the trustee of the express trust. Where the trust has to be construed by the court, implied from the facts available, judicial decisions have indicated the law of the State to govern the trust relationship. In fact, judicial decisions preceded legislation in time and have formed the basis for the present law. The manner of creation of these trusts has been broached in chapter II. Particular consideration has been given to the origin of the trust concept in so far as the administrator is a bishop in the Catholic Church. This relationship will be given particular treatment in this chapter.

For the creation of the trust, the trustee is conveyed the legal title and the equitable title remains in the beneficiary. The beneficiary is often called the *cestui que trust*. The beneficiary

---

[125] Mood v. Methodist Episcopal Church South, 289 S.W. 461 (Com. App., 1927).

[126] Summerhill v. Wilkes, 153 S.W. 492, 63 Civ. App. 456 (1910).

[127] Perry v. Long, 222 S.W. 2d 460 (Civ. App., 1949) citing Revised Statutes Articles 1397, 7425-7425b which state that trustees are not agents but principals, and are liable to beneficiaries for breach of duty.

[128] Richardson v. Prospect Hill Missionary Baptist Church, 7 S.W. 2d 179 (Civ. App., 1928).

must be made evident in the act establishing the trust.[129] The duties of trustees are not merely passive. That is, the mere possession of the legal title for the benefit of another is not the only purpose of the trust relationship. The duties encompass more than the duty to refrain from interfering with the complete use by the beneficiaries of the trust property. Rather, there exists an express and implied active trust in religious and charitable associations which arises by express agreement or by a construction of such a trust by law from the words or the acts of the parties.[130]

The trustee of an active trust has duties, obligations, powers and compensation generally determined in the trust instrument. If not, then the words or actions that established the trust as well as statutory regulations deserve consideration. The first principle governing the actions of a trustee is that he is to act as an ordinary prudent man in conducting his own affairs. He is required to act at all times with the utmost good faith and he is not permitted to justify failure by saying that no one asked him to protect the trust.[131] However, this does not give him the same freedom that a prudent business man has in the conduct of his own affairs. He is forbidden to enter into speculation according to one decision even though he has the obligation to invest the funds.[132]

In dealing with a trust fund, the trustees' own personal interests and opportunities for gain must be cast completely aside. Absolute and scrupulous good faith is the very essence of the obligation. In administering the fund, he must act for the beneficiaries and not for himself in antagonism to their interests.[133] If the trustee sold to another from whom he re-

---

[129]Miller v. McDonald, 235 S.W. 2d 201 (Civ. App., 1950); Wacasey v. Wacasey 256 S.W. 1020 (Civ. App., 1925).

[130]42 Tex. Jur. 600, 604.

[131]McMullen v. Sims, 37 S.W. 2d 141 (Civ. App., 1933) reversing 22 S.W. 2d 313, the trustee omitted to invest funds; cf. Lowry v. Gallagher, 190 S.W. 2d 165 (Civ. App., 1945).

[132]Murphy-Bolanz Land and Loan Co. v. McKibben, 236 S.W. 78 (Com. App., 1922) affirming 221 S.W. 650.

[133]*Loc. cit.*

ceived a benefit or a commission of some type, the sale might be contrary to the interests of the beneficiaries. The facts would have to determine if there were in fact any detriment to the interests of the beneficiaries.

Courts do not generally favor the power to sell the property, unless expressed in the trust.[134] However, the power to sell or encumber under a passive or secret active trust is given statutory recognition in order that an innocent person will not suffer.[135] The power to mortgage is not favored if this might lead to the destruction of the trust.[136] The trustee can never sell the property of the trust to himself. This is impossible since he is the legal title holder. If there were any authorization for such a transaction, the conveyance would have to be made by an indirect method.[137]

Although the trustee cannot delegate another to administer the trust, he is not forbidden to employ agents. Agents cannot be employed in such a way that the trustee circumvents the law forbidding the delegation of full administration of the trust. Agents can be employed only in those ways in which they are customarily employed in business transactions. When agents are employed, the trustee is not liable for their acts. In fact, he is not even liable for being negligent in choosing the agents.[138]

An account of all transactions must be given in an accurate manner. However, this does not require that the trustees keep a record of all such transactions. It does mean that all transactions that are not accounted for will be the responsibility of the trustee.[139]

Even if it is not mentioned in the trust itself, the trustees are deserving of compensation for their services. The com-

---

[134]First Church of Christ, Scientist v. Snowden, 276 S.W. 2d 571 (Civ. App., 1955), denied the power of sale to the trustee in order that the trust would not be destroyed.

[135]Revised Statutes Article 7425a.

[136]Humphries v. Wiley, 76 S.W. 2d 793 (1934).

[137]42 Tex. Jur. 420.

[138]42 Tex. Jur. 717.

[139]42 Tex. Jur. 722.

pensation must be reasonable, while considering the responsibility and the degree of care and labor required. The trustee is permitted to credit payments, taxes, insurance, necessary repairs and expenses reasonably undertaken.[140]

Beneficiaries are not without remedies for maladministration of a trust. All remedies given by law to creditors are at the disposal of the beneficiaries. The court of equity will appoint a receiver of trust property when necessary, for example, when the trustee has been guilty of so mixing the trust funds that the specific property cannot be traced. If he has lost the funds by poor, reckless investments, he will be liable to the beneficiaries.[141]

The removal of the trustee may be accomplished for a good cause. The cause might be the act of showing hostility to the beneficiary or to the interest of the beneficiary. In general, the power of substitution belongs only to the court. The trustee may substitute another for himself only if that is expressly permitted in the trust. When another is substituted, he has all the powers of the original trustee.[142]

Trusts do not fail because the trustee fails to accept. The court will appoint a trustee. The trustee may be a corporation when it is acting within the purposes of the corporation, if the corporation has a permit to transact business in Texas.[143] The trustee may resign at any time but he is accountable for transactions down to the time of resignation and for proper disposition of the trust property upon resignation. If the trustee is an appointee by operation of law, such as the Attorney General, he may not resign at any time but only when the law permits.[144]

This law on trust is applicable to all trust relationships.

---

[140]Slay v. Burnett Trust, 143 Tex. 621, 187 S.W. 2d 377 (1945).

[141]42 Tex. Jur. 760-764; Murphy Bolanz Land & Loan Co. v. McKibbin, 236 S.W. 78 (Com. App., 1922) affirming 221 S.W. 650.

[142]42 Tex. Jur. 625.

[143]42 Tex. Jur. 622.

[144]Republic National Bank and Trust Co., 74 S.W. 2d 461 (Civ. App., 1935).

However, the law varies when express stipulations are in the trust instrument or the words and facts from which the trust is construed. When a trust is created in favor of a religious society, the implied conditions must include the rules and regulations of the religious society.

C. Trustee in the Catholic Church

The bishops of the Catholic Church in Texas are considered as the trustees of the Church. Church property is held in this manner by the respective dioceses and archdioceses: the ordinary of the place has the legal title to the property, the equitable title is in the Roman Catholic community in Texas. Fundamentally, the principles governing this trust is no different than that governing the trust relationship in other unincorporated religious associations. The power of the ordinary will be determined by the instrument of trust, the laws of the State and the rules of the Catholic Church.[145] The laws of the State of Texas concerning trusts have been indicated in the preceding sections. These laws apply to the trust relationship that exists in the Catholic Church with variations being found because of the nature of the Catholic Church. The express trust will be enforced according to the peculiar statutes governing that trust. If a donor desires to specify a trust, the donor should be specific in the instrument in which the trust is created. The ordinary of the place will be obligated by the law of the Church and the law of the State on trusts in order to enforce the trust.[146]

The rules of the Catholic Church, that is the law of the

[145]Clark v. Brown, 108 S.W. 421, reversed on other grounds in 102 Tex. 323, 116 S.W. 360, 29 L.R.A. (N.S.) 670 (1909); First Baptist Church of Paris v. Fort, 93 Tex. 215, 54 S.W. 892 (1898); First Church of Christ, Scientist v. Snowden, 276 S.W. 2d 571 (Civ. App., 1955). Cf. Blanc v. Asbury, 63 Tex. 489, 51 Am. Rep. 666 (Com. App., 1885); Olcott v. Gabert, 23 S.W. 985, 86 Tex. 121 (1893) reversing Gabert v. Olcott, 22 S.W. 286 on other grounds; Cussen v. Lynch, 245 S.W. 932 (1922).

[146]Peace v. First Christian Church of McGregor, 20 Civ. App. 85, 48 S.W. 534, (1898); Jarrell v. Sproules, 20 Civ. App. 387, 49 S.W. 904 (1898); cf. canons 1513-1517.

Church concerning the powers of the bishop have been given judicial recognition.[147] The first case in which the Catholic Church was a party, gave recognition to the trust relationship that was created or recognized by the legislative grant of the State of Texas. This grant bestowed those church properties held under the former governments to the Church. The State did not consider the bishop as a corporation sole but rather as a trustee for the Catholic Church.[148]

The case of Blanc v. Asbury concerned property that had been conveyed to the Bishop for the use of the church in Hempstead.[149] The Bishop had the church built and gave certain lots to the builder to pay for the construction of the church. This conveyance was challenged by the parishioners. The court held that the purpose of the original conveyance to the bishop was to build the church. To secure this purpose, much was left to the discretion of the bishop, both by the deed of conveyance and according to the laws of the Catholic Church. Therefore, the conveyance from the bishop to Asbury was upheld.

In reaching the decision the court declared:

> . . . in securing that object (building a church in Hempstead), much was left to the discretion of the bishop, who, as head of the church in the diocese, had the necessary power as supplemented by the conveyance, to manage the property in such a manner as his judgment might approve as the best in securing the object intended, and in promoting the welfare of the church at Hempstead. . . . it is

[147] Blanc v. Asbury, 63 Tex. 489, 51 Am. Rep. 666 (Com. App., 1885).

[148] Blair v. Odin, 3 Tex. 288 (1848); cf. McMullen v. Hodges, 5 Tex. 34 (1852).

[149] 63 Tex. 489, 51 Am. Rep. 666 (Com. App., 1885): the conveyance stated: "To have and to hold unto him, the said Claudius M. Dubuis, for the use aforesaid, and his successors and his or their assigns, forever. It is hereby declared that the premises herein described are granted the said Claude M. Dubuis for the purpose of erecting thereon a Roman Catholic Church, and other buildings pertaining thereto, or to be exchanged or used in the purchase of other property in the town of Hempstead for said purpose."

> a matter of historical and common knowledge, that the form of government in the Roman Catholic Church is an episcopacy, and in which the diocesan bishops possess enlarged powers, respecting the temporal as well as the spiritual affairs of the church, in their respective dioceses.[150]

The case of Olcott v. Gabert concerned a return of land by Bishop Gallagher to a donor who had become bankrupt when the Bishop foresaw that the Church would not be able to use the land. The donor was the Houston and Texas Central Railway Company. The railroad went bankrupt in 1889 and the land was returned to the receiver, Olcott, who entered a trespass to try title suit. This action is used to clear titles.[151]

Bishop Dubuis had resigned the see of Galveston at the time of the case and the administrator was Bishop Gallagher.[152] The donation had been made in 1881 to Bishop Dubuis. The court considered the capacity of Bishop Gallagher to give the land back to the railroad. In order to solve the question: does the bishop of the Roman Catholic Church have the power to convey land once given to the Church back to the donor, the court repeated the words of the court in Blanc v. Asbury:

> It is a matter of historical and common knowledge that the form of government of the Roman Catholic Church is an episcopacy in which the diocesan bishop possess en-

[150] *Loc. cit.*

[151] Gabert v. Olcott, 22 S.W. 286 held that the bishop gave Olcott a legal title in trust for the railroad, therefore, Gabert received a clear title in the execution sale. Olcott v. Gabert, 23 S.W. 985, held that the bishop gave Olcott a legal title but not in trust, therefore, Gabert did not receive a clear title. Both courts agreed that the donation of the land from the railroad gave legal title to the bishop for the use of the Catholic Church. The deed stated in the words of grant. "to Claude M. Dubuis, Bishop of Galveston, and his successors in office, for the use of the Catholic Church." This put complete legal title in the bishop without a condition to use the land for a church or even for church purposes. The court neither affirmed nor denied that the bishop was holding in trust for the Church.

[152] *Official Catholic Directory, 1953*: C. M. Dubuis was consecrated on Nov. 23, 1862, resigned in 1882 but remained with the title of Bishop of Galveston until 1892 when he was promoted to an archbishopric in

> larged powers respecting the temporal as well as the spiritual affairs of the church in their respective dioceses. It could not be lightly assumed that the Bishop acted without authority. The presumption is that public officers do as the law and their duty require. The members of the Roman Catholic Church are found in every part of the world, and their interests, temporal and spiritual, are looked after by a well-disciplined hierarchy, consisting of functionaries of successive grades, whose respective powers are accurately defined, and among themselves well understood. In such a case, in the absence of proof to the contrary, the presumption that everything has been rightfully done ought to apply with peculiar force.[153]

The court then stated that it recognized that Bishop Gallagher was acting as administrator. Bishop Dubuis had given Bishop Gallagher the power of attorney to perform all administrative acts for him. The court stated that even in the absence of such power of attorney, Bishop Gallagher, as a coadjutor bishop had the power to make the conveyance. The coadjutor was described as one who is appointed to perform the functions of a regular bishop who is old and infirm. Therefore, by the fact that Bishop Gallagher was the "administrator Bishop," the court inferred that Bishop Gallagher was charged, as coadjutor to Dubuis, with the administration of the affairs of the see.[154]

The bishop, as trustee, has been held to be a person capable of suing and being sued for the interests of church property.[155]

France. He died on May 21, 1895 in France. Nicholas A. Gallagher, was appointed as administrator to the see of Galveston in 1882, consecrated titular bishop of Canopus, April 30, 1882, succeeded to Galveston on December 16, 1892.

[153]Olcott v. Gabert, 23 S.W. 985 (1893).

[154]*Loc. cit.*: The return of the land was considered an act that the bishop might hold binding in conscience but which is not binding in civil law.

[155]Jung v. Neraz, 71 Tex. 396, 9 S.W. 344 (1888): Jung owned 4 acres of land next to church property destined for a cemetery. An injunction was granted against Bishop Neraz because of the proximity of the cemetery to the residence of Jung.

The members of the church can challenge an action of the Bishop if they can show that it affects a property right. In the case of a priest who contested the bishop's right to remove him, the court held that there is a presumption that an order of suspension by a bishop is regular. In absence of facts clearly showing an irregularity, the court will not interfere.[156]

Title to the land in Cussen v. Lynch had been conveyed to the Bishop of Dallas by the following words of grant: "to the Right Reverend Catholic Bishop of Dallas, and his successors in office of bishop and their assigns." The priest had been appointed to the town of Canadian, but after a breach of discipline, the bishop ordered him to leave. The court declared that the civil courts will not assume jurisdiction in cases involving only ecclesiastical questions. A civil right of property must be involved and the right to the possession of the church in Canadian was involved in this case.

The bishop had legal title and right of possession ordinarily follows the legal title. Cussen had a right dependent on the settling of the ecclesiastical question. Citing Brown v. Clark and Watson v. Jones, the court stated that:

> It is generally conceded that when an ecclesiastical question has been decided by an ecclesiastical tribunal, properly constituted and proceeding in accordance with the rules prescribed by the organization, such decisions are binding upon the civil courts in the trial of the dependent property rights.[157]

As to the question of jurisdiction of the ecclesiastical court or the regularity of the proceedings, the court said:

> It is not to be supposed that the judges of civil courts can be as competent in ecclesiastical law and religious

[156]Cussen v. Lynch, 245 S.W. 932 (1922): the court observed that the plaintiff, Father Cussen, would have had recourse to a higher ecclesiastical tribunal if he had chosen to take recourse. Therefore, even if the preceding were irregular, this recourse must be used. The case thoroughly reviewed the canonical procedure for suspending a priest and for removal of a pastor.

[157]*Loc. cit.*

> faith of all these bodies as the ablest men in each are in reference to their own. It would, therefore, be an appeal from a more learned tribunal to one which is less so.

Therefore, in case of doubt, where the ecclesiastical tribunal is not clearly without jurisdiction, the decisions of the ecclesiastical tribunal as to its own jurisdiction and the regularity of its proceedings should receive great weight.[158]

The final case showing the extensiveness of episcopal power in the eyes of the courts of the State of Texas is the case of the Community of Priests of St. Basil v. Byrne. Byrne was the Bishop of Galveston who sought the return of land that had been conveyed to the community by his predecessor, Bishop Gallagher, for the purpose of building a school. The community maintained a school for some years, then moved, and sold the property[159] The bishop held the land in trust for the benefit of the Church in Waco. The deed conveying the land to the community for the maintenance of a school was held to be a gift. A clause in the conveyance to the effect that the community was to return the land in the event that they could not maintain a school was not contrary to the gift. The community had conveyed the land to another in order to move the school. The court observed that the then bishop, Gallagher, had consented to the conveyance and thereby waived the reconveyance agreement. It seems that this action of the bishop might have induced the court to hold that the conveyance from the bishop to the community was a pure gift. Be that as it may, the case indicates that the bishop is conceded extraordinary powers as a trustee which is not conceded to any other trustee in a trust relationship.

From these cases, it is evident that a conveyance to the ordinary, as the bishop or archbishop of a diocese, and to his successors in office, and their assigns forever, indicates a charitable trust. This trust is conceived irrespective of the intentions of

[158]*Loc. cit.*

[159]255 S.W. 601 (Com. App., 1923) reversing 236 S.W. 1016 (Civ. App., 1922); Bishop Byrne was appointed July 18, 1918; died April 1, 1950.—*Official Catholic Directory, 1953.*

the grantor, because of the nature and functions of the named dignitaries as an ecclesiastical administrator under the precepts of Canon Law.[160] This type of conveyance is presently used by the diocese and the archdiocese in Texas. However, it is advisable to indicate more exactly the nature of the use by stipulating that the property is granted "for the use of the Roman Catholic Church."[161] The addition of those few words necessary to stipulate the use might save inestimable time, work and money in the future.

The observation has been made that this general practice of holding the property in the name of the ordinary, as trustee for the Church in his respective diocese, may have certain difficulties. When the ordinary raises money, he may use the entire trust, that is, all the property of the diocese, in order to secure the loan. Therefore, all the property could be reached in equity in satisfaction of a judgment recovered against the bishop as trustee. Further, the debts of one parish or group of parishes would be the debts of every parish and the inefficient operation of one parish would be visited upon the whole diocese. This situation would be true even if the bishop did not pledge the whole of the trust as security for a debt. The reason is that as long as the trust fund is for the same purpose, that is, the Roman Catholic Church, all the property is automatically joined. This effect of having the whole of diocesan property subject to judgment executed against one diocesan property would not occur if the conveyances described the use more particularly.[162]

The suggestion has been made that every conveyance stipulate the use for which the property is to be employed with great exactness. Therefore, the conveyance in the Blanc v. Asbury case would be used as a model. It could be observed that in that instance, the court allowed the Bishop complete freedom to dispose of the property by force of the powers that he has as a Roman Catholic Bishop.[163] Every parish should

[160]Olcott v. Gabert, 23 S.W. 985 reversing 22 S.W. 286 (1893).

[161]Cf. *Mode of Tenure, Survey,* p. 160.

[162]*Loc. cit.*

[163]Blanc v. Asbury, 63 Tex. 490, 41 Am. Rep. 666 (1885).

have the title to its properties in the name of the parish. This is not possible without incorporating the parish. Therefore, this system would designate the use for the particular parish with the title being held in the name of the bishop.[164] By the power of vigilance, which the bishop has over the parishes, permission for the alienation of the property can be given. It would be contrary to the law of the Church if the bishop were to encumber the property of one parish by the contraction of a debt for another parish. Consequently, the State laws should not visit these debts upon another part of the trust held by the bishop according to the present system of tenure in Texas. The corporation sole is not to be desired, nor is incorporation according to the present statute in Texas. It would seem clarity in the status of church property might be obtained if a new corporate status were permitted by the laws of Texas.

---

[164]Canon 1538: the administrator of the moral person places the property under a mortgage, with the permission of the ordinary. By canon 1519, the ordinary is to maintain vigilance, but he is not to directly administer the properties of parochial moral persons. The respective moral persons are to be placed under determined administrators, such as pastors.

CHAPTER V

TAX EXEMPTION

There is no place in the political or legal philosophy of the State of Texas for the recognition of one religion in preference to others. Nor does the State consider that any religion is a perfect society, sovereign in itself. Consequently, the Republic declared in the Bill of Rights that "No preference shall be given by law to any religious denomination or mode of worship over another."[1] However, at a later date the State Constitution of 1876 imposed upon the legislature the duty to pass such laws as necessary to protect equally every religious denomination in the peaceful enjoyment of its own mode of public worship.[2]

Therefore, granting that every religion is considered equal in the legal system of the State, the State has willed to obligate itself to protect religious denominations in the peaceful enjoyment of public worship. It would be virtually impossible for religions to sustain the many temporal goods required for the peaceful enjoyment of public worship if the State imposed taxes upon these temporal goods.

Taxation is a necessary power of the government in order that it might have those means necessary for governing the State. The Supreme Court of the United States has declared that taxes are necessary to the existence and the prosperity of a nation so that taxes have the power to keep alive.[3] In an earlier case, the same Court had aptly called the power to tax the power to destroy.[4] Both of these assertions are equally true and the State must not hastily grant tax exemptions to all who desire

[1] 1 Gammel 1082, Constitution of 1836.

[2] Article 1, section 6.

[3] Nicol v. Ames, 173 U.S. 509 (1899).

[4] McCulloch v. Maryland, 4 Wheaton 316 (1819).

the exemptions. History illustrates the manner in which pressure groups have obtained tax exemptions to the detriment of the common good. Therefore, the State has limited tax exemptions by firm constitutional restrictions.[5]

In general, the States of the United States exempt religious societies from taxation. The policy of exempting religious societies from taxation began in the colonial governments. The churches were instrumentalities of the States and it would have been unsound for the State to tax its own instrumentality. This reason also prevailed in the Spanish dominions where the State supported the Church. However, when the established churches vanished, tax exemption for religious societies remained.[6]

The reasons for these tax exemptions of religious societies had to be re-evaluated. It has been asserted that those properties devoted to charitable and educational purposes are justifiably granted tax exemptions because they are public in nature. The similar privilege granted to church properties, not patently public in nature, must be justified on other grounds. The reason given for this assertion is that it is not in the domain of the government to give religious culture or instruction.[7] Although it is true that church properties are not patently public in nature, religious organizations are of a definite benefit to society. There is no religious society that does not benefit mankind in some way. The christian religion has elevated the civilization of the West to a high level. Similarly the forerunner of christianity, judaism, greatly promoted the social and moral welfare of the Jewish people. Even today, these religious groups give a moral and spiritual instruction that it is impossible for the State to give but which is necessary for the proper functioning of the State.[8]

Therefore, the States of the United States exempt religious societies from taxation as a matter of public policy in order to

[5]Cf. Interpretative Commentary to Article XII, section 1, of the Constitution of 1876. Railroads were granted exemptions that were then unnecessary.

[6]Zollman, p. 328.

[7]*Ibidem,* p. 365.

[8]Coquia, p. 106.

promote the common good.[9] The extent of the tax exemption varies with the respective States. Certain activities, such as religious schools, are exempted by every State.[10] The granting of these exemptions is generally and uniformly upheld by the court as being constitutional and valid.[11] This holding is a denial of the contention that the granting of tax exemptions to religious societies is a form of State aid.

If the granting of tax exemptions were a form of State aid, the exemptions would fail. The first and fourteenth amendments to the Constitution of the United States prevent the States from establishing a religion or State church and from aiding any church or religious body by the appropriation of public money. Consequently, the exemption would be unconstitutional if it were State aid in the sense that it violated the constitution of the United States. A study has found that the primary objectives of the State in this matter is:

> not . . . a form of State aid, in the usual sense of those words; it is an inducement or encouragement held out by the State to private persons, or private corporations, to establish or maintain institutions which are of benefit to the State.[12]

Article I. Church on Tax Exemption

Ecclesiastical immunity from taxation is of ancient origin. It has been said that our ancestors considered the goods of the Church as the goods of God Himself, and, as such, wholly withdrawn from the power of princes, and free, consequently,

---

[9] *Corpus Juris* (71 vols., New York: American Law Book Co., 1934), Vol. LXI, 256 ff. (Hereafter cited as 61 Corpus Juris 256.)

[10] F. F. Beach and R. F. Will, *The State and Nonpublic Schools*, with particular reference to responsibility of State departments of Education, U. S. Department of Health, Education, and Welfare, Misc. No. 28 (Washington, D. C.: United States Government Printing Office, 1958), p. 13. (Hereafter cited as Beach-Will.)

[11] 61 Corpus Juris 256.

[12] Beach-Will, p. 19, citing a report of Charles William Eliot on "The Exemption of Church Property, and the Property of Educational, Literary and Charitable Institutions."

from secular taxation. Severe ecclesiastical penalties sanctioned this immunity, and in spite of resistance here and there, it was generally recognized.[13] This concept that the goods of the Church were the goods of God Himself developed in the centuries that immediately followed the Edict of Milan. The Edict of Milan in 313 marked the end of the Roman persecution of the Church. Constantine the Great decreed that Catholic Churches would be freed from the obligation of paying tributes to the Empire. Subsequent emperors, with the exception of Julian the Apostate, continued the policy of Constantine until the Thirteenth and Fourteenth centuries.[14]

In these centuries, a violent reaction to the immunities of the Church began to foment. The princes of the various kingdoms were disregarding the claims of the Church almost entirely so that by 1296, the princes were demanding the most abundant subsidies from individual churches.[15] The Church had practiced the paying of tithes to the States. Besides the payment of this tenth part of its revenues, the Church usually contributed generously to national emergencies. These payments were at first free and spontaneous. Later it was requested by the kings and authorized by the Pope and the Bishops. At times it was of obligation because of an urgent necessity. But the Church reserved the basic right to consent or refuse to the payment of the tax.[16]

With the vicissitudes of history, the political society ceased to recognize the Church as a supernatural society, independent of the power of the State. Whereas Boniface VIII had insisted upon the immunities of the Church, the Council of Trent merely recommended that the kingdoms exempt church properties from taxation. The numerous concordats that were entered into in

---

[13]C. Journet, *The Church of the Word Incarnate,* (4 vols., London and New York: Sheed and Ward, 1954), I, p. 202, footnote 2. (Hereafter cited as Journet.)

[14]Coronata, *Ius Publicum,* n. 151.

[15]Wiggins, p. 16.

[16]*Loc. cit.* Cf. Coronata, Ius Publicum, n. 147. Both authors comment on the famous Bull *Clerici laicos,* of Pope Boniface VIII, which forbade the payment of taxes without submitting the cause to Rome.

the last few centuries between the Church and the States of Europe, make little mention of this immunity from taxation. The present Code of Canon Law utters scarcely a word, although some authors have deduced a canonical assertion of immunity from certain canons.[17] The argument is that the Church was constituted a perfect society by its Divine Founder, and as such, is able to acquire, hold and administer property independently of all civil power. To impose a tax by law is a sign of jurisdiction and of true power over the subject in question. The State does not possess such a power with regard to the Church and ecclesiastical property.[18]

Canonists distinguish church property with respect to immunities in a threefold manner:

> 1) that property which directly and immediately is rereferred to divine worship and is so deputed by a blessing or consecration. This includes churches, cemeteries, altars, sacred vessels and so forth.
>
> 2) that property owned by an ecclesiastical moral person which is directly destined for the sustenance of the ministers of the Church and only indirectly destined for divine worship. This includes the lands that support the Church or furnish a dwelling place for ministers.
>
> 3) that property owned by physical persons, such as the bishop or pastor, for their sustenance as ministers, and is thus only indirectly destined for divine worship.[19]

The goods of the first class are wholly withdrawn from the dominion of the State so that the State may exercise no power of jurisdiction over these goods without the consent of the Church. The consent of the Church will be given in those cases where the State makes just demands to exercise its power over

---

[17]Coronata, *Ius Publicum,* n. 147. Cf. canons 1495, 1499, 1518.

[18]Murphy, p. 8. In the *Syllabus of Errors,* Proposition 30 of the condemned propositions reads as follows: "Ecclesiae et personarum ecclesiasticarum immunitas a jure civili ortum habuit."—Denzinger-Bannwart-Umberg, *Enchiridion Symbolorum Definitionum et Declarationum de Rebus Fidei et Morum* (editio vigesima sexta, emendata et aucta, Barcelona: Herder, 1951), n. 1730.

[19]Coronata, Ius Publicum, n. 166.

ecclesiastical temporalities of this category.[20] This doctrine is certain and must be held by all Catholics as to goods of this category. As to goods of the second and third class, there is no certain doctrine that is held by all canonists. Goods of the second class are held and administered according to the laws of the Church and are church goods in the strict sense. It must be held that the laws of the State should give recognition to the laws of the Church concerning these goods.[21] As to goods of the third class, these are church goods only in the wide sense and are not considered as church goods by canon law.[22]

The origin and nature of this immunity from taxation is explained by numerous theories. A rejected theory is that which professes open Regalism. According to this theory, the State grants or abrogates tax exemption as it wills. This is a denial of the fact that the Church is a perfect society, completely independent of civil power.[23] Other theories profess the origin of the immunity to come formally from the divine law, either the natural or positive divine law; or from the divine positive law fundamentally, and from the ecclesiastical or civil law formally.

These are summarily presented in the following manner: the natural law, which is evidenced by the common practice of all peoples of all times to consider sacred things, persons and places as immune from being used for the support of the community, insists upon this immunity from taxation for church goods. The divine positive law, which is evidenced in Matthew XVII, 24, insists upon the immunity of church goods from taxation. In this verse, Christ indicated that as the Son of God, He was free from taxation and similarly, His Church, which is Christ's Body upon earth, should be exempt.[24] In support of these arguments are the documents of the Church which have

---

[20] *Ibidem,* n. 167; Journet, p. 203, footnote 1.

[21] Coronata, *Ius Publicum,* n. 169.

[22] *Ibidem,* n. 168. Cf. canon 1499, §2.

[23] *Ibidem,* n. 150; *Syllabus of Errors, Propositions* 30 and 31.

[24] *Ibidem,* n. 151. The passage from Matthew referred to a tax being paid to the temple.

strongly insisted upon the immunity of certain properties of the Church from the jurisdiction of the civil powers. These documents date from the early centuries.[25]

An argument in support of these broached by canonists to favor exemption of church properties from taxation, is that given by the civil law. This argument states that religious groups give a moral and a spiritual instruction that it is impossible for the State to give but which is necessary for the proper functioning of the State.[26] Consequently, the court in Texas has said that:

> The granting of tax exemptions involves a balancing of factors affecting the public good . . . in the case of certain institutions, such as religious and educational organizations, the theory of benefit to the public good in allowing tax exemption is fairly clear.[27]

Article II. Texas on Tax Exemption

In many States of the United States, tax exemptions are explicitly granted by the constitution, in others, by legislative enactment only. Texas, with many other States, gives constitutional authorization to the legislature to exempt certain properties from taxation.[28] In consequence of this authorization, the legislature of the State of Texas has explicitly exempted schools, churches, dwelling places for ministers of churches or religious societies, endowment funds of institutions of learning and religion and the buildings for the same, cemeteries, public charities, and the buildings and lands belonging to such charities. These exemptions of the legislature have been granted in view of the common good.

At times, the legislature may have granted exemptions that were not authorized by the Constitution. In those cases, the judiciary seeks to harmonize the constitutional intent with the

[25] *Ibidem*, n. 149.

[26] Coquia, p. 106.

[27] Dickinson v. Woodsmen of the World Life Insurance Society, 280 S.W. 2d 318 (1955).

[28] Beach-Will, p. 19.

legislative enactment. If it is not possible to reconcile the two, the legislation is void and the tax exemption fails. This article will present the constitutional authorization, the legislative enactments and the judicial interpretations of the two. At the same time, the position of the Church will be alluded to and where necessary, clarification of church law on property will be included.

Section 1. Constitutional Power

The Constitution of the State of Texas authorizing the legislative power to grant certain tax exemptions, reads as follows:

> All occupation taxes shall be equal and uniform upon the same class of subjects within the limits of the authority levying the tax; but the legislature may, by general laws, exempt from taxation public property used for public purposes; actual places of religious worship, also any property owned by a church or by a strictly religious society, and which yields no revenue whatever to such church or religious society; provided that such exemption shall not extend to more property than is reasonably necessary for a dwelling place and in no event more than one acre of land; places of burial not held for private or corporate profit; all buildings used exclusively and owned by persons or associations of persons for school purposes and the necessary furniture of all schools and property used exclusively and reasonably necessary in conducting any association engaged in promoting the religious, educational and physical development of boys, girls, young men or young women operating under a State or National organization of like character; also the endowment funds of such institutions of learning and religion not used with a view to profit; and when the same are invested in bonds or mortgages, or in land or other property which has been and shall hereafter be bought in by such institutions under foreclosure sales made to satisfy or protect such bonds or mortgages, that such exemption of such land and property shall continue only for two years after the purchase of the same at such sale by such institutions and no longer, and institutions of purely public charity; and all laws

exempting property from taxation other than the property above mentioned shall be null and void.[29]

This original authorization appeared in the Constitution of 1876 and subsequent amendments have not changed the article substantially. In 1907, endowment funds were permitted to be exempted from taxation.[30] In 1913, an act was passed to exempt the Young Men's Christian Association and the Young Women's Christian Association. In 1926, the act was declared invalid as contrary to the constitution.[31] Therefore, the State amended the constitution in 1928 to exempt such institutions. Similarly, the court had permitted the taxation of a Methodist parsonage in 1918,[32] and the State amended the Constitution to exempt the dwelling places of ministers.[33]

Section 2. Rules of Interpretation

In accordance with the authorization of the Constitution, the legislature has enacted Statutes to permit the exemption of religious, educational, charitable and other works of a similar nature. These statutes are the law and only fail if they surpass the power granted to the legislature. By force of the doctrine of "stare decisis," this legislation is to be measured with the constitutional authorization in a definitive manner by the courts of the State. The doctrine of "stare decisis" means that the law is declared by a court of competent jurisdiction authorized to construe it. That construction of the law by the court is in evidence of the law until changed by competent authority, in the absence of palpable mistake or error.[34]

Fundamental rules of interpretation of the tax exemption statutes are as follows:

---

[29]Article VIII, Section 2.

[30]Interpretative Commentary to Article VIII, section 2.

[31]City of San Antonio v. Y.M.C.A., 285 S.W. 844 (Civ. App., 1926).

[32]Trinity Methodist Episcopal Church v. City of San Antonio, 201 S.W. 669 (1918).

[33]Interpretative Commentary to Article VIII, section 2.

[34]*Black's Law Dictionary*, p. 1652, "stare decisis." Cf. discussion on common law in Chapter I.

1) There is no exemption unless the legislature acts in passing the general laws of exemption. In case of doubt as to whether a particular institution is exempt, the taxing power is favored.[35]

2) The legislative power to grant the exemption as well as the exemptions that are granted by the legislature must receive a strict construction.[36]

3) The courts have indicated that the legislative definition should be given effect;[37] but the same courts have refused to permit an enlargement of the exemptions.[38]

In order that a tax exemption may be of benefit to an association, the organization or person desiring the exemption must file a complete itemized statement of all of said property without regard to the kind of property, with the Tax Assessor of the County in which such property is situated. All property that is not so listed is to be assessed and the Tax Assessor is to make levy upon the same and collect the tax.[39] The one who claims a tax exemption has the burden of proof to show that the property is exempt.[40] Further, the person or persons claiming the exemption must own the property and make actual, direct and exclusive use of the same. Preparation for use is equivalent to actual use under the terms of the statute. The renting to another or the permission to use by others not making use of the property for a tax exempt purpose is forbidden.[41] These

[35]Jones v. Williams, 121 Tex. 94.

[36]City of San Antonio v. Y.M.C.A., 285 S.W. 844 (1918); Little Theatre of Dallas v. Dallas, 124 S.W. 2d 867 (1939).

[37]Scott v. All Saints Hospital, Episcopal, 203 S.W. 146 (Civ. App., 1917); State v. Settegast, 227 S.W. 253 (Civ. App., 1920) reversed in 254 S.W. 925 (Com. App., 1923).

[38]City of Houston v. Scottish Rite Benevolent Association, 111 Tex. 191, 230 S.W. 978 (1921).

[39]Revised Statutes Article 7150.

[40]Little Theatre of Dallas v. Dallas, 124 S.W. 2d 867 (1939).

[41]Benevolent and Protective Order of Elks v. City of Houston, 44 S.W. 2d 488 (Civ. App., 1931); Malone-Hogan Hospital Clinic Foundation, Inc. v. City of Big Spring, 288 S.W. 2d 550 (1956); William M. Stecks, "Tax Exemption of Public Charity under Texas Constitution," 7 *Baylor Law Review* 494 (1955).

general principles will be applicable to every tax exemption granted by the legislature. They must be applied to every piece of legislation that affects the exemption of the particular activities to be considered in the following sections.

Section 3. Exemptions Granted for Religious, Educational and Charitable Purposes

A. Religious Purposes

The Constitution authorized the legislature to exempt the actual places of religious worship and the dwelling places of ministers from taxation.[42] In accordance with their legislative power, the legislature enacted the following statute:

> . . . actual places of religious worship, also any property owned by a church or by a strictly religious society, for the exclusive use as a dwelling place for the ministers of such church or religious society, the books and furniture therein and the grounds attached to such buildings necessary for the proper occupancy, use and enjoyment of the same, or which yields no revenue whatever to such charitable or religious society; provided that such exemption as to the dwelling place for the ministers shall not extend to more property than is reasonably necessary for a dwelling place and in no event no more than one acre of land.[43]

Subsequently, the constitution was amended so that the legislature could exempt the properties of religious, educational and physical development associations from taxation. The legislature expressly exempted those associations in 1931.[44] This legislation has been interpreted as declarative of the exemptions permitted by the constitution and not an extension of the powers given to the legislature.[45]

There have been no attempts to tax actual places of religious worship that have reached the courts. As a consequence, no judicial definition has been given of an "actual place of re-

---

[42]Article VIII, section 2.

[43]Revised Statutes Article 7150.

[44]*Ibidem,* §2a.

[45]City of Houston v. Cohen, 204 S.W. 2d 671 (1948).

ligious worship." In a case in which the issue concerned the use of a public school building for religious purposes, the court asserted that a place of worship is one in which the worship might be indulged in so continuously and in such a manner as to be characterized as a place set apart for worship.[46] In deciding whether or not a place is an actual place of religious worship, the court will follow the general rules, regulations and constitutions of the religious society in question.[47]

The law of the Catholic Church treats of "sacred places" in canons 1154 through 1196. A "sacred place" is defined as that place destined for divine worship or the burial of the faithful, by a consecration or blessing prescribed for this purpose by approved liturgical books.[48] A "church" is understood to be a sacred structure devoted to divine worship for the principal purpose of being used by all the faithful for public divine worship.[49] Another place of public worship is the "oratory," defined as a place devoted to divine worship, not however principally for the purpose of serving the faithful in general for public religious worship.[50] Oratories are classified as public, semi-public and private or domestic. There are relatively few private oratories. Private oratories are erected in pivate houses only for the benefit of a family or private person.[51] An oratory is public when all the faithful have a legitimately established right of having access to it at least at the time of divine services; it is semi-public, if the oratory is erected chiefly for the convenience of some community or group of the faithful who use it. The semi-public oratory may not be freely available

[46]Church v. Bullock, 104 Tex. 1; 109 S.W. 115; 16 L.R.A. (N.S.) 860 (1909).

[47]Clark v. Brown, 108 S.W. 421; Brown v. Clark, 116 S.W. 90, 102 Tex. 323 (1909); Olcott v. Gabert, 23 S.W. 985, 86 Tex. 121 reversing 22 S.W. 286 (1893); First Christian Church v. Peace, 48 S.W. 534, 20 Civ. App. 85 (1898).

[48]Canon 1154.

[49]Canon 1161.

[50]Canon 1188, §1.

[51]Canon 1188, §2.

to everyone.[52] Both of these are "actual places of religious worship" and as such should be exempt from taxation.

The State courts recognized the exemption of the dwelling places of ministers in the case of the State v. Methodist Episcopal Church et al.[53] The State entered a suit to recover taxes due and owing upon a Methodist parsonage. The Methodist church contended that the parsonage was used solely for the residence of the pastor who was necessary for the church. Further, the parsonage was adjacent to the church and was used by the pastor to further the work of the church, which was both religious and charitable work. The State admitted these facts and the court held the parsonage to be exempt from taxation.

Four years later, the State attempted to tax another parsonage of the Methodist Church. In this case, the parsonage was also used solely as a residence for the pastor and at the same time to further the religious and charitable works of the church. However, the parsonage was not adjacent to the church building but was separated from it. Because of this separation, the parsonage was declared taxable.[54] As a result of this decision, the State amended the Constitution in 1928 so that the legislature might grant exemptions to all dwelling places for ministers provided the property was no more than what would be reasonably necessary. In no case, should the exemption extend to more than one acre of land. Consequently, the legislature passed the exemption, adding only that the books and furniture in those buildings are also exempt.[55]

In determining what dwelling places are exempt, it is necessary to investigate each religious society to ascertain who are the ministers. It might be argued that the courts have determined who are the "ministers" of the Catholic Church in the case of Olcott v. Gabert. In that case, the court asserted that ministers are those in whom the ministerial functions are

[52] *Loc cit.*

[53] 163 S.W. 628 (1914).

[54] Trinity Methodist Episcopal Church v. City of San Antonio, 201 S.W. 669 (1918).

[55] Revised Statutes Article 7150.

vested and in the Roman Catholic Church that is a priest subject to the control of the bishop. However, this was a trespass to try title case and only the powers of the bishop to convey the land were at issue. The allusions to the minister were explanatory statements at the most.[56]

The "ministers" of the Catholic Church are numerous. Canon 108 states that those who have been bound to the divine ministry by at least the reception of first tonsure are called clerics. But these clerics do not all belong to the same church. There is a division into a sacred hierarchy of orders, and in this sacred hierarchy, the sanctification and the salvation of the faithful is promoted through public worship and the administration of the sacraments. There is a division of the hierarchy by reason of jurisdiction in that the faithful are brought to eternal life by the power of governing which is exercised.[57]

The difficulty that lies in restricting the meaning of the word "ministers" to those persons indicated in canon 108 is that only clerics participate in the power of orders or jurisdiction in the Church. Therefore, for a more complete concept of ministers in the Church who should be included under the concept of the tax exemption statute, the theological concept must be brought in to extend this canonical concept. The Code envisions the laity as teachers of catechism and as such, they have a canonical mission in the broad sense to act as ministers of the word of God.[58] Similarly, the laity at times participate in the administration of the property of the Church. The laity does not by this fact participate in the jurisdiction of the Church but they do act in a sense as ministers.[59]

It does not seem that the tax exemption statutes would exclude the merely temporal administrator. But the law certainly includes those who teach the Word of God. In many religious

[56] 86 Tex. 121, 23 S.W. 985, reversing 22 S.W. 286 (Civ. App., 1893).

[57] Abbo-Hannan, I, 161.

[58] Canon 1333; Bouscaren, pp. 688, 689.

[59] Cf. B. F. Deutsch, *Jurisdiction of Pastors in the External Forum,* Catholic University of America Canon Law Studies, n. 378 (Washington, D.C.: The Catholic University of America Press, 1957) pp. 153 ff.

societies, the ministers perform no other tasks. These societies lack the concept of a sacramental system or of any ritually performed actions. It is definitely not sufficient to say that ministers in the Catholic Church are only the priests who are subject to a bishop.[60] Those priests are ministers of the church but the statement excludes the bishops who are also ministers and in a higher degree. Further, there are certain clerics who are not subject to the bishops of the Church but are only subject to the Pope in Rome and their respective religious superiors. These clerics are also ministers of the Church in the strictest sense of the word.[61]

Consequently when the situation arises that a determination must be made as to who is a minister of the Catholic Church, all of these many concepts must be weighed. Experts must be drawn from the Church itself in order that the court might understand the various distinctions used in canonical and theological terminology.[62] Thus the court has remarked that:

> The members of the Roman Catholic Church are found in every part of the world, and their interests, temporal and spiritual, are looked after by a well-disciplined hierarchy, consisting of functionaries of successive grades, whose respective powers are accurately defined, and among themselves, well understood.[63]

The extent of the exemption to both the actual places of worship and the dwelling place of the minister is to include the grounds necessary for access to the church, or from one part to another, and to permit the passage of sufficient light and air. The ground is necessary if it is destined to provide appropriate

---

[60]Olcott v. Gabert, 86 Tex. 121, 23 S.W. 985, reversing 22 S.W. 286 (Civ. App., 1893).

[61]Canons 615, 618.

[62]Cf. Journet, pp. 187 ff. gives more of a theological concept to the ministry in the church and the concept is broader than the canonical concepts.

[63]Olcott v. Gabert, 86 Tex. 121, 23 S.W. 985, reversing 22 S.W. 286 (Civ. App., 1893); cf. Blanc v. Asbury, 63 Tex. 490 (1885).

ornamentation. Thus, a vacant lot was considered as necessary to the proper use of a church.[64]

The religious society that claims the exemption must comply with the basic rules noted in the introduction to these sections. That is, the itemized list of the property must be filed with the Tax Assessor in the County in which the property is situated. The property must be owned by the religious society itself and subjected to actual, direct and exclusive use by the religious society that seeks the exemption.

The Catholic Church considers cemeteries as "sacred places" and as such, cemeteries should be exempt from taxation.[65] The State of Texas exempts cemeteries operated by religious organizations without a view for profit. These are not exempted because of their religious purposes but more because of the charitable purpose. The statute exempts cemeteries and all lands used exclusively for graveyards or grounds for burying the dead, except such as are held by any person, company or corporation with a view to profit or for the purpose of speculating in the sale thereof.[66]

B. *Educational Purposes*

The several States of the United States exercise powers in the regulation of schools subject only to the provisions and interpretations of the Constitution of the United States. Two decisions of the Supreme Court of the United States have defined and upheld the basic rights of the non-public school. The Dartmouth College case in 1819 upheld the right of an educational institution to exist as a private corporation.[67] A century later, in 1926, the Supreme Court had under consideration the Compulsory Education Act of the State of Oregon. In order to comply with this law of the State of Oregon requiring attendance at school, students were to go to public schools only. Attendance at private or parochial schools would not suffice. This was held to be an unreasonable interference with the liberty

---

[64] City of Houston v. Cohen, 204 S.W. 2d 671 (1948).

[65] Canon 1154.

[66] Revised Statutes Article 7150, §3.

[67] Dartmouth College v. Woodward, 4 U.S. (Wheaton) 310.

of parents and guardians who must direct the upbringing ot their children.[68]

A special committee on Education reported to the President in 1956 that:

> From the beginning of our national history, private and church-related schools have been a very real and potent part of our national life. It is a matter of settled constitutional law in the United States that it is the right and privilege of parents to send their children to such schools. It is a necessary corollary that private groups, religious or other, have a right to establish schools of their own.[69]

The States recognize that these private ventures into the field of education should be encouraged. Therefore, exemptions from taxation are granted to those so doing.[70]

By virtue of the power granted the legislature to exempt schools from taxation, the following statute was enacted:

> . . . all public school houses . . . all public colleges, public academies and all academies and all endowment funds of institutions of learning and religion not used with a view to profit, and when the same are invested in bonds or mortgages, and all buildings used exclusively and owned by persons or associations of persons for school purposes; provided that when the land has been, or shall hereafter be, bought in by such institutions under foreclosure sales made to satisfy or protect bonds or mortgages in which said endowment funds are invested, that such exemptions of such land and property shall continue for two years after the purchase of the same at such sale by such institutions and no longer. This provision shall not extend to leasehold estate of real property held under authority of any college or university of learning.[71]

The practice of exempting schools from taxation is of early origin in Texas. In 1850, the members of the Know-Nothing

[68]Pierce v. Society of Sisters, 268 U.S. 535 (1926).

[69]Beach-Will, p. 8.

[70]*Ibidem,* p. 19.

[71]Revised Statutes Article 7150.

party vigorously attacked the proposal to grant state aid to all schools that would give free education to the youth of the State. The proposal was defeated. But at the same time, irresponsible attacks against religious freedom, especially that of the Catholic Church, were made by the same Know-Nothing party. This was repudiated by the non-Catholic populace.[72] Although the proposal for state aid failed, the proposals for tax exemption succeeded and this was used as a means to encourage educational enterprises.[73]

The court succinctly stated the reasons for granting tax exemptions in the last century in the case of Cassiano v. Ursuline Academy:

> Those who, from charitable considerations, to forward, sectarian views, or for private profit, have organized or conducted schools, have assisted the state in the performance of a duty it owes to its citizens, which cannot be too thoroughly performed, and which the state has never assumed that it had either the means or the machinery of doing sufficiently well without private assistance. The Ursuline Academy is performing its part in this branch of the public service, and it should rather be encouraged by aids, than impaired in its usefulness by a tax upon its pitiful revenues.[74]

This policy has been reaffirmed in recent decisions of the State courts.[75]

---

[72]Fitzmorris, p. 84, gives an interesting discussion from the newspapers of the day relating the arguments of Sam Houston against the possible encroachment of Catholic schools if such state aid was granted. Sam Houston had united with the Know-Nothing party for other political purposes, and was undoubtedly infected with the poison of their propaganda.

[73]Harris v. Ft. Worth, 142 Tex. 600, 180 S.W. 2d 131 (1944) reversing 177 S.W. 2d 308 (Civ. App., 1944) on an endowment fund of Texas Christian University.

[74]64 Tex. 673 (1886).

[75]Harris v. Ft. Worth, 142 Tex. 600, 180 S.W. 2d 131 (1944) reversing 177 S.W. 2d 308 (Civ. App., 1944); Smith v. Feather, 229 S.W. 2d 417 (1950) affirmed in 234 S.W. 2d 418 (1950); State v. University of Houston, 264 S.W. 2d 153 (Civ. App., 1954).

The exemptions of these educational institutions extends to all the land and buildings used in operating the institutions as well as the endowment funds which the institution might possess. However, an endowment fund that consists of property is exempt only for the two year period specified in the statute.[76]

The term "school" has been defined as an institution devoted to instruction to improve the mental, rather than the physical faculties of the scholars. It is immaterial that the object of the founders is to propagate sectarian doctrine.[77] However, the statutory exemption extends to any association engaged in promoting the religious, educational and physical development of boys, girls, young men or young women.[78] A recent case has considered a school offering a three year course in commercial art with the award of a certificate at the end of three years as a "school" within the terms of the act.[79]

The word "building" has been construed to embrace the land used in connection with it. The ground used for the recreation of the students and to supply the school table with vegetables, which was necessary and used for the purpose and contributed to the economical running of the school, was exempted.[80] But land used only for the purpose of supplying the table of the school, though contiguous and connected therewith, was not within the clause exempting the lands from taxation in a subsequent case. The amount of land so used was 499 acres and this probably contributed to the adverse decision.[81]

Property is "owned" for school purposes within the language of the exemption when the owners themselves use it for the purpose of operating a school. The courts emphasize the principle that the owner could not take advantage of the exemption

---

[76]Harris v. Ft. Worth (*loc. cit.*).

[77]Cassiano v. Ursusline Academy, 64 Tex. 673 (1886).

[78]Revised Statute Article 7150, §2a.

[79]Smith v. Feather, 234 S.W. 2d 418 affirming 229 S.W. 2d 417 (1950).

[80]Cassiano v. Ursuline Academy, 64 Tex. 673 (1885).

[81]St. Edward's College v. Morris, 82 Tex. 1, 7 S.W. 512 (1891).

and rent to others for profit. Nor could another lease from the owner for the purposes of operating a school in order that the owner might claim the exemption.[82] The property must be used exclusively for the purpose by the owners of the property. The exemption becomes effective when the preparations to use the property for school purposes are begun, not when the property comes into one's possession; nor does one have to wait until actual operation is begun to claim the exemption.[83]

The Attorney General has given opinions stating the position held by his department concerning the exemptions granted property used for educational purposes. A use of property owned by the Catholic Church for both a school and a chapel is exempt.[84] He also considers oil royalties from land and land surface as exempt from ad valorem taxes when the land comprises the campus of and is owned by a non-profit educational college operated by a religious organization, and is wholly used and dedicated to educational activities.[85]

The concept of the "endowment fund" has been given a liberal interpretation. A fund that was invested in bonds and mortgages was given to Texas Christian University in Fort Worth. Notes secured by mortgages were included in the fund. The income from these notes went to a common fund that was to be given to the University at a later date. The court considered these an endowment fund even though not invested by the University but acquired while invested by force of the grant. The reasoning of the case was based upon the fact that the amendments to the Constitution and enactments of the legislature evince a liberality in granting exemptions from taxation of property used for education or religious purposes.[86]

---

[82]Red v. Morris, 72 Tex. 554, 10 S.W. 681 (1889); Red v. Johnson, 53 Tex. 284 (1868); Smith v. Feather, 234 S.W. 2d 418 affirming 229, S.W. 2d 417 (1950).

[83]Smither v. Feather (*loc. cit.*).

[84]*Opinions of the Attorney General, 1943*, No. 0-4909 (Austin, Texas, 1944).

[85]*Ibidem, 1952*, No. V-1568.

[86]Harris v. Fort Worth, 142 Tex. 600, 180 S.W. 2d 131 (1944) reversing 177 S.W. 2d 308 (Civ. App., 1944); cf. City of San An-

The position of the Church on the maintenance of private schools is well known in the United States. The Bishops of the United States asserted in 1919 that:

> The Church in our country is obliged, for the sake of principle, to maintain a system of education distinct and separate from other systems. It is supported by the voluntary contributions of Catholics, who at the same time, contribute as required by law to the maintenance of public schools. It engages in the service of education a body of teachers who consecrate their lives to this high calling; and it prepares, without expense to the State, a considerable number of Americans to live worthily as citizens of the Republic. . . .[87]

A denial of tax exemption would ultimately lead to the downfall of most private schools with great detriment to the welfare of the State. It would be hard to understand how such a burden would not be in violation of the freedom to practice religion assured in the 1st amendment and extended to the citizens of the states in the 14th amendment. It would practically deny Catholics the opportunity to fulfill a most grave obligation to provide to the best of their ability for the religious and moral as well as for the physical and civil education of their children, and for their temporal well being.[88] Similarly, the Constitution of the State of Texas would be violated if tax exemptions are denied for the legislature has the duty to pass those laws necessary to protect equally every religious denomination.[89] However, the policy that has been followed in the State of Texas in this matter of tax exemptions has been most beneficial to the free practice of religious beliefs in the education of the child.[90]

---

tonio v. Y.M.C.A., 285 S.W. 844 (Civ. App., 1926) denying exemption, with section 1, this chapter.

[87] *Our Bishops Speak, 1919-1951* (Milwaukee: Bruce Publishing Co., 1952), p. 59.

[88] Canon 1113; cf. canons 1372-1375, for particular legislation on education.

[89] *Bill of Rights,* Article I, section 6.

[90] Beach-Will, pp. 2 ff., gives interesting statistics indicating that

C. Charitable Purposes

Tax exemptions of charitable associations is almost universal in the United States, but the statutory and constitutional exemptions are far from uniform. In colonial America, such exemptions were justified for churches because they were governmental agencies.[91] Subsequently, the States came to realize that private works of charity prevented many persons from becoming charges on the State and therefore, the exemptions were extended to include charitable associations. These private institutions that engaged in charitable activities considerably lessened the burden of taxation. Not only were activities assumed that would have fallen to the State, but private charitable organizations ordinarily performed works that the State could never assume. This has been said to be a good bargain for the State in that part of the work was done in consideration of the tax exemption. The State would suffer great detriment if these organizations were abolished and the work were thrust upon the State. The cost would far exceed the loss suffered by granting the exemptions.[92]

The Constitution of 1876 permits the legislature of the State of Texas to grant exemptions from taxation to purely public charities. In accordance with this power, the following statute was enacted to exempt property:

> All buildings belonging to institutions of purely public charity, together with the lands belonging to and occupied by such institutions, not leased or otherwise used with a view to profit, unless such rents and profits and all moneys and credits are appropriated by such institutions solely to sustain such institutions for the benefit of the sick and

---

nonpublic schools constitute 14.6% or 4,339,163 of the total elementary and secondary enrollment in the continental U. S. as of February, 1957. Enrollment in Catholic schools make up 88.93% of this number of 4,339,163. On the University level, 46.06% of the total enrollment of universities are to be found in nonpublic universities.

[91] Zollman, p. 328.

[92] *Ibidem,* p. 327; Commonwealth v. Young Men's Christian Association, 116 Ky. 711, 76 S.W. 522, 25 Ky. Law Rep. 940, 105 Am. St. Rep. 234 (1903).

> disabled members and their families and the burial of the same, or for the maintenance of persons when unable to provide for themselves, whether such persons are members of such institutions or not. An institution of purely public charity under this article is one which dispenses its aid to its members and others in sickness or distress, or at death, without regard to the poverty or riches of the recipient, also when the funds, property and assets of such institutions are placed and bound by its laws to relieve, aid and administer in any way to the relief of its members in want, sickness and distress, and provide homes for its helpless and dependent members and to educate and maintain the orphans of its deceased members or other persons.[93]

It has often been stated that both the Constitutional authorization to grant exemptions and the legislative enactments granting the exemptions are to be interpreted strictly.[94] But judicial decisions have been liberal in concluding that private ventures into the field of charitable activities are purely public charities as intended by the statute. In general, the court merely enunciates the wording of the statute, describes the activities of the organization under consideration, and if there are evidences of charitable works, without a corresponding gain for private individuals or associations, the organization is considered as exempt.[95] However, the courts have declared that charitable purposes are the relief of poverty, advance of education, promoting religion, promoting health, and fostering governmental or municipal purposes or any other purpose beneficial to the community.[96]

A purely charitable purpose was evident in the Santa Rosa

[93]Revised Statutes Article 7150, §7.

[94]Cf. City of Houston v. Scottish Benevolent Association, 111 Tex. 191, 230 S.W. 978 (1921).

[95]Santa Rosa Infirmary v. City of San Antonio, 249 S.W. 498, reversed in 259 S.W. 926 (Com. App., 1925); Hedgecroft v. City of Houston, 244 S.W. 2d 632 (1951) reversing 239 S.W. 2d 828; cf. Malone-Hogan Hospital Clinic Foundation, Inc. v. City of Big Spring, 288 S.W. 2d 550 (1956).

[96]Moore v. Sellers, 201 S.W. 2d 248 (1947); Taysum v. El Paso Nat'l Bank, 256 S.W. 2d 172 (Civ. App., 1952).

Hospital case concerning the Sisters of Charity of the Incarnate Word, incorporated under the laws of Texas. The hospital of the sisters, incorporated in a separate charter, was a purely charitable organization by force of the charter and its operation. The charter stated:

> the purpose of this corporation shall be both benevolent and charitable, and especially for the acquisition of, or the erection of and the maintenance of a hospital in the city of San Antonio, Bexar County, Texas, at which the members of the corporation will administer to the sick, the infirm, the helping of the maimed and the afflicted of all creeds, colors and nationalities . . etc.

The court asserted that the facts supported the announced intention in this charter.[97]

While it is true that the tax exemption legislation is to be interpreted strictly, the courts should not strive to limit the legislature to a literal reiteration of the Constitution; but those activities that aptly fit into the spirit of the constitutional authorization should be construed as validly exempted. Zollman considers this the duty of the court for the literal construction would often destroy the true intent of the law.[98] The courts have so acted in the interpretation of the word "purely." This word excludes all notion of private gain.[99] However, the exemption is not lost to hospitals merely because the patients must pay for the accommodations according to the quality of the accommodations.[100] This is not operating the charity for profit when whatever surplus is received is placed in a general fund for other charitable works.[101]

---

[97] 249 S.W. 498 reversed in 259 S.W. 926 (Com. App., 1924).

[98] *American Church Law,* pp. 324-325.

[99] Malone-Hogan Hospital Clinic Foundation, Inc. v. City of Big Spring, 288 S.W. 2d 550 (1956): the court said that the statute was adopted from Ohio law and the construction put on the statute by Ohio courts was also adopted. The word, "purely," was so construed by Cleveland Osteopathic Hospital v. Zongerle, 153 Ohio St. 222, 91 N.E. 2d 261 (1950); Gerke v. Purcell, 25 Ohio St. 229 (1874).

[100] Baylor University v. Boyd, 18 S.W. 2d 700 (1930); Baptist Memorial Hospital v. McTighe, 303 S.W. 2d 446 (1957).

[101] *Loc. cit.*

The courts have permitted a reasonable compensation to those running a hospital when the organization was notably a charitable organization.[102] But when there is an apparent private scheme, the court will not permit the exemptions to apply.[103] The courts would probably presume a charitable activity in those organizations such as the Salvation Army and Catholic hospitals. But a hospital operated by a group of private individuals who might have monetary interest therein, would have a more difficult burden of proof.[104]

The charitable institution must be owned by the association claiming the tax exemption.[105] Mere ownership will not suffice, there must be bona fide necessary preparations in being in order that the exemption will apply.[106] This preparation for actual use of the land or buildings for charitable purposes need not be performed by the association seeking the exemption but the land must be owned by them. When the property is in actual use, that use must be exclusively that of the charitable institution.[107]

There is a group who claim that tax exemptions are State aid. Therefore, the exemptions are conceived as a support of religion. The group suggests that the State itself should bestow upon all citizens those services rendered by the charitable societies. They will not admit that the works of charity that society has need of cannot be adequately given either by the State or by charitable organizations of a private nature. Consequently, both must exist and neither should seek the elimination of the other.

---

[102]City of San Antonio v. Salvation Army, 127 S.W. 860 (Civ. App., 1922).

[103]Malone-Hogan Hospital Clinic Foundation, Inc. v. City of Big Spring, 288 S.W. 2d 550 (1956), concerned a group of doctors that ran the hospital. The court noted that the salary was a means of securing the profits of the hospital.

[104]Cf. Raymondville Memorial Hospital v. State, 253 S.W. 2d 1013 (1954).

[105]Dickinson v. Woodsmen of the World Life Insurance Society, 280 S.W. 2d 318 (1955).

[106]Hedgecroft v. City of Houston, 244 S.W. 2d 632 (1951).

[107]*Loc. cit.;* Morris v. Lone Star Chapter No. 6, Royal Arch Masons, 68 Tex. 698, 5 S.W. 519 (1876).

Pope Pius XII remarked upon the excessive trust that is placed in State charities. In consequence, this situation arises: the trust in the State demands excessive taxation and compromises the rights of private property and even reaches the rights of the person and the family. The Pontiff stated:

> In not a few nations the Modern State is becoming a gigantic administrative machine, which extends its hands over almost all phases of life. It seeks the domination of all things: the different political segments, the economical and the social aspects, the intellectual life of men, and even life and death, so that all life is under its administration. It is no wonder, then, that in this climate of the impersonal, which tends to penetrate and involve all phases of life, the sentiment of the common good is dulled in individual consciences and the State is consequently losing its primary character of a community of citizens.[108]

Every moral person in the Church exists for a charitable or religious purpose.[109] They make possible the performance of one or more of the divinely established functions of the Church. These functions include the religious government of the members of the Church in the exercise of spiritual and temporal charity toward men. The very purpose of the preaching of the Gospel is to bring the Good News of salvation and sanctification to all men. Love of neighbor in this life is more evident in those who externally manifest that love in works of charity. The members of the Church realize that love of neighbor is what urges others to lives of prayer and more intimate worship to bring all men to Christ. Thus, the Church intends to insist upon its freedom from taxation which might easily result in confiscation of the temporal goods with which the Church militant is enabled to worship, teach and practice brotherly love.[110]

---

[108]*Radiomessage of 1952—Acta Apostolicae Sedis, Commentarium Officiale,* (Romae: 1909-), XLV (1953), 37.

[109]Canon 100, §1.

[110]Cf. Canons 1255, 1322, 1327, 497, §2, 1473, 1489 and 1499. Cf. Murphy, pp. 20-22.

CONCLUSIONS

I. *Historical Conclusions:* The Catholic Church was recognized as a juridical entity that functioned independently of the State under the regimes of Spain and Mexico. The sovereign State of Texas has not granted this recognition to the Catholic Church but the State has permitted the Church to function without being hampered by the law. (pp. 3-52.)

II. *Legal Conclusions:* Christ established the Catholic Church as a juridically perfect society. Consequently, the Universal Church has the right to acquire, hold and administer whatever property is necessary for the purposes for which it is founded. This includes the Church's power to found subordinate moral personalities with the same rights to acquire, hold and administer property independently of the authority of the civil power. (pp. 53-75.)

In order to function as a juridical society in the State of Texas, the Church must be given the legal capacity by the laws of the State. This is the common law doctrine adopted in all the States of the United States. (pp. 76-86.) The Catholic Church is desirous of receiving a legal status before the laws of the State that is completely compatible with the nature of the Church. The present statute for incorporating religious societies might be broad enough to permit the incorporation of the Catholic Church and all its properties in Texas. However, the statute is vague in its terms and the following difficulties might arise:

> 1) In forming the corporation, will the members of the local parish be able to choose a board of trustees superior to the ordinary or the pastor?
>
> 2) Will the supervisory power of the local ordinary be given full cognizance when the local administrators perform acts which are invalid or illicit at Church law?

3) Would there be a great danger of interference by the members of the local parish or the diocese and by the State through the Attorney General's office with the supervisory power of the Bishop or the administrative power of the Pastor?

The statute permits the charter to include the constitutions, rules and regulations of the religious society as a constituent part of the charter. Therefore, the statute seems sufficiently broad. However, since there is doubt, it would be better if a statute were passed that would favor incorporating of a hierarchial religious society. (pp. 90-95; 115-119.)

The trust relationship that presently exists permits every religious society to function according to its particular nature by force of judicial recognition. However, the Catholic Church expects each moral person in the Church to have title to its own property. The moral person is to have one or more persons as the administrator. The local ordinary is to have broad powers of supervision but he is not to act as the administrator. Therefore, the trust relationship in effect contradicts the Church law on property because it makes the local ordinary the legal owner of the property with the power and the duty to administrate the property. (pp. 95-115.)

It must be admitted that the Catholic Church is at present functioning in the spirit of its laws if not to the letter. Therefore, unless a corporation statute were passed that would be fitted to the nature of the Catholic Church, it is better to keep the present system of holding in trust. The advantage of having a statute according to which the church is incorporated is that there is more stability and certainty before the law. (pp. 79-79e; 115-120.)

As to the acquisition of property, the Catholic Church, as every other religious society in Texas, has the capacity to acquire property by every means permitted to others. The following observations may be made between the law of the Church and that of the State as to the acquisition of property:

1) Prescription or Adverse Possession:

a) A prescriptable object: The law of the State

would not permit prescription or adverse possession of an object not subject to prescription by the laws of the Church except in the case of sacred things. (pp. 133, 151, 164, 47-52, 216-238.)

b) Good faith is required to be present in the prescription of personal property and also for real property, except in the case of the 10 and 25 year statutes. (pp. 133, 150, 164-168.)

c) Just title is required by Church law, but only for the curative statutes in State law. (pp. 133, 164.)

d) Just possession is required by the law of the State for the curative statutes and for personal property. (pp. 133, 151, 164.)

e) The time: there is no recognition given to Church law forbidding prescription of certain properties before thirty years of adverse possession.

2) The State law will not enforce bequests or legacies in favor of pious causes that do not conform to the solemities of State law.

Other than these, there seem to be no patent variances in the law of the Church and the State on acquisition.

The tax exemptions which are granted in the State of Texas are in complete conformity with the doctrine of the Church on such immunities.

APPENDIX

In 1955, the legislature of the State of Texas passed a new corporation act for profit associations which is called the Texas Business Corporation Act. The reasons for the passing of this new act are to be found in the desire of the state to accommodate its laws to modern business practices and to eliminate certain outmoded restrictions formerly placed upon profit corporations. Similarly in 1959, the Texas Legislature acted to render the corporation laws for non-profit associations more adaptable to modern practices and to eliminate unnecessary restrictions. Certain aspects of the new law are vast improvements over the former law. However, the Catholic Church has not benefited by these changes for the difficulties in incorporating under this law remain practically the same for the Church. A summary of these points are herein indicated.

The new law offers definitions of various technical terms found therein.[1] These definitions are not found in the old law. The old law specifically determined the purposes for which a corporation could be formed.[2] However, the new law states a very general purpose for which a private non-profit association may incorporate:

> Such purpose or purposes may include, without being limited to, any one or more of the following: charitable, benevolent, religious, eleemosynary, patriotic, civic, missionary, educational, scientific, social, fraternal, athletic, aesthetic, agricultural and horticultural; . . .

The act specifically states that a non-profit corporation may be organized for any lawful purpose or purposes, which pur-

[1]*Texas Non-Profit Corporation Act,* Article 1.02, Vernon's Texas Session Law Service (Kansas City, Mo.: 1959) pp. 286. (Hereafter cited Article 1.02, etc.)

[2]Revised Statutes Article 1302.

poses shall be fully stated in the articles of incorporation.[3] This purpose clause is a vast improvement in that the corporation will be able to encompass many acts and activities in a single charter, thereby eliminating the need for many charters to permit the same organization to perform many charitable activities

The general powers have been clarified and in part extended. Of particular note is the fact that the corporation now may have perpetual succession,[4] whereas it formerly could exist for only fifty years before it had the obligation of filing again to succeed to itself.[5] The general powers are:

> 1. To have perpetual succession by its corporate name, unless a limited period of duration is stated in its articles of incorporation.
> 2. To sue and be sued, complain and defend, in its corporate name.
> 3. To have a corporate seal . . .
> 4. To purchase, receive, lease, or otherwise acquire, own, hold, improve, use, or otherwise deal in and with, real or personal property, or any interest therein, wherever situated, as the purposes of the corporation shall require.
> 5. To sell, convey, mortgage, pledge, lease, exchange, transfer, and otherwise dispose of all or any part of its property and assets.
> 6. To lend money to, and otherwise assist, its employees, but not its officers and directors.
> 7. To purchase, receive, subscribe for, or otherwise acquire, own, hold, vote, use, employ, mortgage, lend, pledge, sell or otherwise dispose of, and otherwise use and deal in and with, shares or other interests in, or obligations of, other domestic or foreign corporations, whether for profit or not for profit, associations, partnerships, or individuals, or direct or indirect obligations of the United States or of any other government, state, territory, government district, or municipality, or of any instrumentality thereof.

---

[3]Article 2.01.

[4]Article 2.02, A, (1).

[5]Revised Statutes Article 1320 (1).

8. To make contracts and incur liabilities, borrow money at such rates of interest as the corporation may determine, issue its notes, bonds, and other obligations, and secure any of its obligations by mortgage or pledge of all or any of its property, franchises, and income.

9. To lend money for its corporate purposes, invest and reinvest its funds, and take and hold real and personal property as security for the payment of funds so loaned or invested.

10. To conduct its affairs, carry on its operations, and have officers and exercise the powers granted by this Act in any state, territory, district, or possession of the United States, or any foreign country.

11. To elect or appoint officers and agents of the corporation for such period of time as the corporation may determine and define their duties and fix their compensation.

12. To make and alter by-laws, not inconsistent with its articles of incorporation or with the laws of this state, for the administration and regulation of the affairs of the corporation.

13. To make donations for the public welfare, or for charitable, scientific, or educational purposes and in time of war to make donations in aid of war activities.

14. To cease its corporate activities and terminate its existence by voluntary dissolution.

15. Wherever included in the foregoing or not, to have and exercise all powers necessary or appropriate to effect any or all of the purposes for which the corporation is organized.

16. Any religious, charitable, educational, or eleemosynary institution organized under the laws of this State may acquire, own, hold, mortgage and dispose of and invest its funds in real and personal property for the use and benefit and under the discretion of, and in trust for any convention, conference or association organized under the laws of this State or another state with which it is affiliated, or which elects its board of directors, or which controls it, in furtherance of the purposes of the member institution.

17. To pay pensions and establish pension plans and pension trusts for all of, or classes of its officers and employees, or its officers or its employees. B. Nothing in this

> article grants any authority to officers or directors of a corporation for the exercise of any of the foregoing powers, inconsistent with the limitations on any of the same which may be expressly set forth in this Act or in the articles of incorporation or by-laws or in any other laws of this State. Authority of officers and directors to act beyond the scope of the purpose or purposes of a corporation is not granted by any provision of this Article.[6]

Certain protective measures are found in the old law but they have been deleted in the new. These provide that the Board of Trustees shall not usurp the functions of any officer in-charge and state that all secular control is to be in the domain of this board but not spiritual control. In fact, the old law would forbid the Attorney General from inspection of purely religious matters when it becomes necessary for him to intervene in the temporal affairs of a religious association incorporated under the law.[7]

A fundamental complaint to the old law on incorporation is still valid. That is, the law envisions every "church" as being guided by the members who can elect and depose their leaders at will. This weakness of the law is latent in the requirement that the only way incorporation is possible is for the majority to vote for incorporating. Incorporators in the new law are:

> A. Three (3) or more natural persons, two (2) of whom must be citizens of the State of Texas, of the age of twenty-one (21) years or more may act as incorporators of a corporation by signing, verifying, and delivering in duplicate to the Secretary of State articles of incorporations for such corporation.
>
> B. Any religious society, charitable, benevolent, literary, or social association, or church may incorporate under this Act with the consent of a majority of its members, who shall authorize the incorporators to execute the articles of incorporation.[8]

Assuming that the act of incorporation could be effected, the

[6] Article 2.02, A, B.

[7] Revised Statute Article 1397; 1398.

[8] Article 3.01, A, B.

requirement of annual elections, the requirement to fill vacancies amongst the directors by a vote of the members, and the general approach to providing for leaders of such organizations were odious to the concept of an hierarchical church under the old law.[9] However, the new law seems to permit an establishment of a board of directors and officers which can be adapted to the administrative requirements of an hierarchical church. Thus, the board of directors or trustees of religious, charitable, educational or eleemosynary institutions may be affiliated with, elected and controlled by a convention, conference or association organized under the laws of this State or another state, whether incorporated or unincorporated, whose membership is composed of representatives, delegates, or messengers from any church or other religious association.[10]

The new law provides that:

> The articles of incorporation of a church may vest the management of the affairs of the corporation in its members. If the church has a board of directors or *similar body,* it may limit the authority of such board to whatever extent as may be set forth in the articles of incorporation or by-laws.[11]

It might be assumed that the bishop or the pastor could be the board of directors as is indicated by the next section of this Article:

> In the case of a corporation which is a church, the Board may be designated by any name appropriate to the customs, usages, or tenets of the church.[12]

The new law provides that a church need not have the officers required for other organizations but that its duties may be vested in the board of trustees or other designated body in any manner provided for in the articles of incorporation or the

[9]Cf. Articles 1323, et alii.

[10]Article 2.14, B.

[11]*Ibid., C.*

[12]*Ibid.,* D.

by-laws.[13] Thus, the hierarchical church could establish a board of directors with definitive powers according to the laws of the church who would be able to elect, classify and remove directors according to such laws.[14] Vacancies are likewise filled by the board of directors.[15] The only question that might be asked is this: "Could the Bishop act according to the laws of the Church to depose a pastor of an incorporated Church if he was not joined by the other members of the board, even though the laws of the Church are part of the by-laws set up in the articles of incorporation?" The answer would seem to be in the negative because of the quorum required for a meeting of the board of directors and because of the need for a majority vote required in any action by such a quorum.[16]

The comments made in the text on dissolution of corporations, either voluntary or involuntary are in general valid both for the old and the new law. The new law has the improvement in that where an involuntary dissolution occurs, the assets are to be applied to a similar religious or charitable purpose.[17]

In conclusion, the new law is a great step forward and seems to be adaptable to the Catholic Church. However, it is to be hoped that the State will see fit to pass a new law along the lines of the model New York law which will be more easily and surely adaptable to the incorporation of diocesan and parochial properties of the Roman Catholic Church.[18]

[13]Article 2.20, D.

[14]Article 2.15, A. B. C. D.

[15]Article 2.16.

[16]Article 2.17.

[17]Article 7.06, B, (3).

[18]Cf. pp. 79 *sqq. supra.*

BIBLIOGRAPHY

SOURCES

Acta Apostolicae Sedis, Commentarium Officiale, Romae, 1909-1929; Civitate Vaticana, 1929-

Acta et Decreta Concilii Plenarii Baltimorensis Tertii, A.D. MDCCCLXXXIV, Baltimorae: John Murphy, 1886.

Acta Sanctae Sedis, 41 vols., Romae, 1865-1908.

Black, H. C., *Black's Law Dictionary,* 3. ed., St. Paul: West Publishing Company, 1933.

Canon Law Digest, The, edited by T. Lincoln Bouscaren, 4 vols., Milwaukee: The Bruce Publishing Co., 1934-1958.

Bouvier, John, *Law Dictionary and Concise Encyclopedia,* 2 vols., St. Paul, Minn.: West Publishing Co., 1914.

Code Iuris Canonici, Pii X Pontificia Maximi iussu digestus, Benedicti Papae XV auctoritate promulgatus, Praefatione, fontium annotatione et indice analytico-alphabetico, ab Emo Petri Card. Gasparri auctus, Romae, 1917.

Codicis Iuris Canonici Fontes, cura Emi Petri Card. Gasparri editi, 9 vols. Romae (postea Civitate Vaticana): Typis Polyglottis Vaticanis, 1923-1939 (Vols. VII-IX, ed. cura et studio Emi Iustiniani Card. Seredi.)

Concilii Plenarii Baltimorensis II, In Ecclesia Metropolitana Baltimoriensi habiti, Acta et Decreta, Baltimorae: Joannes Murphy, 1868.

Concilium Plenarium Totius Americae Septentrionalis Foederatae, Baltimori Tributum, Baltimori: Joannes Murphy, 1852.

Corpus Juris, 71 vols., New York: American Law Book Co., 1939.

Corpus Juris Secundum, 95 vols., Brooklyn: American Law Book Co., 1939.

Denzinger, H., Bannwart, C., Umberg, J., *Enchiridion Symbolorum Definitionum et Declarationum de Rebus Fidei et Morum,* editio vigesima septima, augmentata, Barcelona: Herder, 1951.

Hernaez, Javier, S.J., *Collecion de Bulas Breves,* 2 vols., ed. A. Vromont, Brussels: 1879.

Laws of Texas, 1822-1905, Gammel, H. P. N., 10 vols. and index, Austin, 1906.

Magnum Bullarium Romanum, 8 vols., Luxemburgi: 1727.

Southwestern Reporter, St. Paul: West Publishing Co.

Texas Digest, 1840 to date, 42 vols, and index, St. Paul: West Publishing Co.

Texas Jurisprudence, 43 vols., San Francisco: Bancroft-Whitney Co., 1935.

Texas Non-Profit Corporation Act, Vernon's Texas Session Law Service 1959, Kansas City, Mo.: Vernon Law Book Co., 1959.

Texas Probate Code, Vernon's Statutes, 1956 Supplement, Kansas City, Mo.: Vernon Law Book Co., 1956.

Texas Reports, Cases adjudged in the Supreme Court of the State of Texas and published by the State of Texas at Austin.

Vernon's Annotated Revised Civil Statutes of the State of Texas, Revision of 1925, Kansas City, Mo.: Vernon Law Book Co., 1945.

Vernon's Texas Statutes, 1948 Kansas City, Mo.: Vernon Law Book Co., 1948.

REFERENCE WORKS

Abbo, John A.-Hannan, Jerome D., *The Sacred Canons,* 2. ed., St. Louis: B. Herder Book Co., 1957.

Aigler, Ralph W., Bigelow, Harry A., Powell, Richard R., *Law of Property,* St. Paul, Minn.: West Publishing Co., 1942.

Barker, E. C., *The Father of Texas,* Austin: The Steck Co., 1935.

Beach, F. F.-Will, R. F., *The State and Nonpublic Schools, with particular reference to responsibility of State Departments of Education, U. S. Department of Health, Education, and Welfare,* Misc., No. 28, Washington, D. C.: United States Government Printing Office, 1958.

Bouscaren, T. Lincoln—Ellis, Adam C., *Canon Law, A Text and Commentary,* 3. revised ed., Milwaukee: The Bruce Publishing Co., 1957.

Brown, Brendan, *The Canonical Juristic Personality with Special Reference to its Status in the United States of America,* The Catholic University of America Canon Law Studies, n. 39, Washington, D. C.: The Catholic University of America, 1927.

Byrne, Harry J., *Investment of Church Funds,* The Catholic University of America Canon Law Studies, n. 309, Washington, D. C.: The Catholic University of America Press, 1951.

Cappello, Felix, *Summa Iuris Canonici,* 3 vols., Vol. II, 4. ed. Romae: Apud Aedes Universitatis Gregorianae, 1945.

——*Summa Iuris Publici Ecclesiastici,* 5. ed., Romae: Apud Aedes Universitatis Gregorianae, 1943.

Castaneda, Carlos E., *Our Catholic Heritage in Texas,* 6 vols. in 7, Austin: Von Boeckmann-Jones, 1950.

Cleary, J., *Canonical Limitations on the Alienation of Church Property,* The Catholic University of America Canon Law Studies, n. 100, Washington, D. C.: The Catholic University of America, 1936.

Columbia-Viking Desk Encyclopedia, 2 vols., New York: Viking Press, 1953.

Comyns, Joseph J., *Papal and Episcopal Administration of Church Property,* The Catholic University of America Canon Law Studies, n. 147, The Catholic University of America Press, 1942.

Coquia, Jorge R., *Legal Status of the Church in the Philippines,* Washington: D. C.: The Catholic University of America Press, 1950.

Coronata, M. Conte a, *Institutiones Iuris Canonici, Introductio: Ius Publicum Ecclesiasticum,* Romae: Marietti, 1948.

——*Institutiones Iuris Canonici,* 3. ed., 5 vols., Taurini-Romae: Marietti, 1947-1952.

Deuther, C. G., *John Timon,* Buffalo: 1880.

Deutsch, Bernard F., *Jurisdiction of Pastors in the External Forum,* The Catholic Universities of America Canon Law Studies, n. 378, Washington, D. C.: The Catholic University of America Press, 1957.

Dignan, P. J., *A History of the Legal Incorporation of Catholic Church Property in the United States,* New York: Kenedy, 1935.

Doheny, W. J., *Church Property: Modes of Acquisition,* Catholic University of America Canon Law Studies, n. 41, Washington, D. C.: The Catholic University of America, 1927.

Five Great Encylcicals, New York: Paulist Press, 1931.

Fitzmorris, Sister Mary Angela, *Four Decades of Catholicism in Texas, 1820-1860,* Washington, D. C.: The Catholic University of America, 1926.

Gettys, W. E., *Texas,* New York: Hastings House Publishers, 1940.

Goodwine, J. A., *The Fight of the Church to Acquire Temporal Goods,* Catholic University of America Canon Law Studies, n. 131, Washington, D. C.: The Catholic University of America Press, 1941.

Gomez, R., *Las Leyes de Indias y el Derecho Ecclesiastico en la America Espanola e Islas Filipinas,* Medillin, Columbia: Ediciones Universidad Catholica Bolivariana, 1945.

Hannan, Jerome, *The Canon Law of Wills,* The Catholic University of American Canon Law Studies, n. 86, Washington, D. C.: Catholic University of America, 1934.

Heston, E. L., *The Alienation of Church Property,* The Catholic University of America Canon Law Studies, n. 132, The Catholic University of America Press, 1941.

History of Texas Land, General Land Office, Austin, 1958.

Journet, C., *The Church of the Word Incarnate,* 1st of 4 vols., London and New York: Sheed and Ward, 1954.

Lamadrid, R. S., *El Concordato Espanol de 1753,* Doctorate Thesis in the Gregorian University, Rome.

McCaleb, W. F., *Spanish Missions of Texas,* San Antonio: The Naylor Co., 1954.

McManus, James, *The Administration of Temporal Goods in Religious Institutes,* The Catholic University of America Canon Law Studies, n. 109, Washington, D. C.: The Catholic University of America, 1937.

Martin, Thomas O., *Adverse Possession, Prescription and Limitation of Actions, The Canonical "Praescription,"* Catholic University of America Canon Law Studies, n. 202, Washington, D. C.: The Catholic University of America Press, 1944.

Mitchell, A., *Corporations,* Law Review Series, Austin: Hemphill's Book Store, 1956.

——, *Personal Property,* Law Review Series, Austin: Hemphill's Book Store, 1956.

——, *Real Property,* Law Review Series, Austin: Hemphill's Book Store, 1957.

Mode of Tenure, Roman Catholic Church Property in the United States, A Survey by the Legal Department, National Catholic Welfare Conference, Washington, D. C.: 1941, Supplement, 1954.

Mundy, J. E., *Ecclesiastical Property in Australia and New Zealand,* Catholic University of America Canon Law Studies, n. 387, Washington, D. C.: Catholic University of America Press, 1957.

Murphy, J. P., *The Laws of the State of New York Affecting Church Property,* Catholic University of America Canon Law Studies, n. 388, Washington, D. C.: Catholic University of America Press, 1957.

Official Catholic Directory, 1953, New York: P. J. Kenedy & Sons.

Opinions of Attorney General of Texas, Austin, Texas.

Our Bishops Speak, 1919-1951, Milwaukee: The Bruce Publishing Co., 1952.

Perez, L., *Iglesia y Estado Nuevo, los concordatos ante el moderno derecho publico,* Madrid: Ediciones Fax, 1940.

Prescott, W. H., *Ferdinand and Isabella,* 1st ed., 1837, by Prescott; New and revised ed., J. F. Kirk, Philadelphia: Lippincott, 1883.

Regatillo, E. F. & Zalba, M., *Theologia Moralis Summa,* 3 vols., Madrid: Biblioteca de Autores Cristianos, 1952-1954.

Restatement of the Law of Trusts, 2 vols., St. Paul: American Law Institute, 1935.

Stenger, J., *The Mortgaging of Church Property,* Catholic University of America Canon Law Studies, n. 169, Catholic University of America Press, 1942.

Texas, Compiled by Workers of the Writers' Program of the Works Projects Administration in the State of Texas, W. E. Gettys, Director, New York: Hastings House, 1940.

Wiggins, Urban C., *Property Laws of the State of Ohio Affecting the Church,* Catholic University of America Canon Law Studies, n. 367, Washington, D. C.: Catholic University of America Press, 1956.

Woywod, Stanislaus-Smith, C., *A Practical Commentary on the Code of Canon Law,* 2 vols, New York: Joseph F. Wagner, Inc., 1948.

Yoakum, H., *History of Texas,* 2 volumes, New York: 1856.

Zollman, C., *American Church Law,* St. Paul: West Publishing Co., 1933.

ARTICLES

Cahill, W. H., "The Dedication of Property to the Fixed Patrimony of a Church," *The Jurist,* XVII (1957), 133-156.

Gilmer, "Early Courts and Lawyers of Texas," *Texas Law Review,* XII (1934), 435.

Hall, Ford W., "An Account of the Adoption of the Common Law of Texas," *Texas Law Review,* XVIII (1950), 801.

Markham, E., "The Reception of the Common Law of England in Texas and the Judicial Attitude toward that Reception, 1840-1859," *Texas Law Review,* XIX (1951), 904.

Martin, Paul, "Property Rights Among Factions in Independent Churches," *Baylor Law Review,* VII (1955), 425,

McGrath, John J., "Canon Law and American Church Law: A Comparative Study," *The Jurist,* XVIII (1958), 260-278.

Stecks, William, "Tax Exemption of Public Charity under Texas Constitution," *Baylor Law Reveiw,* VII (1955), 494.

Stumberg, G. W., "Testamentary Dispositions and the Conflict of Laws," *Texas Law Review* XXXIV (1955), 28.

CIVIL LAW CASES CITED

(Texas Cases)

African Methodist Episcopal Church v. Independent A.M.E. Church, 281 S.W. 2d 758 (Civ. App., 1955).

Alexander v. Bowers, 79 S.W. 342 (1904).

American Insurance Co. v. Edwards, 78 S.W. 2d 1020 (Civ. App., 1935).

Ballard v. Ballard, 296 S.W. 2d 811 (1956).

Baptist Memorial Hospital v. McTighe, 303 S.W. 2d 446 (1957).

Barker v. Hazel, 219 S.W. 874 (1920).

Baylor University v. Boyd, 18 S.W. 2d 700 (1929).

Benavides v. Garcia, 290 S.W. 739 (Com. App., 1926).

Benevolent and Protective Order of Elks v. City of Houston, 44 S.W. 2d 488 (Civ. App., 1931).

Blair v. Odin, 3 Tex. 288 (1848).

Blanc v. Asbury, 63 Tex. 489, 51 Am. Rep. 666 (1885).

Belcher v. Cassidy, 62 S.W. 924 (1894).

Boysles v. Gresham, 260 S.W. 2d 144 (Civ. App., 1953) rev'd on other grounds in 263 S.W. 2d 935 (1954).

Brown v. Warfield, 234 S.W. 2d 264 (Civ. App., 1950).

Brown v. Weir, 293 S.W. 916 (1927).

Cassiano v. Ursline Academy, 64 Tex. 673 (1873).

Chapman v. 1st National Bank 275 S.W. 498 (Civ. App., 1927).

Chevalier v. Wilson, 1 Tex. 161 (1846).

Church v. Bullock, 104 Tex. 1, 109 S.W. 115, 16 L.R.A. (N. S.) 860 (1909).

City of Anson v. Arnett, 250 S.W. 2d 450 (1953).

City of Dallas v. Cochrian 166 S.W. 32 (Civ. App., 1914).

City of Houston v. Cohen, 204 S.W. 2d 671 (1943).

City of Houston v. Scottish Rite Benevolent Ass'n, 111 Tex. 191, 230 S.W. 978 (1921).

City of San Antonio v. Salvation Army, 127 S.W. 860 (Civ. App., 1912).

Clark v. Brown, 108 S.W. 421 (Civ. App.) rev'd in Brown v. Clark, 102 Tex. 323, 116 S.W. 360, 24 L.R.A. (N.S). 670 (1909).

Community of St. Basil v. Byrne, 236 S.W. 1016 (1922).

Cranfill v. Haydin, 22 Civ. App. 656, 55 S,W. 805 (1896).

Crossland v. Dunham, 135 Tex. 301, 140 S.W. 2d 1095 (1940).

Cussen v. Lynch, 245 S.W. 932 (1922).

Davis v. Gulf Ry. Co., 196 S.W. 603 (1920).

Davis v. Skipper, 83 S.W. 2d 318 (1936).

Davis v. Turner, 148 S.W. 2d 256 (Civ. App., 1941).

Dickinson v. Woodsmen of the World Life Insurance Society, 280 S.W. 2d 318 (1955).

Firestone Service Stores v. Darden, 96 S.W. 2d 316 (1936).

First Baptist Church of Redland v. Ward, 290 S.W. 828 (Civ. App., 1927).

First Baptist Church v. West, 120 S.W. 2d 528 (1939).

First Church of Christ, Scientist v. Snowden, 276 S.W. 2d 571 (Civ. App., 1953).

Fort v. First Baptist Church of Paris, 55 S.W. 402 (Civ. App.) modified 93 Tex. 215, 54 S.W. 892, 49 L.R.A. 617 (1898).

Frost Nat. Bank v. Boyd, 188 S.W. 2d 199 (Civ. App., 1945) aff'd in 196 S.W. 2d 497 (1946).

Gabert v. Olcott, 22 S.W. 286, rev'd in Olcott v. Gabert, 23 S.W. 985 (1893).

Gerking v. Fort Worth National Bank, 284 S.W. 2d 791, (Civ. App., 1955).

Gibson v. Morris, 31 Civ. App. 645, 73 S.W. 85 (1903).

Greer v. Lafayette County Bank, 47 S.W. 737 (1887).

Grigsby v. Reid, 105 Tex. 597, 153 S.W. 1124 (1913).

Haggset v. Dallas Mortgage Securities Co., 110 S.W. 2d 135 (Civ. App., 1937).

Harris v. Fort Worth, 142 Tex. 600, 180 S.W. 2d 131 (1944) revg. 177 S.W. 2d 308 (Civ. App., 1944).

Hedgecroft v. City of Houston, 244 S.W. 2d 632 (1951).

Herrington v. Williams, 31 Tex. 448 (1870).

Hillebrand v. Brewer, 6 Tex. 45 (1850).

Holloway Seed Co. v. City Bank, 47 S.W. 95 (1887).

Holman v. Hopkins, 27 Tex. 38 (1863).

Hopkins v. Upshur, 20 Tex. 89, 112 S.W. 433, aff'd in 102 Tex. 519, 119 S.W. 1139 (1904).

Humphries v. Wiley, 76 S.W. 2d 793 (Civ. App., 1934).

Inglish v. Johnson, 95 S.W. 558, 42 Civ. App. 118 (1890).

Jarrell v. Sproules, 20 Civ. App. 387, 49 S.W. 904 (1889).

Johnson v. Hocker, 39 S.W. 406 (1885).

Jones v. Hilliard, 63 S.W. 2d 909 (1934).

Jones v. State, 45 S.W. 2d 612 (1932).

Jones v. Williams, 121 Tex. 94 (1923).

Jung v. Neraz, 71 Tex. 396, 9 S.W. 344 (1888).

Kelly v. Curry, 75 S.W. 2d 109 (1935).

Laird v. Bass, 50 Tex. 412 (1878).

Lake v. Hood, 79 S.W. 323, 35 Civ. App. 32 (1894).

Lightfoot v. Poindexter, 199 S.W. 1152 (Civ. App., 1920).

Little Theatre of Dallas v. Dallas, 124 S.W. 2d 867 (1939).

Lowry v. Gallagher, 190 S.W. 2d 165 (Civ. App., 1945).

McCall v. Capers, 105 S.W. 2d 323 (1937).

McCamey v. Hollister Oil Co., 241 S.W. 689 aff'd in 115 Tex. 49, 274 S.W. 562 (1926).

McDowell v. Harris, 107 S.W. 2d 647 (1936).

McMullen v. Hodges, 5 Tex. 34 (1852).

McMullen v. Sims, 37 S.W. 2d 141 (Civ. App., 1933) rev'ing 22 S.W. 2d 313.

Macedonia Baptist Church v. Farm and Home Sav. and Loan Ass'n, 110 S.W. 2d 1012 (Civ. App., 1941).

Magnolia Petroleum Co. v. Jackson, 82 S.W. 2d 1011, (1935).

Malone-Hogan Hospital Clinic Foundation, Inc. v. City of Big Spring, 288 S.W. 2d 550 (1956).

Means v. Robinson, 7 Tex. 502 (1852).

Methodist Episcopal Church South v. Clifton, 34 Civ. App., 248, 78 S.W. 932 (1894).

Methodist Episcopal Church v. Roach, 51 S.W. 2d 1100 (Civ. App., 1935).

Miller v. Davis, 136 Tex. 299, 150 S.W. 2d 973, 136 A.L.R. 177 rev'ing 146 S.W. 2d 1006 (Civ. App., 1941).

Miller v. McDonald, 235 S.W. 2d 201, (Civ. App., 1950).

Minton v. Leavell, 297 S.W. 615 (Civ. App., 1927).

Mood v. Methodist Episcopal Church South, 289 S.W. 461 (Com. App., 1927), 296 S.W. 506, modified opinion in 300 S.W. 30.

Moore v. Sellers, 201 S.W. 2d 248 (1947).

Morris v. Lone Star Chap. No. 6, Royal Arch Masons, 68 Tex. 698, 5 S.W. 519 (1876).

Murphy-Bolanz Land & Loan Co. v. McKibbin, 236 S.W. 78, (Com. App., 1922), aff'ing 221 S.W. 650.

Ochoa v. Rogers, 234 S.W. 693 (1923).

O'Connor v. Thelford, 174 S.W. 680 (1915).

Olcott v. Gabert, 86 Tex. 121, 23 S.W. 985, rev'sing 22 S.W. 286 (Civ. App., 1893).

Ortiz Oil Co. v. Luttes, 141 S.W. 2d 1050 (1941).

Parrish v. Looney, 194 S.W. 2d 419 (Civ. App., 1946).

Pascal v. Acklin, 27 Tex. 173 (1863).

Peace v. First Christian Church of McGregor, 48 S.W. 534, 20 Civ. App. 85 (1898).

Perry v. Long, 222 S.W. 2d 460 (Civ. App., 1949).

Powe v. Powe, 268 S.W. 2d 558 (1954).

Raymondville Memorial Hospital v. State, 253 S.W. 2d 1013 (1954).

Realty Trust Co. v. First Baptist Church of Haskell, 46 S.W. 2d 1009 (Civ. App., 1935).

Red v. Johnson, 53 Tex. 384 (1875).

Red v. Morris, 72 Tex. 554, 10 S.W. 681 (1889).

Republic v. Lee, 121 S.W. 2d 973 (1938).

Republic National Bank and Trust Co., 74 S.W. 2d 461 (Civ. App., 1935).

Richardson v. Prospect Hill Missionary Baptist Church, 7 S.W. 2d 179, (Civ. App., 1928).

Roaring Springs Townsite Co., v. Paducah Telephone Co., 164 S.W. 50 (Civ. App., 1914).

Ryan v. Porter, 61 Tex. 106 (1885).

Samuell v. Brooks, 207 S.W. 626 (Civ. App., 1920).

St. Edwards College v. Morris, 82 Tex. 1, 7 S.W. 512 (1891).

San Antonio v. Odin, 15 Tex. 539 (1855).

Santa Rosa Infirmary v. City of San Antonio, 259 S.W. 926 (Com. App., 1924).

Schley v. Courch, 284 S.W. 2d 333 (1955).

Schumann v. Dally, 29 S.W. 2d 422 (Civ. App., 1930).

Scott v. All Saints Hospital, 203 S.W. 146 (Civ. App., 1920).

Scott v. Sterret, 234 S.W. 2d 917 (Civ. App., 1950).

Shaw v. Lone Star Bldg. and Loan Ass'n, 123 Tex. 373, 71 S.W. 2d 863 (1934).

Sikes v. State, 28 S.W. 688 (1893).

Simonton v. White, 53 S.W. 339 (1874).

Slaughter v. American Baptist Publication Society, 150 S.W. 224 (Civ. App., 1910).

Slay v. Barnett Trust, 143 Tex. 621, 187 S.W. 2d 377 (1945), aff'ing 180 S.W. 2d 480.

Smallwood v. Midfield Oil Co., 89 S.W. 2d 1086 (Civ. App., 1935).

Smith v. Feather, 229 S.W. 2d 417 (1950), aff'd in 234 S.W. 2d 418 (1950).

State v. Methodist Episcopal Church et al., 163 S.W. 628 (1914).

State v. Settegast, 227 S.W. 253 (Civ. App., 1921), rev'd in 254 S.W. 925, (Com. App., 1923).

State v. University of Houston, 264 S.W. 2d 153 (Civ. App., 1954).

Summerhill v. Wilkes, 153 S.W. 492, 63 Civ. App., 456 (1900).

Taysom v. El Paso National Bank, 256 S.W. 2d 172 (Civ. App., 1952).

Trinity Methodist Episcopal Church v. City of San Antonio, 201 S.W. 669 (1918).

Toledo Society for Crippled Children v. Hickok, 152 Tex. 578, 261 S.W. 2d 692 (1953).

Toole v. Christ Church, Houston, 141 S.W. 2d 720 (Civ. App., 1940).

Tunstall v. Wormley, 54 Tex. 476 (1882).

Wacasey v. Wacasey, 256 S.W. 1020 (Civ. App., 1925).

Wadlington v. Peoples Baptist Church, 296 S.W. 2d 784 (Civ. App., 1956).

Wallace v. Wells, 228 S.W. 111 (Civ. App., 1924).

Wells v. Sansing, 245 S.W. 2d 964 (1955).

Werner Stave Co. v. Pickering, 119 S.W. 333 (1903).

Williams v. Davenport, 212 S.W. 675 (1920).

Women's Christian Temperance Union v. Cooley, 25 S.W. 2d 171 (Civ. App., 1932).

Woodward v. San Antonio Traction, 95 S.W. 76 (1899).

Y.M.C.A. v. City of San Antonio, 185 S.W. 844 (1915).

(Other Cases Cited)

Antoine et al. v. Esclavos' Heirs, 9 Porter 257 (1839).

Marlin v. Ramirez, 7 Philippines 41, (1906).

Brind v. International Trust Co., 179 Pac. 148 (1919).

Cleveland Osteopathic Hospital v. Zongerle, 153 Ohio St. 322, 91 N.E. 2d 261 (1950).

Commonwealth v. Y.M.C.A., 116 Ky. 711, 76 S.W. 522, 25 Ky. Law Rep. 940, 105 Am. St. Rep. 234 (1903).

Dartmouth College v. Woodward, 4 U. S. (Wheaton) 310 (1818).

Everson v. Board of Education of Ewing tp., 67 S.Ct. 504, 330 U.S. 1, 91 L.Ed. 711, 168 A.L.R. 1392, reh. den. 67 S.Ct. 962, 530 U.S. 855, 71 L.Ed. 1297 (1947).

Gerke v. Purcell, 25 Ohio St. 229 (1874).

Hodgmann v. Cobb, 202 App. Dir. 259, 195 N.Y.S. 428 (1922).

Levy v. Levy, 33 N.Y. 97 (1865).

McCulloch v. Maryland, 4 Wheaton 316 (1819).

Mannix v. Purcell, 46 Ohio St. 102 (1888).

Nance v. Busby, 91 Tenn. 303, 18 S.W. 874 (1891).

Nicol v. Ames, 173 U.S. 509 (1899).

Pierce v. Hill Military Academy and Pierce v. Society of Sisters, 268 U.S. 535 (1926).

Ponce v. Roman Catholic Apostolic Church in Puerto Rico, 210 U.S. 296, 28 S.Ct. 737, 52 L.Ed. 1068 (1908).

Santos v. Holy Roman Catholic and Apostolic Church, 212 U.S. 463, 29 S.Ct. 338, 53 L.Ed. 599 (1908).

Watson v. Jones, 80 U.S. 679, 20 L.Ed. 666 (1871).

ALPHABETICAL INDEX

BIOGRAPHICAL NOTE

Born in Beaumont, Texas, on April 20, 1926, Donald Charles McLeaish received his elementary and secondary education in the public schools of the State of Texas. He attended Tulane University in New Orleans, and Rice Institute in Houston, while in the Navy in World War II. Rice Institute awarded him a Bachelor of Arts degree in 1948. He entered the University of Texas Law School in the fall of 1948, but after four semesters left to study for the priesthood. He studied philosophy at St. Mary's Seminary, La Porte, Texas, now in Houston, from 1950 through 1952. In 1952 the Bishop of Austin sent him to the North American College in Rome, Italy, and he was ordained to the priesthood on July 17, 1955. The following year he received the Licientiate in Sacred Theology from the Gregorian University in Rome. Upon his return to the United States, he was sent by the Bishop of Austin to study at the School of Canon Law of the Catholic University of America, Washington, D. C., in September, 1956. In June, 1957, he received the Baccalaureate Degree, and in June, 1958, the Licientiate Degree, in Canon Law.

CANON LAW STUDIES*

402. Chyang, Rev. Peter B., M.A., J.C.L., Decennial faculties for ordinaries in quasi-dioceses.

403. Gossman, Rev. Francis J., A.B., S.T.L., J.C.L., Pope Urban II and canon law.

404. Love, Rev. Paul L., A.B., J.C.L., The penal remedies of the Code.

405. McLeaish, Rev. Donald C., A.B., S.T.L., J.C.L., The laws of the State of Texas affecting church property.

406. Rodriguez, Rev. Manuel J., Ph.B., S.T.L., J.C.L., The laws of the State of New Mexico affecting church property.

407. Sampon, Rev. Robert G., Ph.B., S.T.L., J.C.L., A comparative study of the First Provincial Council of Milwaukee and the Code of Canon Law.

408. Schreiber, Rev. Paul F., A.B., J.C.L., Canonical precedence.

409. Welsh, Rev. Maurice L., M.A., J.C.L., The laws of the State of Nevada affecting church property.

*For a complete list of the available numbers of this series apply to the Catholic University of America Press, 620 Michigan Ave., N.E., Washington (17), D. C., for a general catalogue.

www.ingramcontent.com/pod-product-compliance
Lightning Source LLC
LaVergne TN
LVHW050242080826
844660LV00012B/583

* 9 7 8 0 8 1 3 2 2 5 6 5 4 *